THE ~~ST~~ORY OF
TOYS
& GAMES

Around the World

THE FASCINATING HISTORY OF
TOYS
& GAMES
Around the World

Warwick Henderson

NH
NEW
HOLLAND

CONTENTS

GAMES IN THE PYRAMIDS, TOYS TO THE MOON

I have collected antique toys, games and other ephemera for more than forty years. Rather than continue to haplessly explain to friends, relations or incredulous visitors why I collected such enthralling items I decided to write a book explaining it.

Children's toys and games have proved a wonderful medium for the artist, designer and toy maker for well over a century and this is now recognized by museums, historians, writers, and collectors throughout the world. Inherent in a toy is the ability to capture elements of history and this was largely the rationale and motivation behind the creation of this book. I have always collected things – for as long as I can remember. From around eight years old I collected vintage lithographed

A busy turn of the nineteenth century French metropolitan scene (diorama c. 1910) featuring figures in period dress, including a tin plate Renault veteran car with chauffeur, a lady cyclist, a girl playing with a hoop, a policeman and bystanders. A superbly detailed toy made by Mignon Toys of France. Photo courtesy Bertoia Auctions, USA.

tins, unusual old bottles, toy soldiers, cereal premiums, cigarette cards, books, postcards, old magazines and, yes, toys. Toys fascinated me for many reasons and while I was not aware of all the 'whys and wherefores' during my childhood of rummaging through bric-a-brac and second-hand stores with my father searching for various treasures, fifty years later I think I know the 'whys and wherefores'. While I still retain some hard-earned childhood collectibles such as a set of **Herald** 1950s toy soldiers, a 1940s *Queen Mary* ship candy jar and early 1950s lithographed paintbox tins, all paid by installments from lawnmowing and

Pontiac, cast-iron, Arcade Toys, USA, 1936, 4 in long (10 cm).

a paper run, my serious collecting really began when, like the boys on the *Meccano* cover (pictured on the next page), I peered into a second-hand toy store one day in 1978 and spotted an aged 1936 Pontiac

Tut-Ankh-Amen's Tomb as discovered by Howard Carter, Churchman cigarette card number 26, 'Treasure Trove' series, 1930s.

Meccano Magazine cover, Christmas 1954.

cast-iron toy car. Following tertiary studies, I had ventured into the art world more seriously, and the sculptural qualities of this toy I found compelling. I knew nothing of the history of the play-worn Pontiac sedan (which I still have) but was hell-bent to discover everything about it. Not only had my interest in collecting been revitalized, but the 'why' to collect had been vigorously stirred, if not shaken.

While this book showcases the many distinct categories of toys I have collected over the past forty years, the focus remains not only on those which to me are unique, stylish and captivating but those which are more straightforward and those toys that quite simply no one else had thought to make. Many are uncommon and valuable, some not so, but they form the sequel to fascinating and ingenious ideas and the dreams of designers, artists and craftsmen who made toys from not only traditional materials such as wood, paper, cardboard, rubber, lead and cast-iron, but more new-age materials and inventions such as celluloid, aluminum, die-cast metal, Bakelite and plastic molding resins. Many of these materials previously undiscovered, were surprisingly used in early toy making, often experimentally, and not everything went to plan or proved smooth sailing. Billiard and pool balls made from celluloid in the nineteenth century reputedly exploded, livening up games considerably. Later, prior to World War II, even more fragile celluloid toys decided to be just as contrary, but this time 'implode' to frustrate children and parents who had parted with scarce Depression-era earnings or pocket money. Cast-iron was not only very heavy but could be notoriously fragile if dropped. Even worse, a cast-iron toy thrown by one child who chose not to use his 'words' but his accuracy, knocked another child unconscious in Auckland in 1959 (Robert Donaldson). Many toys that have survived playground battles and early unsupervised childhood development (and it is surprising how many have) remain artworks in themselves, the

Pool and billiard balls, cast phenolic resin (early period plastics) by Permac, England, c. 1920.

creativity, originality, popularity and quality of the toy enduring well to cement its claim to a place in toy history.

In 1994, a major exhibition mounted at the Katonah Museum of Art in New York was appropriately named *America at Play*, and featured games which epitomized the magnificent 'art' in a toy. Project developer, Mary Lou Alpert said, 'The games are about…culture, history, values, technology and graphic art. Mirrored are…images of life. Over a one hundred year period–this is a prime example of living history. The artwork is eye-catching, intricate and often compelling.'[1] Here Alpert has identified the importance of toys as historical objects, the significance of popular culture then and now. In Chapter 1 we will see for

Plastic cereal premiums 1950s, 2–4 in long (5–10 cm).

Plastic molding resins and color swatches for Monsanto Plastics. 'Here are materials half the weight of aluminum, warm to the touch, sturdy and long wearing with through and through color! (Advertisement, *Fortune* magazine, 1939).

Streamline sports car, molded in blue Bakelite/plastic, Codeg, England, c. 1940. Clockwork with electric lights, 13 in long (33 cm).

example how the discovery of an ancient tomb sparked the creation of 'Egyptomania' and of course, why new toys soon followed.

More recently, in 2016–17 the New Jersey State Museum mounted an exhibition of almost 200 toys which chronicled the history and role of the toy industry in New Jersey, USA. In 1950 New Jersey reputedly contributed one tenth of America's $450 million of gross toy production.[2] The *Toy World* exhibition was mounted not only to celebrate the significant contribution toys made to industry, commerce and employment, but also their contribution to history in general, in and around the eastern seaboard of America. My sojourn through collectible markets and fairs in this region in the 1980s provided me with an abundance of fabulous antique toys for my collection. I left many discoveries behind, however, as my credit card bill at one stage threatened to match New Zealand's budget deficit.

Although dolls and early primitive toys and games have been discovered at ancient burial and archaeological sites, the end of the Industrial Revolution created the platform for advancements in the invention and mass production of toys. Toys are living proof of social changes, trends and fashions, design styles, manufacturing and industrial developments, ostensibly the very fabric of our society. During the course of compiling this book it became apparent the game of tennis has arguably reflected every social issue and several manufacturing advancements to date, from long skirts and bloomers to miniskirts, women's liberation and space-age composition tennis rackets (see chapter 10). While we will see cast-iron soldiers to plastic robots, horse-drawn coaches to streamline convertibles, and an overdressed cyclist to a miniskirted tennis player doll, it is clear these items are no longer just toys but objects that showcase an era or segment of our history.

When astronaut Neil Armstrong took 'one giant leap for mankind' on the moon, science fiction became reality – in one step sci-fi flipped to life imitating art from art imitating life. Millions of creative toys followed based on real history. But similarly to toys, games and decorative items that were inspired by discoveries in the pyramids, an unprecedented sci-fi movie culture exploded, spawning a galaxy of new toys and collectibles. A **Star Wars, Ben (Obi Wan) Kenobi** plastic action figure (made in 1978) sold at auction in November 2017 at Hakes Americana Auction House, Pennsylvania for a record $76,700. A complete chapter in this book (chapter 5) is dedicated to the development of space toys and their collectibility.

The genesis of many toys and games is not solely the domain of real events such as the moon landing or the discovery of Tutankhamun's tomb. Thousands of toys can be attributed to classic books and dime-store novels that eventually morphed into radio shows, television serials, movies or in some cases all three. Several of these authors (and their classic stories) originate from the nineteenth century such as Jules Verne, Zane Grey and HG Wells. For many reasons which will be explored and discussed in this book, the toys inspired by these stories did not appear until the twentieth century or close to the twenty-first century, born from radio, television, or a movie series. The movie and screen play adapted from Jules Verne's classic 1860s sci-fi novel *From the Earth to the Moon* did not appear until 1958, only eleven years before the real event. Davy Crockett and Buffalo Bill television

'Duperite' dancing dolly (detail), crib toy, Bakelite, Modern Plastics [NZ] Ltd, c. 1940s.

Scottish highland band plastic soldiers, Herald, England, 1950s. Originally the Zang Company, England. Zang changed their name and adopted the famous 'Herald' coat of arms and logo in 1953.

Sinnet tennis board game by Chad Valley, England, c. 1930.

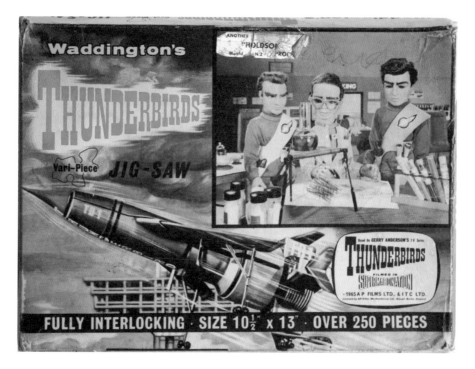

Thunderbirds jigsaw puzzle made by Waddingtons, New Zealand, 1960s, 9 x 7 in (23 cm x 7 cm).

movies based on nineteenth century dime-store novels did not screen until the middle of the twentieth century. Blockbusters such as the *Thunderbirds, Star Trek, Star Wars* and *Toy Story* franchises spawned thousands of toys and collectibles much later in the twentieth century.

A large majority of the toys in this book originate from the writer's forty-year collection. Diversity and the unusual has been the basis of this collection rather than a concentration on one category. While there are various examples from the traditional toy makers from America, England, France and Germany, there are toys from many other countries such as Japan, Spain, Italy, Czechoslovakia, Russia, Denmark, Holland, Australia and New Zealand. The materials used in their manufacture are wide-ranging including pressed-steel, ivory, wood, aluminum, die-cast metal, tin plate, and cast-iron, however early plastic toys are an area that interests me greatly. How many plastic toys pulled from a 1950s Christmas stocking survived until the serving of the Christmas afternoon roast? Although mass-produced, very few of these debut plastic toys have lived to tell the tale of manufacturing with plastic. Early Bakelite toys are another area of interest. Many are quite exquisite and extremely scarce in that Bakelite was used in toy making for such a brief period in the 1930s.

Who would buy toys made from a plastic material? Who were these prophetic and ingenious toy makers, many of whom are now largely forgotten? (see chapter 'Early Period–Late Period Plastic Toys'). Plastic and Bakelite model aircraft were used to assist and encourage the identification of friendly and enemy aircraft during World War II. Immediately following the war, it was 'plastics' that arrived in force, massive injection molding machines armed with tons of plastic molding resins. Seventy years later many now consider plastics are the 'enemy'. Who would have predicted that?

Why collect antique toys is a question often asked, particularly it seems, from those who choose not to appreciate the hobby. While the fascinating history, materials, tactility and design aspects appeal to me greatly there is no doubt nostalgia plays a part. Louis Benech speaking from Christie's in France about a 1930s **Eureka pedal car** about to be auctioned said, '…for me it is a piece that re-

Dusty the miniskirted tennis player, vinyl doll made by Denys Fisher Toys, England, 1970s, 11½ in long (29 cm).

Dreadnought two-stack battleship on tin-plate wheels, tin plate, c. 1910.

awakens an unrealized childhood dream of owning the perfect red car. This isn't (also) just a functioning toy but a work of art.'[3] Obviously, the buyer concurred, paying twice the estimate to €6875. American Dale Kelley, long-term publisher and editor of *Antique Toy World* magazine agrees stating, 'I have talked with many collectors over the years and a large percentage say they collect toys and objects they remember as kids. It seems many collectors are motivated by what they remember as a child or just what they have a passion for.'[4]

Nostalgia is often attributed as the motivation to collect and childhood memories can invoke powerful reactions and emotions. Marcel Proust (1871–1922) said our memories can be like a dispensary or chemical laboratory which hands out a soothing drug.[5] That theory gets a 'like' from me, and famous American artist, poet and toy collector Ken Botto (1937–2008) would surely have agreed. He became so obsessed with his relentless search for antique toys the hobby consumed him. 'I was overtaken by the mania. I became obsessed, a toy junkie always on some crazy search for the next toy fix.'[6]

Molding plastics, line of 150-ton presses, *Mecanno Magazine* cover, December 1946.

Rockets, Missiles and Outer Space, breakfast cereal collector's card album, Flemings Company, New Zealand, 1960s.

Kris Kristofferson immortalized nostalgia when he wrote in his 1970s hit 'Me and Bobby McGee', 'I'd trade all of my tomorrows for a single yesterday'. A single yesterday or cherished memory is not enough however for most collectors – and in the case of antique and collectible toys the choice is almost unlimited. While some collectors may be content with six **Dinky toys,** a 1930s **Ideal Shirley Temple doll** or a battery-operated **Smokey the Bear** coveted from childhood, others have enormous collections of thousands of antique toys. The late Donald Kaufman, a serious American toy collector, collected over 5000 pieces, which took more than three years to eventually auction, contained in five cataloged sales. By April 2011 the 5787 lots had grossed over US$12 million.[7]

An article titled 'Toys Aren't Just Kids'

Austin saloon, Bakelite and pressed-steel, by Ranlite of England, 1929, 9½ in long (34 cm).

Stuff Anymore' published in 2017 stated, '…according to recent research adults in Britain are buying toys for personal use in record numbers…adults wanting to relive their youth have purchased one in five children's building sets and action figures for themselves.'[8] It also stated that this phenomenon has seen the 'kidult' toy market expand at three times the pace of the wider toy market and the trend is 'possibly a reaction against the stresses of our fast paced lives. Toys are fun and when you are having fun, any stress you are feeling goes away.' Favorite for British 'kidult' buyers were building sets, **LEGO** and **Star Wars** characters, 'as they can evoke a feeling of nostalgia among the more mature fan base…' The article went on to say that *American Demographics* magazine reported '45% of 20,000 adults surveyed nationwide had bought a toy or game for themselves or an adult friend in a typical year.' Early plastic building block sets and their makers are discussed in Chapter 6 (Early Period–Late Period Plastics). It seems then that it is not simply grandparents, parents or hardened collectors buying toys, and according to expert business analysts, the 'kidult' market for new toys is also fueled by nostalgia. I

American plastic brick set by Halsam Products, 1940s Chicago, USA.

Exquisite early nineteenth century tin plate train station by Marklin Toys of Germany.

prefer to leave this 'kidult' aspect of toy collecting to Bill Bryson's analysis in his book *The Lost Continent* when he said, '…I wanted to go back to the magic places of my youth, (read childhood) to see if they were as good as I remembered them.'[9] Perhaps he was analyzing the psyche behind many toy buyers and collectors of the world.

As this book attempts to demonstrate there are many reasons to collect antique toys, games and associated ephemera. I trust the readers of this book will gain more than just a few childhood memories while doing so, even if it is just a fleeting reminiscence of that toy you threw at your brother, sister or cousin. In future please use your words not the toys!

Shirly Temple doll by Ideal Toy and Novelty Company, 1930s.

CHAPTER 1

FUN AND SERIOUS GAMES IN THE PYRAMIDS

If we accept that toys, games and history are inextricably linked then by extension we must assume many toys detailed in this book are related to compelling aspects of history. Napoleon Bonaparte's Egyptian campaign for example (1798–1801) sparked new world interest in the wonder of Egypt and North Africa. In a bloody expedition and crusade in which over 30,000 French soldiers perished in combat or by disease, somewhat paradoxically, his *folie de grandeur* is credited with the birth of Egyptology. Napoleon's substantial army and navy was accompanied by scholars, scientists and artists and among many dubious activities such as plundering countless precious and irreplaceable antiquities, he introduced the printing

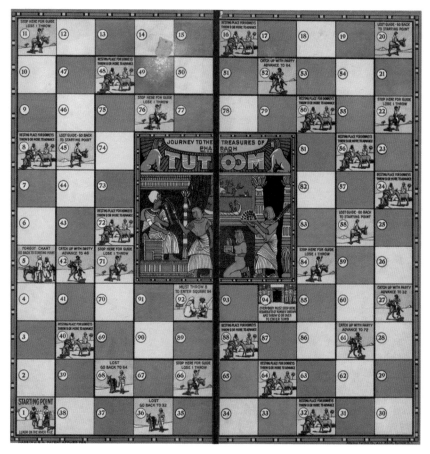

Tutoom board game by All Fair Games (Alderman Fairchild Co.), Rochester, New York, USA, c. 1920s. Photo courtesy Griffiths Institute, University of Oxford, England.

press to Egypt. The British occupation of Egypt (1882–1922) soon revealed the fascinating reality of an ancient civilization surrounded by remarkable structures (pyramids and tombs) and accounts of previously undiscovered mummies, wrapped with priceless personal treasures and jewels. The news of Egyptology and the pyramids soon spread throughout the

Tutoom playing pieces.

'Africa' Round the World playing card game, Pepys Series, c. 1970s.

Discovery of Tutankhamun's tomb, 1922, 'Treasure Trove' collector's card series, number 26, WA & AC Churchman.

Early turned fruitwood top with hand-cut ivory tops, 1½–3½ in (4–9 cm).

world, progressed by rapid development in transport, travel and communication. By the time Tutankhamun's tomb was revealed in 1922, anyone with the means could travel within weeks to Egypt. Egyptomania, a by-product of Egyptology, became larger than life.

Toys and parlor games date back to early civilizations, some 5000 years ago, and this was irrefutable when the intact tomb of King Tutankhamun (ruled 1332–1323 BC) was discovered in Egypt by British archaeologist Howard Carter in 1922. The discovery generated headline news around the world. When asked what he could see after peering through a hole in the wall which he had chiseled open, completely dumbfounded, all Carter could reputedly utter was, 'wonderful things'. He is more likely to have said, 'I think we have just won Lotto', but he definitely stated later, '…as my eyes grew accustomed to the light, details of the room emerged slowly from the mist, strange animals, statues and gold, everywhere the glint of gold.'[10] In a letter to Lord Carnarvon, the long-term sponsor of Carter's search for the tomb, the Egyptian Antiquities Service wrote, '…you have attached your name to one of the greatest discoveries not only in Egypt but in all the domains of archaeology…as for the collaboration of Howard Carter, who has conducted the work through so many years, it is for him the finest crowning of a career and the most astonishing reward that any archaeologist could have.'[11]

Ironically, such was the jumble of artifacts in one room in the tomb, Carter likened his task of cataloging each piece as 'playing a game of "Spilikins"', a recently patented name for the game we commonly know as **pick-up sticks** or **jackstraws.** Apart from the incredible golden treasures

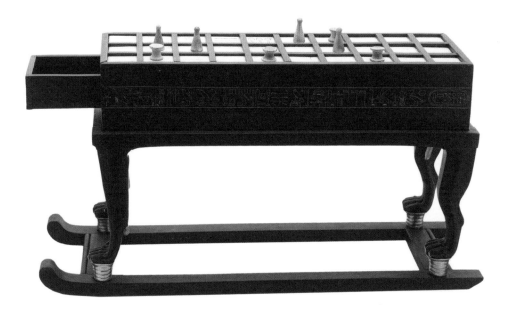

Senet game table with ivory playing pieces, collection Egyptian Museum, Cairo. From the Tomb of Tutankhmun, photo Ayman Khoury.

and everyday objects found in various rooms of the tomb, Tutankhamun's games such as **senet** (game of passing) were discovered, which were placed to enable him to play and 'pass' to the afterlife, which was a significant aspect of Egyptian culture and religion – indeed the very genesis for the construction of the pyramids and tombs hidden nearby or within.

The discovery of these tombs became more frequent in the nineteenth century, culminating in the revelation of incredible treasure troves in the early twentieth century. Apart from revealing 'time warps' which contained chariots, stunning paintings, statues, solid-gold figurines and elaborately gilded 'designer' furniture, they included everyday objects such as parlor games, dolls and tops. Even pharaohs and their families loved their toys. An iconic painting concealed in the tomb of the Egyptian Queen Nefertari (1295–1255 BC) which was discovered in 1904, depicts the good lady playing the game of **senet.**[12]

Queen Nefertari (1295–1255 BC) playing senet.

Am Duat (the Egyptian mahjong) promotional brochure by Chad Valley Games, c. 1923/1924.

This game had previously been identified incorrectly by some experts as **chess** or **draughts.**[13] **Senet** was not just a game privy to pharaohs, kings and queens. Egyptologists confirm game-board designs have been discovered carved on outside stones and walls of tombs that they maintain were completed by pyramid builders, workers and artists during their lunchtime or afternoon tea. A **senet** game board etched onto a child's learning slate is a prized exhibit held in the Egyptian Museum, indelible proof of the significance and depth of popularity of the game.

There were four game boards found in King Tutankhamun's tomb, but undeniably the most outstanding was a **senet** game pictured here. The importance of this game was highlighted by its very aesthetics and construction, where the elaborate double-sided ebony and ivory game box had been mounted on an elegant stylized feline 'paw-foot' stand. This had then been fixed to a matching sled to enable the game to be perfectly balanced and be moved around as well. Parts of the stand were gilded while the feline (leonine or leopard) paws were carved from ebony. The four sides of the box featured artistic hieroglyphic inscriptions which refer to the owner himself, early toy collector and boy king, Tutankhamun. Although Tutankhamun reigned for ten or so years, he was apparently only about nineteen years old when he died, unpleasantly of disease or violently, perhaps in battle, hunting; or possibly even squabbling over the rules or result of a game…teenagers. Experts remain unclear on his exact age or cause of death.

While the game's stick-like dice were eventually discovered on the ground, sadly the ten or fourteen playing pieces (five or seven playing pieces per player) were missing. Carter speculated that they were probably made from silver and gold and had been stolen in earlier tomb raids, as this chamber showed evidence of a much earlier break-in, possibly thousands of years before his discovery. Ironically, the game on the reverse of the inlaid game box consisting of twenty squares was called 'robbers' or synonymously 'twenty squares'. This magnificent table-mounted game is one which would be eagerly sought by collectors today, but it is now housed safely in the Cairo Museum, labeled with a date of 3100 BC. Similar full sets with playing pieces discovered in other tombs are held in the collection of the Cairo Museum.

Earlier, Carter had discovered another outstanding and elaborate board game he called **Dogs Contra Jackals,** now more commonly known as **Hounds and Jackals** (tomb of Reny-Seneb, twelfth dynasty BC). The superbly carved ivory peg-type playing pieces consisted of five jackal-headed pieces and five dog-headed pegs. These fitted into holes on the playing board similarly to a cribbage board. The elaborate ivory, ebony and sycamore board is unusually torso shaped and mounted on a table not unlike the senet game. The rules of the game are still subject to debate but the object seems to involve moving the pieces up to the top of the centrally located palm tree. Pieces could possibly move up or down, similar to **snakes and ladders.**

The discovery of the tomb sparked an unprecedented popular Egyptian movement during the Art Deco and flapper period of the 1920s and 1930s. An introduction to the Victoria and Albert's *Art Deco 1910 to 1939* exhibition in 2003 stated '…generic Egyptian imagery and motifs such as lotus flowers, scarabs, hieroglyphics, pylons and pyramids rapidly became popular. They covered everything…In fashion design Egyptomania was ubiquitous and sometimes bizarre; a Mummy's wrap was even all the rage in the 1920s.'[14] Application for King Tut inspired products apparently swamped the patents and trademarks office including designs for jewelery, handbags, garments, soaps and games. An unusual beetle-style car was even manufactured in the 1930s in the USA named the **Scarab.** Rather ugly, less than 100 were produced. A well-constructed, pressed-steel clockwork toy **Scarab** car made at the time by **Buddy L Toys** USA fared little better and even now these are not popular with antique toy collectors. Designed also in the 1930s, but in Germany, another 'beetle-style' car would prove infinitely more successful and enduring. King Tut, as a spoiled teenager, would have loved a VW Beetle, providing several more horsepower than his gilded

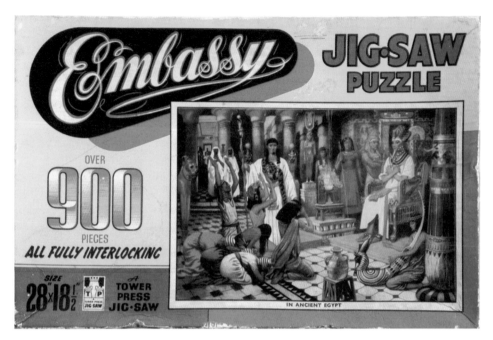

In Ancient Egypt, large-scale jigsaw puzzle by Tower Press, England, c. 1950s, 28½ x 18½ in (72 x 47 cm).

chariot, which he no doubt 'drifted' around the pyramids, much to the consternation of his mother. The VW Beetle car has endured, creating a comprehensive collectible genre to this day.

Fascinating stories and legends surround the discovery of the tombs; particularly regarding the unwrapping of the mummy and the possibility of a curse upon all those who entered the tombs, or indeed disturbed any mummies or personal items. The stories of thefts and trade in stolen artifacts including mummies are well recorded and discussed, which inspired many of the

books, movies, video and other games on the market today.

There is a history of crossover or, at worst, cheating by game manufacturers themselves when it came to companies leaping on the bandwagon during this period. Prior to the advent of television sets and movie theaters, parlor games were a lucrative business for the big toy manufacturers such as **Chad Valley, Spears, Parker Brothers** and **Milton Bradley** and the decades 1880 to 1940 became the 'golden age' of board and card games. It seemed all bets were off in the rush to produce a new or popular game; nothing seemed sacred. **Spilikins,** mentioned earlier as a name used for **pick-up sticks,** was a title originally given to cribbage pegs. **Cribbage,** incidentally, derives from a seventeenth century English card game called **noddy.** We now know where the little man in the red and yellow car inherited his name from; crucial information surely for upcoming pub quiz nights and games of 'trivial disputes'. It is also possible the 1920s strategy peg-style board games such as **Pegity** and **Spoil Five** by **Chad Valley** of England were influenced by the **Dogs and jackals** game Howard Carter had discovered. To confuse the issue further, **Spoil Five** is actually a traditional 500-year-old Irish card game (see picture).

One of the most attractive examples of a game that appeared soon after Carter's discovery was one rather creatively named **Tutoom.** Based on a snakes and ladders concept the game board is centrally decorated with a stylish poster-like Egyptian court scene that is titled 'Journey to the Treasures of the Pharaoh Tutoom'. The playing squares are illustrated with intrepid tourists, most wearing pith helmets while mounted on donkeys. Many of the penalty squares on the board state 'Lost', or 'Lost Guide – Go Back to Start', but playing the game proved decidedly less risky than the real adventure. Some tourists apparently ended up lost, deceased, and later sold as 'Egyptian mummies' to unsuspecting punters when the demand for mummies reached the heights of popularity. Made by **All Fair Games** USA in 1923, this game would make a fine addition to any toy, game or Egyptology collection. An example is held by the Griffith Institute's Egyptian collection at the University of Oxford in England.

Another game possibly produced after the discovery was **Am-Duat** by **Chad Valley** of England in 1923–24. In the promotional brochure (pictured) the game is advertised as the 'Egyptian mahjong'.[15] Typical of **Chad Valley** games, a fine illustration has been designed for advertising purposes. To my knowledge, the game is even rarer than **Tutoom.** I have never seen this game in forty years of collecting and wonder if it was ever put into production for retail sale. **Chad Valley,** along with other toy makers, made several versions of **mahjong** at this time.

Soon however, and perhaps more influentially, 'talkies' or movies were launched, particularly horror films such as *The Mummy* (1932) starring Boris Karloff, *The Mummy's Hand* (1940) together with three sequels, *The Mummy's Tomb* (1942),

The Mummy's Ghost and *The Mummy's Curse* (1944). Pioneering French filmmaker Georges Melies directed a silent movie *Cleopatra's Tomb* as far back as 1899, however, no copy of the movie has survived. On a lighter note, the popular comedy trio The Three Stooges starred in a comedy titled *We Want Our Mummy* in 1939. It is worth noting it is not just new merchandising, period classic toys and games such as Tutoom and senet which are valuable and collectible. In 1997 a collector paid a world record US$453,500 for an original one sheet movie poster of the 1932 *Mummy* movie. For toy, game and movie production relating to the Egyptian phenomena and Tutankhamun however, these early movies proved to be just a curtain-raiser to a manufacturing boom which gathered pace right up to and including the twenty-first century. In 2017 *The Mummy* was remade starring Tom Cruise. Widely panned by critics, one stated, 'It is one thing to excavate iconography of old Hollywood, it's another to exploit it. This isn't film making, its tomb raiding.'[16]

While accusations of exploitation in the motion picture industry are nothing new, toy merchandising has also become inextricably linked to blockbuster movies and their sequels, particularly from the late twentieth century, as chapters in this book illustrate. The *Indiana Jones* movie franchise, based on the globetrotting adventures of an archaeologist, launched four sci-fi adventure movies beginning with *Raiders of the Lost Ark* in 1981, with a fifth Indiana Jones movie planned for 2020. The success of the movies was phenomenal, with the first earning US$389.9 million on the back of an US$18 million budget. Despite the myths and speculation regarding curses and misfortune befalling those associated with Tutankhamun, Howard Carter's discovery just seems to keep on giving. Carter, who was portrayed in two *Indiana Jones* movies, died in 1939, a famous and wealthy man. Harrison Ford and Steven Spielberg likewise have earned a fortune from the movies inspired by Carter's dogged archaeological discovery in 1922. Harrison Ford is a trustee on the governing board of the Archaeological Institute of America, which promotes awareness of archaeology and assists in the prevention of looting and illegal trade in antiquities. Perhaps they may consider taking action against one of the latest *Mummy* movies, launched in 2017.

Some decades after Egyptomania blossomed and *The Mummy's Curse* was screened, 'Tutmania' was raised to a new level in the 1970s when unprecedented exhibitions of treasures, including the senet

VW Beetle car, FunHo! Toys (Underwood Engineering Co. Ltd, New Zealand), die-cast, 1960s, 2 in long (5 cm).

table game, toured Europe, America and Canada. These touring exhibitions are now variously regarded as the first commercial blockbuster public gallery/museum shows. Over one and a half million people visited the exhibitions in England, but all records were erased when the treasures toured eight cities in America in 1975 to 1979. Negotiated during a softening of political relations between two fractious nations, such was the concern for the safety of the collection, a US Naval stores vessel, the *Sylvania*, was one of the ships requisitioned to transport the priceless items on their final journey to America. In an amusing but satirical take on the method of transport employed to avoid an aircraft hijacking or crash, a *Vanity Fair* journalist wrote, 'Tutankhamun artifacts made their way across the Mediterranean sharing cargo space with refrigerated boxes of hamburger patties. In America the "Boy King" would at last encounter his real afterlife, albeit a rather different one than the ancient Egyptians had imagined.'[17]

The resulting exhibition phenomenon was also certainly not what the young pharaoh would have dreamed of in his afterlife either. 'King Tut' worship was greatly enhanced well beyond his lifetime when reputedly over eight million people visited the exhibition in America. Commercial worship eventually overran the integrity of the exhibition however and, like many blockbuster touring museum and gallery shows mounted in the late twentieth century, they became a fad at worst, or an overblown, entertaining commercial enterprise at best. An avalanche of souvenirs and commercial 'Tut kitsch' was produced which groveled as low as unlicensed t-shirts reading 'Hands off my Tuts'.

Appearing on the credit side of the ledger however were several accessible and reasonably authentic representations of the feature game found in the tombs, **senet**. Although just one of the outstanding objects in the exhibition, it was produced in the form of a board game by **Cadaco Inc.** of Chicago in 1976–77, the appropriately illustrated box depicting the golden mask and other treasures featured in the touring exhibition. Similarly to many traditional board or parlor games, **senet** involves a large degree of strategy and luck. A number of Egyptologists have claimed to have interpreted the rules to the game including Peter A Piccione from the University of Chicago, 'after an exhaustive study of ancient hieroglyphic documents'.[18] Most seem to agree on the basics which include the object of passing your five pieces 'off' the board while occupying key positions for as long as possible to enforce the opponent into an inferior and dangerous position (rules on reverse of box cover). Space 27 of the 30 is a key position, the ancient symbol depicting water or an obstacle which must be 'passed' in order to be 'born again', or move to the afterlife. A similar but more sophisticated senet board game was made by the **Kirk Game Company** in 1978 titled **Passing Through the Netherworld.** The board pictured here is beautifully illustrated with thirty illustrated spaces, bookended by a male and female Egyptian dressed in finery and various period adornment. There are a few variations from the **Cadaco** game such as a trap and safe spaces. A comprehensive rule book, which includes further academic research and information is included, written by the designer and archaeologist Timothy Kendall at the time from the Museum of Fine Art, Boston.

Previous to the touring shows landing in the USA, Milton Bradly, in 1971, manufactured a game which was arguably one of the precursors to video gaming named **Voice of the Mummy.** The game included a battery-operated record to be engaged when the player landed on a square. A lever was then hand operated whereby the recording delivered instructions to the player or players, which determined the next moves. The object of this interactive game is to proceed up the hazardous three-level pathway, collecting jewels on the way. The first to arrive at the mummy secures the great jewel and the protective Evil Cobra Spell. The game was beset with technical problems and now of course seems very outdated. By 1983 their opposition, Parker Brothers, had produced a video game named **Tutankham** (see picture). It was promoted in advertising as the 'Home Video Game you've waited 3000 years for'. The theme of the game was similar to **Voice of the Mummy** where hazards and guards required neutralizing to capture the keys to the treasure tomb.

Egyptomania, which blossomed in the 1920s, later reborn through blockbuster touring exhibitions fifty years later, also infiltrated popular music. The 1974 popular hit song recorded by Maria Muldaur, 'Midnight at the Oasis', refers to a romantic evening in the sand dunes after the camels have been sent to bed. In 1977

Spoil Five peg board game with wooden playing pieces by Chad Valley, England, c. 1920s, 13 x 10 in (33 x 23.5 cm.)

Jonathan Richman's catchy instrumental 'Egyptian Reggae' reached number five on the UK pop charts.

In September 1986 American pop-rock band The Bangles released 'Walk like an Egyptian', which by December had become a smash hit, climbing to the pinnacle of the Billboard Hot 100 in the USA. It remained number one for four

Advertisement for *Tutankham*, Atari video game, 'The home video you've waited 3000 years for', Parker Bros/Sears USA, Konami Industry Company, 1982, 1983.

King Tut's Game, Senet, The Game That King Tut Played, by Cadaco Ellis, Chicago, USA, c. 1976/1977.

weeks. The record covers feature Egyptian imagery and hieroglyphics.

Since and during the touring exhibitions, several of which continued until 2015, for better or worse the significance of the senet game has been lost somewhat in the translation to commercial reproduction. For the Egyptians, in particular the pharaohs and their royal families, the game was inextricably linked to sacred beliefs and religion and partaking in the game and successfully 'passing' square 27 was as good as the promise of a quick chariot ride to the 'afterworld'. Nevertheless, the revival of Egyptian-inspired games, books and movies has continued unabated. Blockbuster shows such as *Indiana Jones* movies, *Lara Croft: Tomb Raider*, *Lara Croft Tomb Raider – The Cradle of Life* along with similarly themed movies resurrected an interest in the genre, as did a trilogy of books, *The Kane Chronicles* written by Rick Riordan between 2010 and 2012.[19] These books and movies inspired a complete new range of toys, video games and interactive books. Currently on the market are not only several senet games but Egyptian collectible figurines, stickers, an Egyptian mummy excavation kit and, right on trend, a children's book of Egyptian tattoos to enable pre-schoolers to achieve that 'look cool' effect to impress their mates or the boy or girl next door. Toy giants **LEGO** and **Playmobil** launched impressive lines of Egyptian-themed toy sets. **Playmobil's** items for example include a chariot set, a temple set, a tomb with treasure, sphinx with mummy, a pharaoh's temple and a pharaoh's pyramid, all with detailed figurines and accessories. Wow! Another recently produced game is **Imhotep, Builder of Egypt,** a board game which was nominated as one of the top toys of 2016.[20] The comprehensive kit includes a finely illustrated box, board, cards and finely crafted playing pieces. Why didn't they have toys like that when I was a kid? The revival of these toys and games can be counted as one of the many positive outcomes from the phenomena that was the discovery of King Tutankhamun.

Despite the question marks over 'disturbing the dead', the tombs have nevertheless revealed not only stunning artworks and treasures but a fascinating time capsule of the life and times of the pharaohs, upon which their comparatively recent discovery sparked not only a comprehensive fashion and design movement, but the reproduction and revival of a game long forgotten. As we have seen, more recently many new and more accessible educational and interactive

games and toys have since been created, many borne from movie franchises. Despite discoveries, controversies, curses, tomb thefts, myths, blockbuster movies and claims of exploitation, it is more probable the young pharaoh King Tutankhamun and his followers would be heartened to know that their spirit is at least alive and well in the twenty-first century, particularly through the creative and inventive Egyptian inspired toys currently available for all to enjoy.[21]

Passing Through the Netherworld by Kirk Game Company, designed by Timothy Kendall, USA. World reknowned Egyptologist, archaeologist and anthropologist.

CHAPTER 2

GO WEST YOUNG MAN, GO WEST!

Similarly to the phenomena that became Egyptomania, the nineteenth century American West genre, born from fabled legends established during the volatile and rapidly expanding frontier settlements of North America, over time provided unparalleled inspiration for toy makers throughout the world.

The cowboys, outlaws, gunslingers, homesteaders, lawmen, Indians and Chiefs were popularised initially through dime-store novels, Wild West shows, and early Western writers such as Zane Grey. Zane Grey (1872–1939) published an iconic Western novel *Riders of the Purple Sage* in 1912 and he reputedly became the first millionaire author. Movie mogul William Fox bought the movie rights in 1916 and eventually fifty of Grey's novels were turned into 112 movies.

Hopalong Cassidy tin target game, Toy Enterprises of Chicago, USA, 1940s.

Before long Westerns turned out movie and radio stars such as Tom Mix, Gene Autry, Roy Rodgers, Hopalong Cassidy, The Lone Ranger and Tonto. Toys in their thousands soon followed. **Hopalong Cassidy** movies began in 1933 although the genesis of the character was based on a fictional cowboy created by writer Clarence E Mulford in 1904. William Boyd (1898–1972) gained the legendary part

In the 1950s and 1960s the Western genre infiltrated popular culture extensively.

William Boyd (Hopalong Cassidy) collector's card, c. 1930s, 5½ x 3½ in (14 x 9 cm).

Lone Ranger board game front cover, Parker Brothers, USA, 1938.

after agreeing to give up drinking and his slothful ways, which were ironically features of the hard-bitten wooden-legged roughrider that Clarence featured in his original short stories and novels. At length sixty-six 'Hoppy' movies were produced which portrayed a reinvented laconic, silver-haired, Stetson-wearing clean-cut cowboy hero, lavishly 'tooled up' while mounted on his famous steed Topper. In the 1940s, somewhat presciently, Boyd purchased the radio and television rights to the films and the 'Hoppy' character, whereby he was soon to cash in on the Western's television boom of the 1950s, eventually screening fifty-two half-hour shows. He was one of the first Western stars to take advantage of merchandising and product endorsement and he quickly became a millionaire. William Boyd literally became a legend in his own lifetime appearing on the cover of *Time* magazine in November 1950, *Life* magazine in June 1950, and *Quick* magazine, among others. The tin target game pictured was made by one of his authorized companies, Toy Enterprises of Chicago, USA. The stylized and panoramic imagery on this target game is typical of the clear, simplified and more modern poster-style artwork of the 1930s and 1940s period. There are many specialist **Hopalong Cassidy** memorabilia collectors who pursue the myriad of 'Hoppy' toys which are regularly traded and auctioned today. His elaborate and highly decorated toy six-shooters and holsters are particularly coveted. Boyd died in 1972 a wealthy and highly respected businessman and cowboy actor.

The Lone Ranger, created by writer Fran Striker and radio-station owner George Trendle in 1933 was a staunch hombre, portrayed as an ex-Texas Ranger, tough enough to sort out any troublemakers, outlaws or Indians, together with his sidekick Tonto. It is possible Striker and Trendle gained inspiration for their masked man from Texas Ranger Hero Captain Hugh, who featured in Zane Grey's 1915 book, *The Lone Star Ranger*. Johnston McCully's masked man **Zorro** may have provided some ideas as well but **Hopalong Cassidy,** over time, proved more endearing and enduring. There were at least six **Lone Ranger** movies made, the latest in 2013 starring Armic Hammer as the **Lone Ranger** and Johnny Depp as Tonto. **The Lone Ranger** game pictured was made by board game giant **Parker Brothers** of the USA in 1938. With a nicely illustrated playing board, the game box includes sophisticated playing pieces with die-cast horses and riders and nickel-plated steel tokens representing **Silver,** the **Lone Ranger's** horse. Luckily for collectors these games are surprisingly attainable, an entry level set valued at around $150. Early 'Hoppy' comics however are a different story, some issues selling for over $3000. The *Lone Ranger Adventure Stories* were published in 1957 by the Western Printing and Lithography Company in Racine, Wisconsin, USA, although the edition pictured here was printed in England by LTA Robinson Limited of London. This book is lavishly illustrated with stills from the 1957 Warner Brothers movie, *The Lone Ranger*, which starred Clayton Moore as the masked man.

Western movie and television screen time exploded exponentially during the 1950s and 1960s, to the extent eight of the ten top-rated television serials in the USA were Westerns. Even theme songs to blockbusters such as *Bonanza*, *Wagontrain*, *Laramie*, *Gunsmoke* and *Rawhide* became either chart toppers or well-known ditties.

Lone Ranger Adventure Stories, Western Printing and Lithography Company, USA, 1957.

The Lone Ranger starring Clayton Moore, 1957, Warner Brothers, USA.

Lone Ranger board game, 18½ x 18½ in (47 x 47 cm).

Laramie Annual, Purnell, London, 1963, 11 x 8¼ in (28 x 21.5 cm).

Zane Grey early movie card To the Last Man, 1924, 7 x 5 in (18 x 13 cm).

Clint Eastwood starred as Rowdy Yates in *Rawhide*, a straight-talking trail boss who eventually transitioned from this successful series to become a movie star and Oscar winning director. Another movie star in waiting was Steve McQueen who played Josh Randell as the Bounty Hunter in a western television series *Wanted, Dead or Alive* (CBS 1958–1961). The hit show *Bonanza* starring Lorne Greene (Ben Cartwright), Michael Landon (Little Joe), Dan Blocker (Hoss) and Pernell Roberts (Adam) boasted over 42 million viewers in the USA alone. Syndicated worldwide, the series won an award as America's favorite television series for 1961–62, running from 1959 to 1973 with 431 episodes, more latterly it would be fair to say, with cheesy and limp storylines. Starring even in 'B' Westerns during this time however seemed no impairment to a successful career, in fact quite the opposite. Ronald Reagan, in true Hollywood fashion, starred in several, eventually becoming the president of America.

A long-playing record *Great Western TV Themes* released in 1969 noted on the sleeve '…Westerns have proved incredibly popular amongst both children and adults alike, they wait patiently, others impatiently with great anticipation for any Western series that is likely to appear before them on their television screens.'[22] Metaphorically speaking, never before had Soule and Greeley's nineteenth century cry to 'Go west young man' been followed with more enthusiasm – a phenomenon one hundred years later.[23]

Western paint box, tin plate, Page, London, c. 1959, 20 in long (51 cm).

Every child of the 'boomer' era probably at one stage during this time had either owned or at least played with a Western-related toy, and virtually every toy imaginable and others that hadn't been, were produced with a Western theme during this golden age of the 1950s and 1960s Westerns. Nothing seemed sacred with items such as wild west cowboy outfits, pistols, rifles, Indian headdress, masks, hats, card games, paint sets, musical instruments, even tents, together with bedsheets, lampshades, and curtains. Superb illustrations are a feature of Wild West ephemera, including books, game box covers and pop-up books such as the one pictured, illustrated by N Dear.

Girls had the option of pink-handled six-shooters with matching pink holsters, boots and clothing, which famous cowgirl/sharpshooter **Annie Oakley,** who in fact dressed more for practical purposes as a sharpshooter in **Buffalo Bill's** Wild West shows, wouldn't have been seen dead in. Born Phoebe Anne Oakley Mozee (1860–1926), the protégé soon became a renowned and relatively wealthy game hunter and showgirl sharpshooter while in her teens, eventually joining **Buffalo Bill's** Wild West shows in 1885. Stunningly attractive, her stage name by then changed to **Annie Oakley,** the American becoming a superstar, traveling across America and eventually to Europe. There Oakley was feted by royalty including Queen Victoria and while in Europe, shot a cigarette from the lips of the future Kaiser of Germany,

Wild West pop-up book, Bancroft, England, 1959, 8 x 9 in (20 x 23 cm).

Wyatt Earp marshall's badge, plated die-cast, Lincoln Toys (NZ), c. 1960s, 2¼ x 2¼in (6 x 6 cm).

Plastic six-shooters, Renwal, USA, 1950s, 2½ in (6 cm) long and 10 in long (25 cm).

Wilhelm II. She reputedly wrote to him later during the First World War I requesting a second shot. While **Annie Oakley's** career predated film and television opportunities, she is remembered not only through an assortment of Western toys over the decade but also in later movies including *Annie Oakley* (1935), played appropriately by a young and beautiful Barbara Stanwick. One standout toy produced, which celebrated Oakley's prowess, was the eponymous **Milton Bradley** board game **Annie Oakley** made in 1955. The game boasts a lavishly illustrated box, playing board and inside box panel (see illustration). Die-cast playing pieces include eight mounted deputies, illustrated die-cast discs and $15,000 in reward money to be handed out by Annie in person when the outlaws are captured.

An earlier but decidedly infamous female gunslinger/ outlaw was **Belle Starr** (1848–1889). While Starr's looks and gun slinging records were no match for the jaw-dropping exploits of **Annie Oakley,** Starr's romantic and knicker-dropping antics far outweighed any other notables from that era. While not her real name either (it was Myra Maybelle Shirley Starr), the woman seemingly associated with or married as many vicious low-lifes and outlaws throughout her tawdry career as possible, including an early association with the outlaw Cole Younger and his gang. While apparently also a crack shot, Starr was usually armed with a Colt 45 and/or a Smith and Wesson pistol, although a bronze statue currently situated in Oklahoma depicts the outlaw brandishing a rifle. Belle Starr was also immortalized in many dime-store novels, movies and television shows including a movie *Belle Starr* in 1941 (Gene Tierney) and another by the same name, unusually starring the elegant Elizabeth Montgomery who appeared in the popular television series *Bewitched*. Despite at one stage being 'Wanted for robbery, murder and treason, dead or alive', Starr is not known to have killed anyone. Her most dangerous enemy possibly transpired to be a disaffected or cuckolded lover, as she was shot from behind while mounted on her horse Venus in 1889 at forty years of age by an unknown assailant. The $10,000 gold coin reward offered by the US government for 'The Bandit Queen' was never claimed.[24] Antique Belle Starr toy guns and ephemera are quite rare.

Quite propitiously, advancements in manufacturing after the Second World War, previously undreamed of, saw Western-themed toys produced by manufacturers virtually worldwide. Japan, tooled up for mass production since the Second World War, was well placed to capitalize and exploit a seemingly unquenchable market. Clockwork and battery-operated toys, many ingeniously produced from recycled tin cans, soon flooded the market with a broad range of western and other themes, largely aimed at the American market. Quick draw gunslingers, drinking and smoking cowpokes, lariat-swinging trail riders and stage coaches crossing the barren plains were produced en masse;

Annie Oakley board game, Milton Bradley, USA, 1955, 18½ x 18½ in (47 x 47 cm).

noisemakers, penny whistles, sheriff's badges, nickel and chrome plated guns and rifles, the possibilities and variations were endless.

An integral part of Westerns, following the advent of color movies and television, was the hardware and other adornments worn by the cowboy and cowgirl actors. Many of the guns used were real, which shot blanks or had been adapted for use in shows. Beautifully engraved pistols and

Peacemaker die-cast cap-gun, Lone Star Toys, England, 8½ in long (22 cm).

The 'Ric-o-Shay' die-cast, Lone Star, England, 1950s, 9½ in (24 cm) long and, 'The Sheriff' cast-iron, J E Stevens, USA, c. 1930s, 8½ in long (22 cm).

the National Cowboy Hall of Fame and Western Heritage Centre in the USA. A fine cast-iron pistol made by **JE Stevens** of the USA in the 1930s is pictured here. The nickel-plated cast-iron is decorated in relief with simulated ivory plastic stocks which are inlaid with simulated rubies.

Antique toy cowboy outfits are extremely collectible, particularly the highly decorated cap guns and matching holsters endorsed by the legendary heroes. Predictably, manufacturers from countries far and wide were quick to join the wagon train or posse to the mother lode of toy sales. In the 1950s a British company **DCML** (Die-cast Machine Tools Limited) seized the opportunity by naming their products **Lone Star,** romantically linking their toy guns and other

rifles were almost de rigueur, some with carved ivory or bone stocks, inlaid with gold or silver. Artistically hand tooled leather holsters, belts and boots added to the glamour. Many of the originals are housed in Western museums such as the Autry Museum of Western History and products with the Lone Star state of Texas in the Wild West. **DCML** also made their cap-gun tooling available to overseas companies under license including France, Spain and Australia, which is where the **Peacemaker** pictured was made. This high-quality nickel-plated die-cast six-shooter is embossed in relief on both sides of the gun including the plastic handle, the star also coming 'straight from the horse's mouth', perhaps to emphasize the message. The holster is made from Australian leather. Another six-shooter, pictured here, labeled 'Ric O Shay' is also a **Lone Star** die-cast cap gun where the barrel is once again lavishly decorated in relief, the grips finished on faux cow horn. These guns were accurate replicas, although cast on a smaller scale to the real hardware. The **Lone Star** company took the initiative to establish a real gun museum to ensure the toys were as accurate and authentic as possible to the originals.

The 'Lone Star State' or 'Texas' in a name, has a dramatic, bloody and legendary history resulting from the Texans' futile battle to defend the Alamo at San Antonio in Texas in 1836. Texas, previously under Mexican rule, claimed independence in 1836 and the siege and desperate fight to hold the fortified mission, while greatly outnumbered, is etched in history. Famous westerners who perished included Davy

Battle of the Alamo, tin plate and plastic playset, marked 'Sears and Roebuck', USA (Marx version).

Crockett, Jim Bowie and Colonel Sam Travis. The battle proved merely a setback however, as that same year the Mexican army under Santa Ana was defeated. Texas became an independent republic with a flag bearing red, white and blue, or a single star or 'lone star' between 1836–1845 before they joined the Union.

Apart from cap guns produced by **Lone Star Products** an extensive range of toys were produced by other manufacturers including toy Bowie knives, **Davy Crockett** fully tasseled dress-up sets, coonskin caps, toy watches, a stage coach, and trading cards depicting the heroes and aspects of the battle. Pictured is a fine boxed 1950s playset **Battle of the Alamo** with figures and accessories marketed by Sears and Roebuck of the USA, similar to a set produced by Louis Marx. Quite unlike the **Lone**

Fort Apache, tin plate and plastic playset by Louis Marx, USA. An impressive set, with tin plate lithographed walls and over 100 accessories.

Native American Indians in a canoe, Timpo Toys, England, variegated plastic canoe, 5½ in long (14 cm) and Cowboy and Indian dime store and cereal premium figurines, 1950s, approx. 2½ in long (6 cm). Cast-iron figurines by Grey Iron, USA, 3 in high (8 cm).

Ranger, Davy Crockett (1786–1836) was a real-life western frontiersman hero, a Lieutenant Colonel in the Tennessee Militia and eventually a congressman gaining a seat in 1825. He was defeated in the 1835 elections. This loss became a catalyst for Crockett's revolutionary ride to Texas and his subsequent heroic demise at the hands of Santa Ana. **Davy Crockett** and the lengthy siege at the Alamo has been immortalized in books, comics, television movies and toys for well over a hundred years. Crockett was first featured in a movie in 1909 (silent) and over twenty movies since. Fess Parker starred in the role in a television series in the 1980s, and two successful Disney movies in 1955 and 1956. The **Davy Crockett** role has been played by actors including John Wayne, Jonny Cash and Billy Bob Thornton. The Sears tin plate **Fort Alamo** set pictured here is similar to many attractive Western tin plate playsets manufactured in America during the height of the Western craze. This set retains its original box which states the contents contain 'over 100 pieces'. The fort and adobe walls are beautifully lithographed and were supplied with plastic figures and other accessories such as ladders, fences with catwalks, a well, flagpole, tin-plate flag, cannons, along with horses and riders. The **Davy Crockett** figure depicts the frontiersman running with his rifle, wearing his traditional coonskin cap, while carrying a turkey he has just caught for supper. As it transpired, it was sadly his last supper.

Texans, in particular the nineteenth century Texas Rangers, earned a reputation for 'true grit', many eventually becoming lawmen or outlaws, fashioned in part by the uncompromising expansive landscape and bloody history of the Lone Star State. Several lines of a nineteenth century poem *The Devil in Texas* provide a somewhat severe literal perspective of the state of Texas about the time **Davy Crockett's** reputation grew to legendary status.

He lengthened the horns of the Texas steer,

he added an inch to the Jack Rabbit's ear,

he put mouths full of teeth in all of the lakes,

and under the rocks he put rattlesnakes,

the rattlesnake bites you, the scorpion stings,

mosquitoes delight you by buzzing his wings,

the heat in the summer's a hundred and ten,

too hot for the devil and too hot for men...' (abbrev.)

The battle for the Alamo and the state of Texas is well remembered through the many, toys, records, movies and games sold well after the victorious battle cry at San Jacinta, 'Remember the Alamo!'[25]

The most accessible and common Western playthings for boys and girls were **plastic dime store or mass-produced cowboy and Indian figurines** (or playsets) that usually appeared armed with pistols, rifles, bow and arrows, knives, tomahawks or lances – armed to the teeth actually – and in a variety of fighting poses.

Red Tomahawk and Soldiers Shooting Indians, gum cards, USA, 1933.

Red Tomahawk and Soldiers Shooting Indians (reverse of cards), USA, 1933, 2¾ x 2½ in (7 x 6 cm).

Scary stuff possibly, but as I remember, not for toddlers or the family dog, who seemed to find them particularly appetizing and chewed on them while teething or ate them in vast numbers. Not however the **Grey Iron cowboys and Indians** from the eponymously named **Grey Iron Casting Company** of Mt Joy, Pennsylvania, USA (1880s–1940). **Grey Iron** made a variety of cast-iron products including toy automobiles, tools, and a large range of toy soldiers including cowboys and Indians until the Second World War. With detailed castings and hand painted they are rather sculptural, like many cast-iron and Bakelite toys as we will see in other chapters.

Over the course of the twentieth century these figurative toys were manufactured in a range of materials including elastolin, aluminum, die-cast, lead, slush-cast metal and of course, from the 1950s, plastic. A few companies such as **Lido, Archer** and **Ajax** from the USA produced sets in plastic in the mid-twentieth century and many, remarkably, have survived, despite the plastic being quite brittle. The aluminum figures are quite rare and were made mainly by French companies **Quirilu, Mignalu** and **Aludo**. A Danish company **Krolyn** also made aluminum figures in the 1950s and three nicely cast and hand-painted aluminum cowboy and Indian figures are pictured in Chapter 4.

The plastic examples are cereal premiums or giveaways, similar to the millions of figures that were made by companies such as **Louis Marx, Ideal Toys** of the USA and **Airfix, Timpo, Britains, Herald, Cherilea,** and **Crescent Toys** of Britain. These toys were often included in sets and accompanied such accessories as forts, cabins, stagecoaches, and teepees with totem poles. The **Wells Fargo stagecoach** pictured was made by **Processed Plastics** USA and is a 1/24 scale toy. **Ideal Toys** in the USA made various versions including a **Roy Rogers** stagecoach and chuckwagon and a Pony Express stage, and most if not all came supplied with figures and accessories. Generally, the sets were unbelievably cheap to buy and extremely good value. A few dollars could buy you a complete set of sometimes up to 100 items. **Louis Marx Company** of the USA (1919–1978) claimed on most packaging or toy boxes they were the 'World's Largest Manufacturer of Toys'. In the 1930s **Lines Brothers (Triang Toys)** made the same claim, however **Marx** were arguably the largest toy manufacturer in the 1950s, which made the question also printed on their toy boxes 'One of the many Marx Toys, have you all of them?', somewhat amusing. Finely lithographed tin toys are also a feature of the legacy **Marx** toys have left for collectors the world over and several of the forts in these playsets are comprised of beautifully illustrated lithographed tin. They were certainly the biggest manufacturer of plastic toy playsets and in 1955 *Time* magazine named Louis Marx 'The toy king'. Western sets **Marx** produced included **Fort Apache, Fort Dearborn, Davy Crockett at the Alamo, The Lone Ranger Ranch, Rin Tin Tin at Fort Apache and The Battle of the Little Big Horn,** among others. The fine **Fort Apache** set illustrated here is contained in an illustrated tin-plate case which folds out to form the fort. The plastic figures and accessories in this set remain in unplayed with, mint condition.

Few people would possibly appreciate or realize now the significance of this **Louis Marx** toy set, inspired by Western heroes around the time of the Battle of the Little Big Horn in 1876. When the pride of the United States Army, the Seventh Cavalry, were effectively wiped out by a combination of Native American Indian tribes, the reverberation felt across the country by settlers and those on top of the totem pole from both nations, could only be described as total horror and anger on one side, and short-lived celebration and trepidation by the other. Newspaper headlines similar to the *Bismark Tribune's* 'Massacred – Gen Custer and 261 men the victims!' soon leaked to the world. The news-breaking event of 9/11 in New York over 100 years later in 2001 would perhaps be a comparable reaction. Led by a brave but overzealous army officer in Lieutenant Colonel George Custer, the unmitigated disaster at the Little Big Horn could be compared to other doomed battles such as Lord Cardigan's Charge of the Light Brigade in the Crimea in 1854, or the Gallipoli allied troop landings in 1915 during the First World War. Custer unwittingly, despite warnings from his chief scout, led his men into a gathering and village of over 1000 warriors. The result was over as one of the warriors described later, 'as quickly as it takes to eat a meal while hungry'. More than 200 cavalrymen were killed including Custer, his brother and a reporter. No soldiers at the Little Big Horn battle survived that day to tell the tale and most bodies were left severely mutilated. While the Sioux, led by warrior Chief Crazy Horse and other tribes, won the battle that day, the victory effectively signaled the beginning of the end for Native American tribes and their happy hunting grounds. From then on in the eyes of the army and many settlers, 'the only good Indian was a dead Indian'. This was an aphorism which developed from General Sheridan's reply to an Indian in 1867 who stated he was 'a good Indian'. Sheridan's response was 'The only good Indians I ever saw were dead.' The bad press and image for the North American native Indian was certainly reflected through toys produced well into the 1950s – Injuns were 'bad medicine'. Two **Western Series trading cards** pictured here dated 1933, one titled 'Soldiers Shooting Indians', depicts soldiers fighting Indians and states none too politely on the reverse, 'In return for the many bloody massacres perpetrated by the Indians, soldiers made punitive attacks on the Indian villages in order to instill in these savages a respect for Uncle Sam's Uniform' (card #239 **Western Series**). A 'real brave Indian' though according to card number 41, was Red Tomahawk (see illustration). 'He became friendly to the whites…and it was he who finally killed [actually assassinated or murdered] Chief Sitting Bull.' The gravity of the Little Big Horn event had faded somewhat by the time the Western boom reached its giddy heights in the late 1950s and 1960s. A nicely illustrated board game, **Battle of the Little Big Horn,** produced by **Waddingtons** of England in 1964 contains rules whereby Custer can defeat the 'Indians' by eliminating three 'Indian Chiefs'. Alternatively, if Custer and three of his officers are eliminated, the Indian side will win. Here it seems a game can change the course of history. The American West and the Battle of the Little Big Horn managed to infiltrate the popular music charts of the 1960s, defying the rise of rock and roll. American singer Larry Vern (V Erickson, 1936–2013) released a lighthearted pop song in 1960 titled 'Mr Custer', referencing the famous

Battle of the Little Big Horn board game, Waddingtons, England, 1964, 19½ x 10½ in (50 x

battle, '…Please Mr Custer, I don't want to go, there's a red skin out there, waiting to cut my hair…' The song shot like an arrow to number one earning Vern a gold disc. Charlie Drake released a song the same year titled 'Please Mr Custer, I Don't Want to Go' that also scored well, reaching number nine on the popular music charts.

Although the **Lone Ranger's** sidekick **Tonto** was a 'good Indian', including a few obligatory or compulsory scouts, it was not until more family-orientated Western television shows such as *Bonanza* in the 1950s and *The High Chaparral* reflected a moral high ground, showing respect and some acknowledgment of Indian rights as the indigenous people of North America. As Westerns became more 'politically correct' and sympathetic to the human condition, toy making soon fell into line. New Western sets appeared such as **Jonny and Jane West,** where a host of other accessories were included in order to survive out on the plains. Some of these included plastic saddles, chaps, bridles, hats, caps (including a coonskin version), a coffee pot and a fry pan for cooking up the buffalo steaks. Cowgirl Jane obviously reflected the flexibility of new soft plastics that had been developed for use in manufacturing, as she could 'pose for you 1001 different ways' according to the blurb on the packaging. Jane was also possibly a contender for the Olympics as a gymnast or perhaps a contortionist as well. While cowboy and Indian sets are not on any child's Christmas shopping lists these days, they definitely remain on others from another generation. Complete sets such as the tin plate **Marx Fort Apache set** are keenly sought by Western genre collectors today.

Despite the explosion of space toys associated with the space race during the 1950s and 1960s, Western themed toys held the drop on space toys during a golden period of toy making. From the 1970s however, the landscape changed dramatically, and space-related and science-fiction toys generated from blockbuster movies such as *Star Trek* and *Star Wars* brought about a decline in the Western-themed toy market. **DCML** of England for example produced more modern-era toy guns and eventually concentrated on the manufacture and export of die-cast toy vehicles while retaining the **Lone Star** logo. While the

Western-themed toy market had effectively galloped off into the sunset by the end of the twentieth century, it left an enduring and wonderful array of playthings and associated items for enthusiastic collectors long after the comparatively narrow history of the true nineteenth century Wild West.

Wild West checkers, fifty plastic playing pieces (figurines), Triang Toys Mini Models Ltd, England, c. 1960s, box 23 x 15 in (58.5 x 38 cm).

CHAPTER 3

TOY HORSES FOR TOY COURSES

It is not surprising that a large percentage of toys in the twentieth century were inspired by motor vehicles, trains, aircraft and spaceships. Transport was a key aspect of life in the developed world, one which evolved from horse-drawn coaches to spaceships orbiting the earth. These fantastic developments were of course all reflected and iconized with virtually every toy imaginable. The horse's influence over

transport and industry faded from the beginning of the twentieth century but endured throughout the decades to follow, mainly through equine sporting events and the games and toys that were subsequently produced.

We have already mentioned the importance of the gallant horse in the nineteenth century (Chapter 2) and much earlier, horses were also employed for

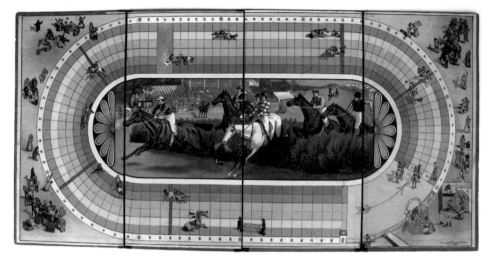

The Game of the Race, magnificently illustrated four-panel board, illustrated on reverse with a similar steeplechase course. Contained in a fruitwood case are six lead horses with removable interchangeable jockeys. Three finely crafted lead fences remain together with a water jump, a wooden shaker and two bone dice. The complete board measures 39 x 19½ in (100 x 49 cm), JW & S Spears, Bavaria.

other purposes, in particular, sports such as hunting, rodeo and racing. Chariot racing by the Romans and Greeks is depicted in ancient buildings and monuments dating back to the second and third centuries, which evolved eventually into today's harness racing, or more commonly known to many as the 'trots'.

Horseracing, colloquially termed the 'sport of kings' became more popular in the middle of the nineteenth century with organized events, particularly steeplechasing, together with flat races. Racehorses and gambling seem inextricably linked, eventually becoming extremely popular, widespread and more organized. Horse-racing games soon followed, which coincided nicely with the advent of more sophisticated mechanical printing processes. Early horseracing mechanical and board games were produced by companies such as **Spears** of England and Bavaria, **FH Ayres** of London, **Jacques** of France, **Wolverine** of America and later giants of board game making such as **Chad Valley** of England and **Parker Brothers** of America.

The superb large, four-panel, nineteenth century board game **The Game of the Race,** pictured here, is beautifully lithographed in full color, which is typical of many games of this period. Hand crafted fruitwood game cases stored the game pieces similar to this set, which hold painted lead race horses, removable painted lead jockeys, fences, bone dice and counters. Note how the jockeys rode upright in the saddle until the early twentieth century until the 'crouch' style of riding became de rigueur and proved crucial to cut seconds off track times.

Around this period **FH Ayres** of London produced a finely crafted hinged and wooden cased roulette-type racing game, **Sandown Race Game,** named after the then recently established famous race track in 1875. In this game the exquisitely illustrated horses with the jockeys in their silks pictured on the segmented rotating wheel are painted by the famous English sporting artist George Finch Mason (1850–1915) (see picture). The horses illustrated are famous race horses of the day, including Mr Pickwick (1878), Maid Marion (1886), Esmeralda, Dorothy, Waverly, and the now not so politically correct Peeping Tom. Interestingly, an example of this game is held in the collection of the Ashburton Museum in New Zealand. It was given to the Bennison children to play with on their long voyage while emigrating to New Zealand in the nineteenth century.

According to museum records however, it was commandeered by shipmates on the journey, which proves toys are not just for children.[26] Sandown's Grand International Steeplechase at the time offered a stake of £2130, a small fortune then and more than the Grand National Steeplechase at Aintree. The stake now totals over £1m.

While the artistically illustrated game boards paint a picture of grandeur embellishing the 'sport of kings', horseracing, similarly to a steeplechase, has experienced its ups and downs with a somewhat checkered career. Hurdle and steeplechase racing specifically are currently under threat and were banned in New South Wales, Australia for example

Sandown race game – roulette-type rotating wheel c. 1890.

Totalizator (the first all-mechanized totalizator), 'This Mechanical Age' cigarette card number 15 of 50, London Cigarette Company, 1937.

in 1997. Protests regarding the cruelty of hurdling and steeplechasing continue to this day, although conditions for the horses have improved somewhat since the nineteenth century. In 1835 a summary of the main steeplechase event at St Albans, England, concluded with the report that, 'King of Diamonds and Predictor had bolted, five horses remained in the brook, Grasshopper was galloped to a standstill, each rider had met with about three falls before the winning post and Payanini was found dead in his box a few days later. Fortunate Youth belied his name finishing last.'[27] Tragedy cruelly mixed with humor but these were the days when primary school children (and

ponies) were sent down mines to work. As late as 1910 steeplechasers in New Zealand could enter 'marathon' races, some up to 40 miles long. The steeplechaser Wanganui won a 40-mile event at Riverton in the South Island of New Zealand in April 1910 and '…ridden by the trainer Sam Trilford arrived at the end of the 40 miles nearly half an hour before anyone else.' He apparently showed no signs of distress. What was he on?[28]

One of the first official race meetings in the South Island of New Zealand was held at Hagley Park, Christchurch in December 1851. The fourth race was the 'Maori Race' with a stake of £3.3s, won by Jack-Fly.[29] Jack-Fly was in fact the only recorded starter, which could indicate some early race fixing. In 1852 over 600 people attended the Canterbury meeting which was reputedly the population of the province. The first all-mechanised totalizator (an Australian/New Zealand invention) was installed at New Zealand's Ellerslie Racecourse in 1913 to coincide with their big Easter Race Meeting (see picture).

While early horse-race games were promoted as exciting and fun for all, incredible race-horse stories are also rife in the annals of horseracing history, none more than one steeplechaser with a New Zealand connection. In 1904 connections shipped a horse, Moifaa, on a tortuous trip to England but the ship was rumored to have been wrecked before arrival. Reputedly the horse then swam 50 miles to an island, was eventually rescued, and to prove the benefits of ocean swimming and training, went on to win the Grand National Steeplechase that year at Aintree. This story, which is buried in several records of racing history (and Wikipedia), according to New Zealand racing historian John Costello, never happened. The feat of victory was certainly newsworthy and true, but the disaster on route was a fabrication by an over-enthusiastic and satirical American journalist. The New Zealand owner, Spencer Gollan, however had the last laugh. He sold the horse to King Edward VII no less, for 2000 guineas.[30]

King Edward VII (1841–1910) was a sportsman, yachtie, racehorse owner and eventually popular king who could be credited with raising the profile and general interest in horseracing in Europe before and during his relatively short reign. He raced the champion horse Persimmon who won both the St Ledger and The Derby in 1896. Famous author GK Chesterton's view of the times was that English people were '…not interested in the equality of men but the inequality of racehorses.' The popularity of parlor games and horse racing saw most game manufacturers produce a horserace game during this golden age of board-game making.

By the time King Edward had passed on in 1910, horse racing became a high profile and newsworthy sport with meetings attracting thousands of punters as well as the aristocracy. Many countries also boasted famous high-stake races, including France's Arc De Triomphe, America's Kentucky Derby and Australia's Melbourne Cup. It was these races which not only contributed to the establishment

New Sporting Game – Neues Sportlpief, AEB Germany, late nineteenth century. Stamped on reverse 'Made in Germany'. Rules are in German and English. The English rules are headed 'For Grown-up People'. The board can be reversed to enable a longer race to be held.

Ascot – The New Racing Game, a wooden cased precursor to Escalado race game. Note the finely crafted wooden and brass crank handle. The horses are lead, one having bolted before the start, Jacques & Son, London, c. 1900, 10 x 3½ in (25 x 9 cm).

of the thoroughbred racing industry, but the wonderful toys and games which followed in their hoof beats, several of which are illustrated here.

Mechanical horserace games were features of early European makers, many set up as clockwork go-round toys, the horses circulating on a pole in the fashion of a fairground ride or merry-go-round. Other mechanical games that followed included the perennial and well-known race game **Escalado** which was operated by a crank that ran and vibrated the

Gee Wiz horse racing game by Wolverine USA, 1925, pressed steel and tin plate with ball bearings and flywheel mechanism to propel tin-plate horses mounted on mahogany wooden frame, 29 in long (74 cm).

horses down the track. A more sophisticated version was produced by the **Wolverine Toy Company** of USA in the 1920s (Wolverine Supply and Manufacturing Company, Pittsburgh, USA). Their mechanical horserace games were named **Gee Wiz,** perhaps a good name for a sprinter. They produced various versions in tin plate and pressed steel with nicely shaped and lithographed tin-plate horses. The tin-plate track and rails are mounted on a wooden base. Unusually, the horses are propelled down the track by steel ball bearings (see illustration). Even larger sets, electrically operated, were made for gaming arcades and casinos. **Wolverine** (1903–1970) made quality toys, particularly during the period this race game was produced. They advertised their games as 'beautifully lithographed in many colors on heavy gauge metal and furnished with durable waterproof lacquer. They are sanitary, can be washed

Race Play by M & L Plastics, Melbourne, Australia, Bakelite c. 1940, horses 3 in long (7.5 cm).

when necessary. They are indestructible and will outlast any cardboard game.'[31] Their claim was quite true if these toys are any example. To confirm the popularity of horseracing at this time **Wolverine** also made **Deck Derby,** a horseracing game especially designed for playing on ocean liners, and **Neck and Neck,** a cheaper action board game. **Wolverine** made some great toys and are a somewhat underrated toy maker from the past.

A rare and early but much simpler version of this game named **Raceplay**

was made during the 1930s in early plastic or Bakelite by **M and L Plastics** of Melbourne. The horses and their jockeys are beautifully molded in mottled Bakelite and the example here is a fine, near-new example in the original box. This game is unique in that it is one of the very few games that has immortalized famous Australian and New Zealand racehorses, not the least being the most famous of all in Phar Lap. Each horse is named on the brown Bakelite finishing gates (as opposed to starting gates) including Phar Lap, Ajax, Carbine, Peter Pan, Windbag, Shannon, Bernborough and Flight. Numerous books and a film were made detailing and dramatizing the tragic story of one of the greatest racehorses of all time. Such was the New Zealand–bred Phar Lap's dominance after winning the 1930 Melbourne Cup, and at one stage winning twenty-three from twenty-six races, bookies would no longer accept bets on the horse and owners and trainers avoided racing against him. Eventually, after eight further wins in a row but handicapped by cruel weights, in 1932 he was shipped via New Zealand to Agua Caliente, Mexico for a specially arranged, unprecedented US$100,000 stakes race, pitted against the best horses available from the Americas. Against all odds, including injury, the majestic horse won in record time to cement his place in history. Two weeks later, not even commiserations from the King of England or America's famous personality of the times, Will Rogers, could console the connections when the horse died tragically in Los Angeles of suspected accidental arsenic poisoning or fatal colic. Ironically, the phenomena of a nation in mourning was repeated some three years later when part Native American Will Rogers himself was tragically killed in an air crash in Alaska in 1935. Lariat extraordinaire, writer, Wild West showman, movie star and people's politician, Rogers had in fact visited New Zealand in 1902 when only twenty-three years old in a traveling circus, billed as the 'Cherokee Kid'. A New Zealand newspaper reported he could lasso 'the business end of a flash of lightning'.[32]

Horseracing and associated games were popular even in times of trouble. The Melbourne Cup in the 1930s was well attended and the talk of Australasia during one of the most depressed economic times in history. Under worse deprivations a popular game titled **Horse Racing Tonight** was invented, developed and later manufactured for sale by prisoners of war in Germany during the Second World War. Pictured, this game was eventually manufactured for commercial sale by quality card and board game maker **Pepys** of England. It is rather sophisticated with cardboard fences, Bakelite shakers, counters, dice, and a detailed, four-panel fold-out race track contained in an illustrated slip case with a betting-rules booklet listing odds. Prisoners of war had more problems than time on their hands, nevertheless as the rules include a statement suggesting that the odds listed in the booklet are the 'Results of over 600 races', at least some fun was obviously experienced during their long and grueling

Phar Lap with regular jockey Jim Pike.

American Crayon Company Old Faithful paint box set advertisement, 1928, New York Toy Fair featuring a colorful race meeting 12 x 8½ in (30 cm x 22 cm).

Horse Racing Tonight four-panel fold-out board in illustrated slip case, six phenolic resin or Catalin horses, cardboard fences, Bakelite counters and shakers, wooden dice, rules book, 47 x 14 in (120 cm x 36 cm). Made by Pepys, England 1940s, designed by POW in Germany.

Catalin and Bakelite horses for Horse Racing Tonight game, c. 1946.

internment. Despite the game's attention to detail, it does however retain a somewhat folk-art charm with quite sculptural Catalin or Bakelite molded horses with integral jockeys mounted on wooden blocks. The number 6 horse would have originally been white but has aged to yellow over time, a common occurrence with formaldehyde molding resins. Pepys also manufactured a similar game, again invented by POWs from Marlag and Milag Nord prison camps in Germany, called **Horsie Horsie.** The game was similar in design without the added adventure or vice of gambling.

Another uncommon race game illustrated here is **Spotto** by **Chad Valley,** made in 1922. Unusually, the horses (or colored discs) are inside the circular board, which is shaken to determine the winners after all bets are placed. The winning horses (colored discs) appear in the placing holes near the bottom of the hollow board. Rules on the reverse suggest odds on which the banker could pay out. An earlier version of this game was produced in France.

A most attractive and appealing horseracing game, illustrated here, **The Lucky Race Game,** was made by **Burnett** of Birmingham, England in the early twentieth century. This superbly lithographed board, shown here, is made of tin plate accompanied by finely lithographed tin-plate horses with 'jockeys up'. The horses, together with dice and counters of bone, are contained in a cylindrical tin-plate shaker. The picturesque steeplechase imagery on the playing board is designed within a sectional horseshoe that numbers up to 100. The rules and title of the board game appear on the reverse – no gambling or betting suggested here though. **Burnett** also made a classically illustrated tin plate snakes and ladders game which was as equally alluring, together with a tin plate draughts or checkers board. A further string to their bow was the production of tin plate and clockwork trucks and cars. While **Burnett** were relatively small in the overall game, they have left a fine legacy of toy making which tin plate toy and game collectors greatly admire and appreciate.

Further evidence of the contribution to experimentation and innovation through toy manufacturing is a French racing game made around the turn of the twentieth century. The horses illustrated here, made as 'flats', have been cut from a translucent celluloid sheet, a somewhat transitional material, which was invented as an alternative to ivory and tortoiseshell, which was becoming too expensive and harder to obtain even 120 years ago. A couple of them are cut from faux tortoiseshell patterned flexible sheeting. Somewhat presciently and possibly because of early 'save the planet' endeavors (but more likely material shortages), these artistically patterned early plastic-type sheets were more commonly used at the time as an alternative to tortoiseshell in the manufacture of combs and to decorate cigarette cases, toilet sets and hair brushes. Here, most unusually, we see toy racehorse playing pieces, true precursors to dime-store plastic soldiers, animals, cowboys and Indians and other figures churned out in their millions

Spotto horseracing/betting game by Chad Valley, 1922, 8½ in diameter (22 cm approx.).

The Lucky Race Game, superbly illustrated two-panel hinged tin plate gameboard, horses, bone dice and counters, the cylindrical container also serves as a shaker. Burnett, Birmingham, England 1903, 11 x 11 in (28 x 28 cm).

Cardigan Bay jigsaw puzzle, Holdson Games New Zealand, c. 1966.

Celluloid horse race game pieces, France c. 1900, 2 ½ in long (6 cm).

Organized harness racing was arranged in Europe and North America in the eighteenth century, the Dutch with the bragging rights having founded trotting and harness racing in New Amsterdam (now New York) in 1810. The slot racing game, pictured, made by Lincoln Toys of New Zealand, is quite rare as it was produced on the back of a crescendo of popularity for slot car racing sets and during a time when harness racing was at a peak with a famous New Zealand/ American pacer, Cardigan Bay. During the 1960s this horse's fame and popularity almost eclipsed that of Phar Lap when he won ten consecutive races amongst forty-three wins, nine seconds and three thirds in Australasia. Eventually leased to famous American reinsman Mr Stanley Dancer, the champion ended his racing days in the USA having won an incredible total of eighty races and becoming the first standard-bred to win over a million dollars. Cardigan Bay appeared on the *Ed Sullivan Show* in 1968 along with The Beach Boys pop band who were also at the height of their fame. As part of the lease agreement, the horse was returned to New Zealand where he retired to Puketutu Island, a retreat and stud farm at the time in the Manukau harbour of Auckland, owned by liquor industry magnate, Sir Henry Kelliher. Pictured is

some fifty years later. The game board which accompanies these horses, while large, is somewhat disappointing, with minimal illustration in green and black. Chapter 6 deals in depth with further wonderful toys made from Bakelite, Catalin and early plastics.

a rare jigsaw puzzle of **Cardigan Bay** made by **Holdson Games** of New Zealand which was produced at the time he achieved the million-dollar mark.

Although electric slot car racing sets were also at the height of their popularity, it is perhaps unsurprising, albeit unusual, that during this wave of general popularity and international fame for Cardigan Bay, a **slot 'harness' or trotting racing set** was produced for the market. Instead of cars we have two pacers, with sulkies (carts) and their reinsmen (drivers) as the main protagonists. As with all slot car sets, they are activated by battery operated controllers, while the rails are electrified. This is a large sized game, the box measuring 27½ inches long (70 centimetres). Although this toy box

Slot horse racing, electric hi-rev slot set, similar to slot cars, 39 x 23 in (99 cm x 58½ cm approx.), Lincoln International New Zealand (made in Hong Kong), c1968. Horses and sulkies 6½ in long (16½ cm).

states 'Made in New Zealand', it is likely the toy was produced in the main in Hong Kong, and boxed and assembled in New Zealand, as with many battery operated or more sophisticated toys marketed and sold by this firm. Unfortunately, similarly with slot car sets, a two-horse race soon induced boredom, which is possibly why these pacers have been raced extremely lightly by their owners. Harness racing or 'the trots', for better or worse, depending on whether you are a horse, a trainer, or a punter, are on the wane in most countries.

The **Jackpot** race game pictured was produced in the 1970s during an anomalous time in the New Zealand thoroughbred industry where the market appeared popular and buoyant, yet provincial racing clubs were losing their grip on the presence of the punter and his gambling dollar. Following a member bringing their attention to the overseas success of jackpot meetings, the Bay of Plenty Racing Club became the first club in New Zealand to introduce accumulator 'on course' jackpot betting on the twenty-second of March 1969. Jackpots entailed selecting the winner of six races on the day (no easy task), however gambling syndicates and betting professionals soon materialized who eventually hit the headlines. The response from the public was phenomenal with courses finding up to 50,000 people queued to obtain jackpot betting slips, when smaller provincial clubs were set up to handle only a few thousand punters.

Jackpot betting run independently by Jockey clubs 'on course' eventually became a victim of their own sensational success and a fraught Te Awamutu jackpot meeting proved to be the final phenomenon. The huge stakes had attracted the attention of the New Zealand Treasury and New Zealand Inland Revenue Department, with whispers of 'black money', tycoon type betting syndicates, wholesale community gambling and tax avoidance. By 1973 racing club managed jackpots were outlawed.

In 1987 Lotto gaming arrived in New Zealand and with all the hoopla, television live draws, and flashy promotions, buying a lotto ticket became as much a part of Kiwi culture as watching the All Blacks and wearing jandals to the barbeque. **Lotto** board games originally introduced in the nineteenth century conversely held little appeal, like many other board games by this time. The **Jackpot** racing game is one of the few reminders of a momentous if not controversial phenomena of horse racing.

While a general decline in support of the racing industry has persisted, particularly with the ever-increasing momentum of government backed Lotto, online sports

The Jackpot race game, Holdson Products New Zealand, c. 1970.

gambling and casinos, thoroughbred racing has in racing parlance 'battled on well' to maintain its popularity. The horseracing games here represent a wide range crafted over a hundred-year period reflecting the popularity and impact of the sport, the fun of having a bet and the history and emotions associated with the horses and their connections. In a resounding acknowledgment of the skill and ingenuity of the manufacturers and designers of these games, collectors worldwide also press on to seek out, celebrate and preserve the games for posterity and hopefully education. Despite world wars, pandemic diseases, revolutionary new methods of transport, economic booms and busts, earthquakes, fixed races, betting plunges, jackpots, bankrupt bookies, horse doping, allegations of cruelty and goodness knows what else, thoroughbred horseracing, breeding and having a bet remain significant industries and popular pastimes which do in fact canter along with us today.

CHAPTER 4

ENDURING FOLK ART, DREAM CARS AND TOYS IN ALUMINUM

Aluminum is a wonder product we now take for granted and similarly to plastics in a historical context, a relatively new material. Unlike plastics, however, aluminum was used sparingly for toys but there are of course exceptions to every rule and toy making in aluminum in New Zealand was, unusually, for one company, the rule for almost fifty years. Aluminum is now widely used in the manufacture of componentry for real vehicles and this usage has an interesting back story, as have the aluminum toys pictured in this chapter. When aluminum was first produced in America in the nineteenth century, it sold for the same price as silver and at one point was valued higher than gold. As a material for general use in manufacturing, aluminum

Bohn advertisement for aluminum bodied vehicles, *Fortune* magazine, USA, November 1945, p. 241.

Wright Brothers biplane, The Flyer, Evolution of Flight, Sanitarium Health Food Co., #33, c. 1960s, 3½ x 2¼ in (9 x 6 cm).

only became readily available in the late nineteenth century and parallels exist here with the invention and development of plastics, which also changed the course of history. One of the first aluminum consumer products was a kettle made by the Pittsburg Production Company and the first aluminum frying pan did not appear until 1890. By 1924 forty companies were registered as manufacturers of kitchenware from aluminum. Teddy Roosevelt (whose name would soon become synonymous with the teddy bear) led his roughriders

into battle in the Spanish American war carrying an aluminum canteen. The new lightweight product was responsible for significant advancements in aircraft design and in fact Orville Wright's first flight was powered by an aluminum engine. Aircraft were soon framed or clad with aluminum and the product's unrivaled qualities were eventually proved beyond doubt when Russia's *Sputnik* became the first spacecraft to orbit the earth.

In 1901 the first aluminum car engine was made by Karl Benz. The Golden Arrow landspeed record car was not surprisingly fitted with an aluminum body in 1929 and although other marques experimented with aluminum bodywork, the higher cost precluded its long-term employment. The postwar 1947 issue of *Fortune* magazine published an article

Pink 'Surrey' Jeep DJ3A/CJ3B 1962–1964 by Tonka Toys, USA, pressed steel and plastic 10 inches long [25cm]. The 'Surrey' Jeep was originally designed for a US postal contract and the surplus Jeeps and parts were transformed into pink Surreys, a combination of the DJ3A and CJ3B.

questioning the longevity of new materials such as aluminum and plastics. 'Cars may be lighter, but they will not be made of aluminum…except for small parts so long as those metals in the raw cost up to 10 times as much as steel…'[33] Paradoxically, in the same issue Bohn Aluminum and Brass of Detroit advertised a futuristic ten-axle (twenty wheels) aluminum bodied road train[34] (see picture).

In the 1950s aluminum was promoted as the new wonder material for external wall claddings. Aluminum siding had already been used twenty years earlier in the construction of the iconic Chrysler and Empire State buildings but fallout from nuclear bombs had hardly settled before aluminum imitation clapboards (weatherboards) were widely promoted. These clapboards were invented by an

Indiana businessman, Frank Hoess who had originally designed them in steel.[35] In 1947 a complete housing development in Pennsylvania was clad in aluminum clapboards. Aluminum windows were first advertised by Premier Metal Products of Arizona in 1947 as 'now an aluminum window for modern homes – a lifetime of loveliness for your home.'[36]

Before long aluminum clapboards became a boom industry, particularly in the north-east region of USA outside the hurricane and storm belt. Existing home owners were also in the firing line from overzealous door to door salesmen and the classic 1987 movie *Tin Men* starring Danny De Vito and Richard Dreyfuss referred directly to the dubious and illegal practices of aluminum siding salesmen during this era.

Henry J Kaiser (1882–1967), major American industrialist and aluminum magnate, ventured into car making in the 1940s, eventually promoting aluminum for use in motor vehicle production. Kaiser was a pivotal entrepreneur, forming Kaiser Aluminum in 1946, eventually cultivating a whole spectrum of industry including mining, production, manufacturing and broadcasting. Kaiser was immersed in building dams and levees from 1931 including the Hoover Dam on the Colorado River, which took six years to build.[37] In a connection as remote as New Zealand he assisted with the design of the major Tiwai Point aluminum smelter which was opened in 1971.

Seventy years ago however Henry J Kaiser decided it was time to build cars, specifically those with aluminum bodies or componentry. The genesis of **Kaiser** cars began when Henry J Kaiser formed a joint venture with

'In a Few Years Aluminum Cars', Henry J Kaiser's aluminum dream cars.

'Aluminum and Glass Car', *Science & Mechanics* article, October 1951, designed by Herb Weissinger and Kaiser Frazer.

Jeep by FunHo! Toys New Zealand (1948–1974), aluminum, 4½ in long (11.5 cm).

1949/50 Kaiser convertible, Toy Founders, Detroit, Michigan, plastic, 8½ in long (22 cm).

The Mattel dream cars, 1953/1954, plastic and tin plate, 10 to 10½ in long (26–27 cm).

Graham Paige Motors in 1945. By 1948 300,000 cars had come off the production line. In an exhibition of further innovation, in 1953 Kaiser built a fibreglass sports car named the Kaiser-Darrin-Frazer 161. He also purchased the **Willys–Overland Corporation**, famous for their World War II 'Jeep'. By 1955 however, **Kaiser Motors** were no longer, despite the fact Kaiser had purchased aluminum processing plants to assist with their car-building venture. An advertisement, illustrated here,

'In a few years aluminum cars' indicates his desire to sell aluminum componentry to the car makers of Detroit. As we will see in Chapter 5, the 1950s announced the arrival of the space age together with spacecraft inspired dream and concept cars. The 1950s dream cars, pictured, tout names such as The Haleakala and The Mehehune, which refer to Kaiser's association with Hawaii, where he resided from 1955. He built the Hawaiian Village Hotel including a large geodesic dome-shaped theater and entertainment center, made, of course, from aluminum and glass. The transportation service vehicles were pink Jeeps, adding a new dimension to his 'general purpose' military-designed runabout.[38] A fine toy model of the pink **Surrey Jeeps** that buzzed around Hawaii made by the significant American toymaker **Tonka Toys** (est. 1946, from 1991, Hasbro) is pictured. **Tonka** purchased two pink **Surrey Jeeps** in 1962 that they used for promotional purposes. The jeeps were originally designed for a USA postal contract that expired in 1959. The surplus jeeps were transformed into pink 'Surreys', the fringed top referring to early horse-drawn vehicles. Launched by **Tonka** in 1962 with a suggested retail of $1.50, the toys today are somewhat undervalued at around $150. The real jeeps featured in the

New Zealand FunHo! Toys, c. 1940s and 1950s – copies of Arcade and Hubley, USA, aluminum, 3½–12½ in long (9–32 cm).

classic Elvis Presley movie *Blue Hawaii* (1961) and 'The King' purchased a Jeep Surrey on his return to Memphis following filming. The restored jeep resides at Graceland to this day. Tonka toy jeeps were also released in conjunction with the John Wayne movie *Hatari*, where the laconic cowboy actor was cast 'ropin and ridin'' wild animals from a Jeep rather than a horse

Ironically, the scarce **Kaiser car** pictured here is made from plastic, and the **Tonka Jeep** pressed steel, probably not materials Kaiser would have necessarily approved of. The toy car is made by **Toy Founders** of Detroit, Michigan and appears to be a 1949/50 four-door convertible. It may have been a promo model as the toy is impressed with the name 'Kaiser' in relief on the trunk (boot). On the other hand, Mr Kaiser may have sanctioned **Fun Ho!'s** aluminum version, although it was an unauthorized and rather crude result, similarly to **Fun Ho!'s** 1948 aluminum **Willy's station wagon** number 172. It is also ironic that a small company from New Zealand progressed to

FunHo! tractor box depicting the home of FunHo! Toys, New Plymouth, with New Zealand's iconic Mt Taranaki in the background.

FunHo! Oliver Tractor (1942–1976), aluminum, 5½ in long (14 cm).

Lincoln Zephyr with trailer (1944–1945) – copy of Hubley Toys models, aluminum, FunHo! Toys New Zealand.

manufacture more cars than Mr Kaiser (albeit toys) in aluminum, which we shall see later in this chapter.

Kaiser has a connection also to the ill-fated **Tucker Motor Car Company** and a sports car designed by Alex Tremalis (1914–1991) who joined **Kaiser-Frazer** in 1951.[39] Tremalis was involved in the design of the famous Cord 810/812, Tucker cars and Fords in 1957. A new sports car was announced by the Kaiser-Frazer Group in 1951 but seemingly a different version of the car appeared in *Science and Mechanics* magazine in October 1951. The article announced 'Kaiser-Frazer plans aluminum-glass car – designed by Herb Weissinger' – also a **Kaiser-Frazer** stylist. The text stated, 'note the predominant fenders and especially the aeronautical treatment of the rear fenders – body would be of aluminum, top of glass and aluminum.'

In 1956/57 Alex Tremalis and Bill Balla designed the futuristic **Ford X 2000** concept car, which was similar to the friction drive toy dream cars, pictured, made by **Mattel** in 1953. The box states 'The Mattel Dream Car – the only car of its kind in the world of toys.' The black version is also made by Mattel and is dated 1954, with a design change to the tail-lights. In 1950 the Kaiser-Frazer Corporation released another car, the eponymous **Henry J**, a low budget car ($1299) for 'less affluent buyers who could only afford a used car', yet for $200 more a Chevrolet could be driven off the showroom floor. In a last throw of the dice, the car was rebranded as an 'All State' and sold through Sears Roebuck & Co. By 1955 **Kaiser Aluminum** effectively removed itself from car making, concentrating on the classic and iconic jeep. By 1970 Kaiser's pet vehicle was owned by **American**

Motors. Despite a relatively shortlived foray into the turbulent automotive world, Kaiser aluminum became one of the top three aluminum producers in the world. Henry J Kaiser even boasts a connection to our Westerns chapter when he funded the popular television Western series *Maverick*. Mr Kaiser was inducted into the Hall of Fame in 2009.

I do not know when the first aluminum toy was produced or who by but while it may seem surprising, it appears the most significant manufacturer of aluminum toys was a company named **Underwood Engineering** from New Zealand. Their toys do however have a direct link to famous toy makers from America and England, which will become clear as the quite bizarre story develops.

Aluminum **Fun Ho!** toys, made by Underwood Engineering since the 1940s are also arguably to date the most significant toys made in New Zealand. The history of the company is quite unusual for several reasons, not the least for the feat of producing cast aluminum toys for over forty years. The other reason, though not so noble, was circumventing copyright by producing copies of toys made previously in America or other countries. While I do not profess to be the first collector of early sand-cast **Fun Ho!** toys (and I am not), I

was one of the first, collecting them from bric-a-brac shops and markets in the late 1970s. My interest stemmed from the fact I had started collecting mainly cast-iron, pressed steel and plastic American toys and realized **Fun Ho!** toys were copies of mainly **Arcade** and **Hubley Toys** from the 1930s. Rather crudely cast in aluminum, I regarded these **Fun Ho!** toys as 'folk art'. By the 1970s these toys from the 1940s and 1950s, previously domiciled mainly in New Zealand preschoolers' sandpits, had survived well but were cloaked in faded and patchy pastel paint, the cast aluminum in some cases smoothed to a shiny patina giving the toy a unique and a very appealing presence to an offbeat toy collector. While mainly transportation toys, there seemed no particular theme to **Fun Ho!** toys, the scale and age completely random from a 6½ inch (17 centimetres) 1929 **Model A Ford** to a 2 inch-long (5 centimetre) tractor. I became somewhat obsessed at one stage, matching the Fun Ho! castings to the original cast-iron toy, which I am sure even fewer (if any) **Fun Ho!** collectors were curious enough to do.

The founder of **Underwood Engineering** and **Fun Ho! Toys** was Jack Underwood (1908–1979), an entrepreneurial character who had previously won a gold medal for model

International panel van (1945–1958) – copy of Arcade Toys van, beside Fun Ho!'s later die-cast toys, FunHo! Toys New Zealand, 9 in long (23 cm).

making while a teenager at Wellington Technical College in 1925.[40] Underwood began manufacturing lead slush cast toys from old imported molds or copied toys from overseas makers such as **Barclay Toys** from the USA and **Britains** and **Jo Hill Company** of England in the late 1930s. Renditions of Barclay's firepumper, streamline racer and stake-bed truck were some of the first vehicles he produced along with toy soldiers, other figures and farm animals.[41]

Toy maker Jack Underwood was a savvy and innovative businessman having already designed an automotive children's safety seat in 1936, which was a market leader for twenty-five years.[42] A game-changer in 1938 for New Zealand manufacturers and importers however was the introduction of import licensing, where local manufacturers would be protected against imports and employment opportunities and regional development could become firmly established. As the proverb goes, 'Man plans, God laughs' and the small matter of a World War curtailed Underwood's plans for toy making considerably. Before long however Underwood found himself in a non-ferrous foundry making aluminum, bronze and brass componentry for military contracts. Every cloud has a silver lining and silver was the color of the material he was to use to conjure up toys for the next forty years.

Eion Young (1939–2014), a New Zealand born motoring author and journalist who wrote for *Autocar* magazine for thirty years, interviewed Jack Underwood's family, who maintained the cast-iron toys which were originally copied in the 1940s were his children's toys.[43] He may have obtained sample import license through his initial company, **Houghton Steel Products,** but by whatever means, the classic Mervyn Taylor designed **Fun Ho!** logo was registered in 1940 and by 1941 **Fun Ho!** produced its first toys, copied largely from **Arcade Manufacturing** of Freeport, Illinois and **Hubley Manufacturing** of Pennsylvania, USA. These toy companies were two of the largest cast-iron toy makers in the USA during the 1920s and 1930s. Countless numbers of these toys were melted down for the war effort in the 1940s and many that remain have become highly prized and valuable. While cast-iron, slush cast and rubber toys from the USA lacked the finesse and detail of their many English, French and German counterparts (e.g. die-cast **Dinky** toys, German and French tin-plate toys), the artistic and sculptural qualities of cast-iron toys in particular hold, for many collectors, more appeal. Many of the sand-cast aluminum toys made by **Fun Ho!** In the 1940s were copies of toys designed and made by **Arcade** and **Hubley** as far back as 1927 and toys produced in the 1930s. These include **Arcade's 1920s dollhouse furniture** (e.g. FH #98) and their **Model A Ford Fordor** (FH #420). Mr Barry Young, a long-time employee of Underwood's, published valuable historical pamphlets in the late 1990s ('Fun Ho! Repro') after the

Advertisement for Bedford truck, 'Buy British' *Truck and Bus Transportation* magazine, April 1957.

Aluminum J2 Bedford tip tray truck by FunHo! Toys of New Zealand, c. 1957–1959, 13½ in long (34.5 cm), the truck is carrying a FunHo! cast aluminum bulldozer. Australia and particularly New Zealand were locked into trade agreements whereby most cars and trucks originated CKD (unassembled) from 'Blighty' (England). Bedford trucks superseded the old underpowered Austins and were a common feature on Australian and New Zealand roads in the 1950s and 1960s.

Arcade's cast-iron Model A Ford (1930) beside FunHo!'s aluminum copy (1964–1965), approx. 6½ in long (16.5 cm).

FunHo! Austin Atlantic, aluminum with yellow casein wheels, early model, FunHo! Toys, 1952–1965, 5½ in long (15 cm).

Fun Ho! Museum opened. He noted that his company copied other toys as late as the 1960s. Among other copies he quotes the **Fun Ho! Dump Truck** #326 (copied from an unidentified English plastic toy) and **Fun Ho! #325, Delivery Truck** (copied from an American **Auburn** rubber toy). The first two aluminum sand-cast toys produced by Underwood were copies of an **Arcade 1937 Oliver tractor** (FH #81, 1942–1976) and a small **Dinky streamline racing car** (FH #76, 1941–1953). The **1937 Arcade tractor** was at this stage quite a recent copy – although they produced it until 1976. Conversely, the **Model A Ford Fordor,** a copy of **Arcade's 1929 Model A,** was not cast until 1964 – and only for one year (see pictures).

Similarly to children of the Midwest and east coast of America who were surrounded by agricultural farming vehicles and implements, farming toys also proved popular with New Zealand children. A multitude of tractors, trailers, implements, road signs and accessories were produced, originating again largely from **Arcade, Hubley** and **SlikToys.** It is believed either the **Hubley, Arcade, Lansing** or **AMT** companies wrote to Underwood at some time requesting that he desist from this somewhat questionable practice.[44] The result however was not what

74

they envisioned when Underwood geared up to produce an even wider range of toys. Now protected by New Zealand's import licensing and tariffs, together with a rather austere and limited range of opposing imports, **Fun Ho!'s** production was able to continue somewhat unabated.

By the end of the Second World War, the **Arcade Manufacturing Company** in the USA had effectively closed, no longer producing cast-iron toys. **Hubley Manufacturing Company** meanwhile changed production methods to die-cast metal and also employed the recently developed product, plastic molding resins. Hubley USA's initial postwar range consisted of their die-cast and plastic **Hubley Kiddie toys** and it was from these toys together with **Slik,** a new range of **Fun Ho!** aluminum sand-cast toys would surreptitiously emerge (e.g. FH #403, 533, 408, 400). Over the years **Fun Ho!** altered some of these toys while also developing some of their own and their dominance in the supply of New Zealand sandpit toys remained fairly impregnable during this postwar period. Underwoods arguably became the largest producer of aluminum toys in the world after **Lancing (Slik Toys)** also converted production to plastic injection molding in the early 1950s.

A dearth of modern cars plied the roads in New Zealand in the 1950s and 1960s, many daily runners dating from the 1930s and 1940s. Most overseas visitors to New Zealand in the two decades after the war expressed amazement at the old cars in daily use in New Zealand. My father ran a 1948 Dodge in 1966 and one of my first cars in 1971 was a 1938 Chevrolet, purchased for $90. I guess, on reflection, we were the Cuba of transportation in the South Pacific. Even so, toddlers in the sandpit would not have squabbled over a **1929 Fun Ho! Ford** in the sandpit in 1964, which would account for the short-lived production run. The model pictured here is a rare mint original which I purchased from Barry Young the day before the opening of the Fun Ho! Toy Museum in 1990. He had found some unpainted castings in a factory crate which had never been assembled or painted. There were three **Model A Ford** cars included which he assembled and painted for the opening of the museum; two were for sale. These are very rare and the value is now equal to an original **Arcade Ford Model A,** despite the fact it is rather a crude casting. Similarly, the **Fun Ho! International panel van,** the **1948 Ford V8 sedan,** the **Lincoln Zephyr with caravan,** are copies of **Arcade** and **Hubley** toys respectively. These are now quite rare and valuable Fun Ho! toys, with the car and caravan quite remarkably now exceeding prices for the original Hubley set. This leaves no doubt there is value, desirability and perennial interest in folk art (see pictures).

In the 1960s **Fun Ho!** entered the world of miniature die-cast production when they bought existing toy tooling from an Australian company, **Streamlux.** These miniature toy vehicles were effectively produced in opposition to, or complementary to, **Lesneys Matchbox Toys,** which had taken the world by storm. Underwood was once again quick to take advantage of bilateral trade agreements and import license restrictions as the toy license available to New Zealand importers fell far below the insatiable demand for both **Matchbox, Dinky** and other toys. The author recalls queuing for two hours outside a Woolworths department store in the early 1960s, clutching his hard-earned pocket money to purchase a maximum of two allocated **Matchbox toys.**

The **Fun Ho!** range of miniature vehicles sold well through retailers and Mobil petrol stations and significant amounts were exported to Australasia. The author completed export documentation for regular shipments to Australia and the Pacific Islands whilst in the employ of Freightways New Zealand Limited in the early 1970s. Some were even shipped to America and the Fun Ho! Museum claims over eight million of these toys were produced between 1965 and 1982.[45] An impressive range of nickel and copper plated miniature vehicles were also produced which are now highly sought by toy collectors (see pictures).

In the 1930s **Lines Brothers** of England claimed to be the largest toy manufacturer in the world. They manufactured a huge variety of toys including trikes, scooters, dolls and dollhouses, as well as pedal cars and prams under the **Triang** and **Pedigree** label. They established branches throughout the Commonwealth, including New Zealand in 1946, and were soon to become the largest importer and manufacturer of these products in New Zealand. The Lines brothers, William, Walter and Arthur, would have no doubt appreciated Jack Underwood's resourcefulness and commitment to his toy development. William Lines was a keen participant in a wide variety of outdoor sports, Walter was a driven businessman and Arthur was known for his sense of humor – which one would hope is compulsory in the toy world. By 1979 however, many traditional toy companies were floundering. It was somewhat poignant that a small manufacturer who

Aluminum pick-up and sedan, Slik Toys, USA, c. 1949, 6¾ in long (17.5 cm).

began making toys in his basement in Wellington some forty years earlier, now found himself in a position to buy the **Lines Brothers' New Zealand business.** To his immense satisfaction, in 1979 Jack Underwood cobbled together a deal, purchasing the total plant and branding of Lines Brothers' Auckland, New Zealand operation. New and colorful labels were developed with a clown depicted holding a triangle within a triangle. Underneath the clown figure were the lyrical words 'Triang by Underwood of Inglewood', referencing the new relationship. Unfortunately, the Underwood Engineering Company's purchase of Lines Brothers brands and the plant in 1979 proved to be somewhat ill-advised. It was soon revealed that much of the plant required new tooling.[46] Fun Ho!'s larger than life founder, Jack Underwood, sadly passed away the same year. By now many light industries in New Zealand were under serious threat after the freeing-up of trade and the eventual abolishment of import licensing. Many toy companies, both in New Zealand and worldwide, were forced to close due to Asian sweatshop mass toy production and the rise in the popularity of computerized gaming. **Lines Brothers** and **Underwood Engineering** also eventually succumbed, and toy production ceased in 1982. The **Fun Ho!** factory in Inglewood closed in 1987 following almost fifty years of production.

1949 Ford single spinner with trailer (1955–1965), aluminum, FunHo! Toys, New Zealand, 12½ in long (32 cm).

Despite this somewhat checkered career, New Zealand's **Fun Ho! Toys** remain largely unique for two reasons. Firstly, the long-term use of aluminum by Underwood Engineering was largely unparalleled in toy-making history. While a few overseas manufacturers such as **AMT** and **Lansing** in the USA produced a range of aluminum toys, the material proved comparatively expensive when cast-iron and then plastic-molding resins became plentiful and more economical. Aluminum was a resource that was readily available to New Zealand manufacturers and aluminum products and raw materials remain a significant export today (over NZ$100 million, 2012).[47] Although the toys were largely based on a

wide range of existing toys designed overseas, the aluminum material has proved hardy and enduring. Many survivors still turn up buried in sandpits, in dumps or under houses or hedges across New Zealand. Only last year I rescued a **Fun Ho! Large Racer #80** buried in a disused daycare sandpit. Cast-iron or pressed steel would not have survived so well as these materials were prone to rust and cracking as well in the case of cast-iron.

Secondly, the rougher secondary castings which compromised the original detail significantly has added an element of folk or naive art to the toys. They remain unquestionably toys to be played with rather than displayed as models, the fate of many **Matchbox** or **Dinky** toys, which were often just displayed or kept in their original boxes. Many Kiwi postwar children (now variously described as baby boomers) harbor a nostalgic connection to **Fun Ho! Toys** which seemingly every New Zealand sandpit could boast. Missing paint, a scratched casting, a cracked green or yellow casein wheel, these characteristics often combine to create an aged patina of flaws which reflect the scars and joys of playtimes past.

The truth is Jack Underwood, in the nicest possible way, was an opportunist who never let the origins or patent on a toy get in the way of a good sand-cast copy for the local market. It could be said he was somewhat audacious by often objecting vigorously in person to the then Department of Trade and Industry, to any applications for the issue of further toy licenses to New Zealand importers or wholesalers. What is undeniable however was his lasting passion for the creation of enduring toys for 'fun and play', which consumed him until the day he died. This is a trait not lost on toy collectors and **Fun Ho!** toys, both sand-cast and die-cast, are now a much sought-after collectible in New Zealand and overseas. Some early **Fun Ho!** sand-cast toys have recently sold for in excess of $3000, surprisingly outstripping international prices for the American cast-iron toys from which they originated. A Fun Ho! Museum was established in 1990, not long after Underwood Engineering Limited effectively closed.[48] Longtime employee and purchasing manager, Barry Young, was instrumental in the establishment of the museum and the resurrection of most of the historical records of the company. While the company has experienced a few metamorphoses, it remains in business today under the stewardship of Richard Jordan. The museum now produces reproductions of many of the earlier and more recent sand-cast toys, some of which are sold to collectors throughout the world.

While earlier I stated I did not know who produced the first aluminum toy, aluminum was in fact rarely used by toy manufacturers apart from Underwoods of New Zealand. Many aluminum toys that have surfaced and I have collected are unlabeled and may have been sample castings, or certainly enjoyed very small production runs.

Two companies that also 'assisted' with **Fun Ho!** production were, the relatively little known American firm, **Slik Toys** of Lansing, Iowa, and **AMT (Aluminum Model Toys)** of Troy, Michigan.[49] The large Iowa toy company **Ertl** (est. 1945) also produced their first farm toys in aluminum during the 1940s. It is possible a few **Fun Ho!** toys originate from their comprehensive range. **Slik Toys Lansing Co.** was a significant maker of cast aluminum toys but by the early 1950s they had switched to plastic injection molding methods. Unusually, prior to toy making, Lansing Co. made pearl buttons. These were made from clamshells dredged from the nearby Mississippi River, but by the 1950s they too would be manufactured from the new wonder material – plastic.

In a somewhat surprising but commendable career change, an Attorney at Law, Mr West Gallogly Snr, launched the **Aluminum Model Toys** company. With connections in the Ford Motor Company he began producing promotional models from aluminum. The sudden availability of aluminum was reputedly due to the scrapping of World War II warplanes. One of his first toys was the 1947–48 **Ford V8 sedan,** which may have been the template for **Fun Ho!'s 1948 Ford V8 sedan #189** (incorrectly listed as a **Ford Mercury** in the Fun Ho! Collectors' reference). **AMT's** next Ford was the newly designed 1949 sedan which reputedly 'saved' the Ford Motor Company from financial ruin. Known in Australasia as the Ford 'single spinner' owing to the chromed bullet nose center grille, the **Fun Ho! #192 Ford Forty Niner** is likely to have originated from AMT's promo. While Fun Ho! took the opportunity to update their Ford as well, possibly courtesy of AMT**,** they did not feel the need to update the caravan they matched with it, mainly because AMT toys did not produce one. In fact, this Ford was to be the final toy AMT manufactured in aluminum prior to their changeover to making the promos in plastic (see Chapter 7). **AMT** were eventually purchased by **Ertl** in 1981. The **Fun Ho! single spinner** was designed with provision for the tow hook, which was mounted on the old 1930s streamline caravan (originally made for their **Lincoln Zephyr FH #110** – see pictures). While Henry Ford II and Mr Gallogly may

have been horrified at Fun Ho!'s somewhat anachronistic duo, Underwood Engineering took the decision in their stride, marketing the combination for ten years.

Another American company, **ER Roach**, based in Mt Vernon, Ohio, were a contemporary of these manufacturers and also dabbled briefly in aluminum, producing a pleasing line of small streamline racers. I am unsure who produced the impressive $10\frac{1}{2}$-inch long (27 centimetres) heavy gauge aluminum record racer, pictured. It is probably from the 1930s but could have been produced in the 1940s, or indeed the 1950s. It has steel disc wheels and although no maker's name is apparent, it is a well-cast toy, quite sculptural, and in fact it feels indestructible. Another unusual aluminum toy car, is a maroon sedan, possibly based on an English **Ford Prefect**. Similarly to the streamline racer, it is made of heavy gauge aluminum and has no markings but is fitted with aluminum cast wheels. **The Realistic Toy Company** from the USA made a **Greyhound bus** but 'realistic' would be stretching a point. **Freidag (1920s racer)** and **Arcade (1935 Pierce Arrow)** also made a few toys in aluminum in the 1930s.

Another aluminum toy maker from New Zealand was **McKenzie and Bannister** from Auckland who produced toys in the 1960s and 1970s. Their toys were gravity die-

Aluminum Racer, a large toy racer (3 ml gauge), maker unknown, c. 1950, 10¾ in long (27 cm).

Stock Car, aluminum, McKenzie and Bannister, New Zealand, c. 1960s, 5½ in long (14 cm).

cast so therefore more refined than the early sand-cast **Fun Ho!** models. The toy pictured here is a rare stock car, similar to the many stock cars which raced on Saturday nights at Waikaraka Park in Auckland. Most of the stock cars were built up from American 1930s coupes, similar to hot rods of the 1960s and 1970s. **Alumcast Products Ltd,** based in Timaru, New Zealand, also made a small range of aluminum toys in the late 1940s labeled **Tiger Toys.**

Many real cars were eventually bodied with aluminum panels, as Mr Kaiser had hoped, particularly in the 1950s, although often the experiments were shortlived. Carl Benz used aluminum in one of his first cars and much later La Gonda and Armstrong Siddeley used aluminum, also for bodywork, during the 1950s. **Fun Ho! sand-cast aluminum toy #305** is very similar to the real **Austin A40 convertible,** which

was aluminum bodied. These cars were designed with the American export market in mind but eventually less than 10,000 were produced. The cars are now regarded as classics with sadly few surviving due to design faults in the bodywork.

Other toys to be produced in significant numbers in aluminum were toy soldiers, particularly those made by French and English companies such as **Mignalu, Domage** and **Cie** (previously **Aludo and Quiralu).** The **Quiralu** brand was started as far back as 1933 by Mr Quirin of Luxeuil in France. His brand name was coined by the first four letters of his name (Quir) and the first three letters of aluminum (alu). In 1946 **Quiralu** switched to plastic manufacturing but aluminum sets could still be found in shops in the 1950s. In 1955 he switched to making 1:43 scale toys from die-cast molds but ceased production in 1959. In 1947

World War I pony [Muleteer] with cannon, Quiralu, French, aluminum, c. 1930s, approx. 3¼ in high (8 cm).

Mr Egar Kehoe from Dorset in England founded a brand named **Wend-al.** Based in Blanford, he sought assistance from **Quiralu** who loaned dies, so most figures are similar to the French toys. Similarly to **Quiralu, Wend-al** produced 200 farm animals to diversify their products but by the 1950s plastic had overtaken lead, cast-iron and aluminum soldiers. **Wend-al** closed in 1956. **Quiralu** also made a fine selection of army motorbikes, some with sidecars, all with removable riders (see pictures). There are, I believe, fine publications written in French recording the production of aluminum toy soldier makers from France[50] and Philip Dean of England published a book on the history of **Wend-al** aluminum figures. I have yet to locate them but I am sure they would be well worth reading to discover more about aluminum toys from Europe.

A selection of aluminum soldiers are pictured here, made by various makers including **Aludo, Quiralu** and **Wend-al.** The aluminum cowboys and Indian figurines made by **Krolyn** of Denmark in the 1950s are quite rare. These I found in a flea market in Melbourne of all places. **Krolyn** reputedly copied elastolin figures for a short period only but they are well cast and painted, wonderful examples of aluminum toys.

There are bound to be many other toys made from aluminum in collections and others waiting to be discovered. These are a selection of toys from my collection. The wonder of aluminum has been indelibly established in the manufacture of componentry for motor vehicles, aircraft, buildings and space rockets. The use of aluminum for the production of beer and soda cans, aluminum foil wrap and window frames is now commonplace. The copper wiring your communication network provider blames for all those computer glitches and gremlins is gradually being replaced with aluminum wiring. Aluminum is now the foremost material, next to steel, used in the manufacture of vehicle engines. Ford's new F150 pickup in 2015 was promoted and advertised as clad in 'military grade' aluminum.

The fact most aluminum toys still survive for collectors to enjoy proves their incredible durability and longevity. Aluminum toys forever?

Military toys made from aluminum by French and English makers such as Quirilu, Aludo and Mignalu, 1930s–1950s, 2¼ in (6 cm) to 3 in (8 cm) long approx.

Western figures, aluminum, by Krolyn, Denmark, c. 1950s, approx. 2–3 ¼ in high (5–8 cm).

CHAPTER 5

TOYS, BOOKS AND GAMES IN A RACE TO THE MOON

In 1969, after *Apollo 11* touched down on the moon, Neil Armstrong shuffled on to the surface and spoke the famous line, 'That's one small step for man, one giant leap for mankind.' Science fiction had become reality. The reality however did not extend to 'oily brown skinned Martians' (HG Wells),[51] or leather bikini-clad aliens emerging from a crater (Ray Cummings) and slapping a parking ticket on the windshield of the 'Eagle' landing craft, or indeed, zapping Buzz Aldrin or his Commander with a **Flash Gordon** type ray gun. Everything was a little anticlimactic and even the rock, dirt and fossil collecting was considered too boring for public viewing. Coincidentally, in a strange twist so often associated with

The Fantabulous Paint Box, tin plate, Lane, England, c. 1960, 14½ in long (37 cm).

HG Wells (1866–1946), science, history and sci-fi author, Carreras cigarette card number 16, 'Famous Men', 1927.

history, Buzz Aldrin was surely destined to land on the moon. His mother's maiden name was Moon.

To suggest however that the whole event was a little too staged and rather pedestrian would be somewhat churlish as there is no denying that the feat of traveling 238,857 miles (384,404 kilometres) and landing on the Moon is not only a watershed moment but, arguably, mankind's greatest achievement to date.

Scientist and author Charles R Gibson in his book *The Stars and their Mysteries* published in 1921 stated, 'We can never hope to fly to the moon…for very many reasons, one of which is the air only goes a comparatively short distance.' He did note however that there is a requirement for heat resistant materials to be fitted to the spacecraft due to the heat of the sun in outer space or the 'ether'.[52] Prior to the

Moon landing in 1969, talk of flying to the Moon and discovering its mysteries was to a large extent held in the domain of science fiction stories, children's books and board games. The few games produced prior to 1930 were inspired by writers such as Jules Verne and HG Wells. Early space board games manufactured include **The Man on the Moon** by **McLoughlin Brothers** of

Flash Gordon rocket fighter, clockwork, tin plate, Louis Marx, USA, 12 in (30 cm), photo courtesy Bertoia Auctions, USA.

Tom Corbett Space Cadet, 'Polaris rocket ship, clockwork, tin plate, Louis Marx, USA, 12½ in (30 cm), photo courtesy Bertoia Auctions, USA.

the USA, **Race to the Moon,** (somewhat optimistically depicting airships, balloons and biplanes), **World to World Airship Race** by the Chicago Game Company in 1913, and **The Moon, Mars and Venus** game, also around 1913 (this game sold for $700 in 2009). These board games in general are extremely rare and collectible, being highly prized by both board game and space toy collectors. A target game **Man in The Moon** was made by early American toy maker **Bliss** in 1885, predating possibly the first space board games known.

Louis Marx produced several superb tin plate clockwork rocket ships in the 1930s and 1950s, along with space guns and other items. Plastic spacemen and Martians were also produced by **Lido** and **Archer Toys** from the 1950s. **All Fair Games,** the maker of the stunning board game **Tutoom,** produced a target game **Race to the Moon** in 1931–32 where a rocket is launched when hit by the spring-loaded ball.

The allure of space ships to the Moon, Moon landings and the yet unanswered question of life on other planets, generated a fascination and complete genre of children's books, magazines, movies, television and radio serials and, of course, wonderfully inventive toys. We will see in this chapter that the discovery and creation of space toys, games, books and other fun items were more exciting for many than perhaps the real event. There is often more fun in the journey to discovery than reaching the destination and wonderfully illustrated toy and game boxes usually promised far more than the game delivered. Perhaps an analogy exists there with the actual moon landing. While this criticism could be true of many toys produced over time, space toys and robots were often the exception to this rule of thumb. We will briefly explore this fascinating history now and the stories and inspiration behind many of the space and sci-fi collectible toys which have appeared on planet Earth.

Prior to radio, movies and television, books and board games (parlor games) were the primary source of indoor entertainment and escape for children. Space travel, or more specifically, the mysteries of the Moon, were topics regularly plumbed and exploited by writers of adventure, mystery and science fiction. Jules Verne (French 1828–1905) could be considered the grandfather of science fiction prose and his enduring classic *From the Earth to the Moon* first published in 1865 is still being reprinted today.[53] It was also published as a 'Classic comic' (No. 105 – see picture) in 1953 and was reprinted twelve times by **Dell** in the same format from 1953 to 1971. Neil Armstrong, the *Apollo 11* commander, acknowledged Verne's prescient novel on the astronaut's return voyage from the Moon in 1969. He also mentioned how Verne's space ship had similarly taken off from Florida and splashed down on return from space in the Pacific Ocean. The wonders of space travel and the possibilities of life on the Moon or other planets expressed in prose and novels

From the Earth to the Moon, Jules Verne, Dell Classic Comic #105, 1953.

Star Wars 'Battlefront' poster. Sci-fi writers such as Jules Verne and HG Wells influenced many later sci-fi movies such as *Star Wars*.

The Moon Voyage, Jules Verne, early twentieth century edition c. 1900, published by Ward Lock and Co., London.

fiction novels. A quite prescient motive advanced to stockholders for backing Brunt's quite bizarre bird-powered flight was the proposal to excavate gold from the mountains of the moon. As we will see, this was an object of the board game **Space Pilot** produced over 200 years later (1951) at the very beginning of the space race.

Verne and Wells though are credited with providing the inspiration for what was arguably the first sci-fi movie, *A Trip to the Moon* (*La Voyage dans La Lune*) directed by George Melies in 1902.

A case could be made also for Baron Munchausen's stories, written by Rudolph Erich Raspe (1736–1794) originally titled *Baron Munchausen's Narrative of his Marvellous Travels and Campaigns in Russia.* The 1786 edition of his book included the bizarre story of the indomitable Baron riding to the Moon on a cannonball in 'Voyage to the Moon with many extraordinary particulars relative to the cooking animal in that planet which are here called the human species.' The fifth edition, published in 1787, has Munchausen (who while a fictional character, was based on a real baron) visiting 'Dog Star' as well. George Melies may well have used Raspe's stories as inspiration for his sci-fi movie as he later produced a short film, *Baron Munchausen's Dream* in 1911. An extremely rare tin-plate toy depicting Munchausen

are not as recent as we may think. Early writers from Gallileo in 1610, Johannes Kepler's *Somnium* published in 1634 (but originally written in 1608 in Latin), Francis Goodwin's *Man in The Moone* in 1683, and Captain Samuel Brunt's (a pseudonym, real author unknown) *A Voyage to Cacklogallinia* in 1727, all speculated about life on the Moon or indeed traveling there, prior to the arrival of the Frenchman Jules Verne and publication of his fantastic science was revealed by Renaud Fournier in 2017. This clockwork toy features Munchausen sitting on a cannonball looking up at two revolving planets or moons. 'When wound, the Baron moves his arms and makes the planets/moons spin above his head.'[54]

The 1874 American publication of Verne's classic book has a rather unusual history. Oddly perhaps, but not inappropriately, the book was translated from the French and published by the American Gun Club. The storyline in the book was fictionally based on the American Gun Club's decision to build a gunpowder-fueled rocket to fly to the Moon. Many of Verne's themes were astonishingly prescient as the motivation to build the rocket came about from the Gun Club's disappointment with a lack of gun play following the end of the Civil War and concern for the club's future. Ironically, Verne himself later became the victim of gun play when his mentally disturbed nephew shot him deliberately in the leg after missing with the first shot. Verne suffered a permanent limp from that day. Other prophecies in Verne's book were also accurate, from his prediction of weightlessness in space and the effects of gravity (no seatbelts required in his space rocket though!), to the use of aluminum in the construction of the space rocket, a virtually unknown material at that time.

Verne's book could well be considered the genesis of all space toys, possibly alongside another early master of science fiction in sci-fi author HG Wells (1866–1946). Wells wrote *The War of the Worlds* in 1898 and he also intuitively wrote of 'liquid fueled' and 'multi stage rockets', not unlike those used to launch men on the Moon some seventy years later. In this classic story, 'oily brown skinned Martians' attack Earth on pylon legged space ships, similar to those seen later in the Star Wars movies of the 1980s. When the novel was adapted for radio in 1938, narrated and directed by Orson Welles, many listeners reputedly panicked, running into the streets due to the 'real' Martian invasion.

An unprecedented number of clever and inventive robot toys and Martian spacemen appeared from the 1950s, most battery operated, many with stunning graphically illustrated boxes. A *War of the Worlds* movie was released in 1953 and a remake by Steven Spielberg in 2005. Wells also wrote *The First Man in the Moon* in 1901, which possibly inspired the **Man in the Moon** board games produced by **McLoughlin Brothers** of America and others around the same time. This game is extremely rare, although one sold for US$1000 in 2010 at auction, well below the $5000–7000 estimate.[55]

Other sci-fi books soon appeared such as Roy Whitman's *Lost on the Moon* (1911), Ray

"Rigged himself up like a tree"

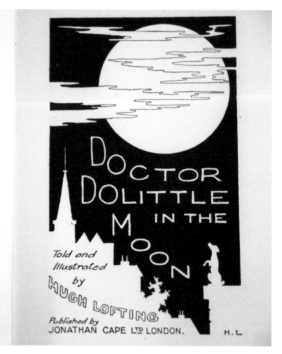

Dr Dolittle in the Moon, Hugh Lofting, 1928–1929, published by Jonathan Cape Ltd, London.

Stewart's *The Surprising Adventures of the Man in the Moon* (1904), Helen Huntington's *The Moon Lady* (1911), and famous classic short story author O'Henry (William Sydney Porter 1862–1910) with stories such as 'Psyche and the Skyscrapers' (1910). In this story he speculated, 'The Philosopher gazes into the intimate heavens above him and allows his soul to expand to the influence of his new view – space too should be the right of his immortal heritage, and he thrills at the thought that someday his

kind shall traverse these mysterious aerial roads between planet and planet.' In 'The Venturers' (1910), he describes 'paralleling the canals of Mars with radium railways.'

In the early twentieth century, Hugh Lofting wrote a children's series of books involving the adventures of Dr Dolittle. Dr Dolittle possessed an uncanny wonderful affinity with animals and most entailed quirky and offbeat animal stories such as *Dr Dolittle's Zoo*, *Dr Dolittle's Circus* and *Dr Dolittle's Garden*. In 1928–29 he wrote *Dr*

Dolittle in the Moon. Here Lofting describes how Dr Dolittle 'could spring 6 or 7 feet in one step…the gravity too was very confusing…walking was no effort at all.'[56]

The Dr Dolittle history has a surprising connection with another sci-fi writer and his boy hero, **Tom Swift.** Swift was an ingenious boy inventor and adventurer who was created originally in 1910 by Edward Stratemeyer, who wrote under the pseudonym of Victor Appleton. The books were first published by his company, Stratemeyer Syndicate, a book-packaging firm where eventually various ghost writers continued under the Appleton pseudonym. His space sci-fi books (see picture) were developed later, in the early 1950s, when the 'space race' began. This second series published as the *New Tom Swift Junior Adventurers* by Victor Appleton II, described exciting adventures such as 'Tom Swift and his Diving Seacopter to the Moon' (1956), 'Tom Swift and Space Solartron' (1958), and 'Tom Swift – Race to the Moon' (1956). The third series published in 1981, were actually set in 'outer space'.

Dr Dolittle and **Tom Swift** crossed paths decades later in 1968 when 20th Century Fox contrived and scheduled a **Tom Swift** movie. Fox had experienced mixed success with a Dr Dolittle movie in 1967 starring Rex Harrison and Richard

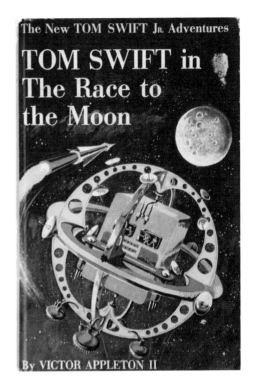

Tom Swift in the Race to the Moon, Victor Appleton II, (Edward Stratmeyer), published by Grosset & Dunlap, USA, 1958.

Attenborough, which was based on Hugh Lofting's 1920s era **Dr Dolittle** books. Because of the mixed success of Dr Dolittle (despite an Oscar nomination for Best Song), Fox decided to 'can' the **Tom Swift** movies. Interestingly, actor Michael Crawford (*Some Mothers Do Have 'Em* and *Phantom of the Opera*) was lined up for the lead role as Tom Swift in a three-picture

Buck Rogers 25th century rocket pistol, Daisy Rifles advert card, 1930s, approx. 11½ in x 8 in (29 cm x 20 cm).

Buck Rogers Rocket Police Patrol, clockwork, tin plate rocket ship, Louis Marx, USA 12 in long (30 cm).

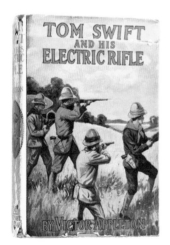

Tom Swift and his Electric Rifle, Victor Appleton (Edward Stratmeyer), published by Grosset & Dunlap, USA, 1911.

trilogy.[57] Surely Frank Spencer and Tom Swift could not have been more light years apart in personality although the thought of a space comedy featuring Frank Spencer rather whets the appetite. Of the two $50,000 airships that had already been built for the movie, one was sold to an amusement park while the other was sold off for parts or props. Even a television pilot for a proposed series that was run in 1983 crashed and burned with seemingly no hope of re-entry to a television audience. Without the potency of movie or television fervor, few Tom Swift toys, apart from the illustrated children's books with colorful covers, survive. Parker Brothers USA produced a Tom Swift board game in 1966 but this game is now scarce and very collectible. It did not sell well, and it seems by the 1960s there was a perception that Tom Swift was somewhat outdated. Despite this, **Tom Swift** stories may have exerted possibly more influence on twentieth and twenty-first century development than any other boyhood hero. Steve Wozniak, co-founder of Apple, credits **Tom Swift** books with inspiring him to become a scientist and inventor. So, as you tap your Apple Mac, text on your iPhone, or power up your iPad, you can thank and pay homage to **Tom Swift** and his creator, Edward Stratemeyer. And brownie points for children's books and toys do not end there. Lee Felsenstein, also credited **Tom Swift** stories for providing the inspiration behind his Taser invention, as well as the Computer Terminal Hard Drive. The acronym 'Taser' originates from the *Tom Swift Electric Rifle*, a story published originally in 1911 (see illustration).[58]

Creative space toys appeared in the late 1920s and 1930s with tin-plate clockwork toys such as **Buck**

Rogers and **Flash Gordon** space rockets. The pièce de résistance among early space toys is a magnificent **War of the Worlds** diorama made by classy toy maker, **Mignot** of France in 1925. This boxed set included a large-tentacled Martian which attacks and devours all earthlings, in this case, earthlings in France. A vast array of ray guns, laser guns and space pistols entered the market, along with early plastic toys such as spacemen, astronauts and Martians by makers such as **Archer** and **Lido Plastics.** A **Flash Gordon** movie serial was released in 1936, which inspired several space toys, and a **Buck Rogers** chemical laboratory set, which is now extremely rare, was produced in 1937 by John F Dille Company of the USA. Many other **Buck Rogers** space pistols were made during the peak of space heroes' popularity, including the sonic ray gun, which doubled as a torch. Illustrated here is a scarce display advertisement for a **Daisy Buck Rogers space-rocket pistol** from the 1930s.

Man from Mars, Martian spaceman wind-up toy, plastic, Irwin, USA, 1950s, 10 in long (25 cm).

Although the genesis of space toys may originate from books, more sophisticated mass-produced space toys were borne out of serials and movies screened in the 1950s. *Forbidden Planet* (1956), now a classic and cult sci-fi movie, launched **Robby the Robot.** The famous and classic **Robby the Robot** toy is now one of the most familiar space toys and has been reproduced many times since it appeared as a stunning clockwork and battery-operated toy from Japan.[59] The timing of the arrival of sci-fi movies and the ability to mass-produce quality tin-plate, battery-operated toys from a rebuilt Japan could not have been better. Space toys comprise a complete collecting genre, but a significant spin-off from this genre

Moon robot Robby Ribbon type, mechanical, tin plate, Yonesawa, Japan, 1960, 10½ in long (27 cm), photo courtesy Lloyd Ralston Auctions, USA.

Jules Verne's *From the Earth to the Moon* starring Joseph Cotton and George Sanders, movie poster, 1958, Warner Brothers, USA.

By Space Ship to the Moon, Jack Coggins and Fletcher Pratt, 1952, Random House, New York and Publicity Products, London.

is toy robots (see pictures). The 1950s and 1960s provided a golden age of space toys as the space race slowly built to a crescendo with the Moon landing in 1969.

Excitement and interest began to increase, not only with books and sci-fi serials, but with technicolor movies. In 1950 two movies were produced by Lippert Productions: *Destination Moon* and *Rocketship*, starring perennial actor Lloyd Bridges (father of Oscar winning actor Jeff Bridges). Despite the rocketship being 'pressurized' and 'gyro controlled', the crew experienced 'nose bleeds and unconsciousness'. Eventually the ship goes off course and ends up on Mars, some 50,000 miles away – perhaps reflecting a contemporary perception of the unlikelihood and difficulty of landing on the Moon.

In 1953 the classic HG Wells 1898 story *War of the Worlds* was released as a movie.

Along with *Forbidden Planet*, this movie is credited with exerting a huge influence on future sci-fi movies (*Star Wars*, for example) and the vast array of ingenious and creative toys which followed. Following the *War of the Worlds* movie, Martian robots were manufactured in their thousands, in varying styles and colors, by companies such as Horikawa of Japan, who made the **Attacking Martian** robots. In 1958 Jules Verne's classic sci-fi story *From the Earth to the Moon* (by then almost 100 years old), was launched as a movie by Warner Brothers (see poster illustration), starring Joseph Cotton and George Sanders.

Another famous children's author who should not be forgotten, is William Earle Johns (1893–1965). Johns was the creator of the famous **Biggles** stories, who also wrote under the pen name William Earle, and later Captain WE Johns. Coincidentally, Johns fought and survived the disastrous Gallipoli campaign in the First World War (fighting for the Norfolk Yeomanry), a large scale and costly military blunder referred to earlier in this book. Eventually, Johns became a real-life Biggles flying ace in the First World War but was shot down and taken prisoner towards the end of the war. As well as his **Biggles** hero stories, Johns wrote a ten-volume science-fiction series between 1954 and 1963, including stories such as 'Return to Mars' and 'To Outer Space'.

If books can be credited as the genesis of the first space movies and space toys, then mention must be made of sci-fi writer Arthur C Clarke (1917–2008) and illustrator Jack Coggins (1911–2006). Clarke's short story *Sentinel* published in 1948 was the basis for the classic movie *2001 A Space Odyssey*, released in 1968 and directed by Stanley Kubrick. Clarke was actually a qualified scientist with a degree in mathematics and physics who eventually served as chairman of the British Interplanetary Society from 1946 to 1947 and 1951 to 1953. The first space flight books he wrote in the early 1950s were mainly non-fiction but he credited 1930s writer David Lasser (*The Conquest of Space*, 1931) with providing the inspiration for his later sci-fi books. Clarke neatly bookended his sci-fi and science career when he was employed as the CBS television commentator for the *Apollo 11* Moon landing in 1969.

Jack Coggins (1911–2006) was a celebrated author and artist who illustrated covers for early 1950s science-fiction magazines, including *Galaxy Science Fiction*, *The Magazine of Fantasy, Science Fiction and Fact* and *Thrilling Wonder Stories*. He completed illustrations for *Life* magazine, *The Saturday Evening Post* and *Yank* magazine, as well as

By Space Ship to the Moon, an illustration depicting exploration of the moon. The spidery legged spacecraft is reminiscent of early French toy maker, Mignot, who made a diorama of HG Wells' War of the Worlds in the early 1900s.

undertaking illustrations on behalf of the US War Department during World War II. Coggins' most illustrious and influential children's book however was *By Spaceship to the Moon*, published in conjunction with author Fletcher Pratt in 1952 (see pictures).[60] Fletcher Pratt (1897–1956) was a well-known military historian who also collaborated with Coggins to write *Rockets, Jets, Guided Missiles and Space Ships*. The depth of detail, accuracy and quality of illustration in these books was quite remarkable, combining depictions and descriptions of astronauts attached by cables to motherships effecting repairs, graphic details of landing equipment, together with operating procedures and appropriately designed apparel. As children's books,

there was a surprising, if not disturbing, military and commercial undercurrent to the storyline whereby the Moon was touted as a military base supported by an underground arsenal and the possible source of huge mineral wealth. Nevertheless, such was the accuracy and prescient nature of the books, NASA used them to illustrate the possibilities of space travel and gain support from Congress for the 1950s American Space Program. Coggins was eventually acknowledged for his contributions, being inducted into the International Association of Astronomical Artists Hall of Fame as 'living legend' and celebrated master of the genre of space exploration art.

Despite television being in its infancy during the aftermath of the Second World War, a remarkable number of sci-fi programs were launched in America almost immediately hostilities had ceased. Four serials spring to mind including *Captain Video* (1949–1955), *Space Patrol* (1950–1955), *Tom Corbett, Space Cadet* (1950–1955) and *Buck Rogers* (1950–1951). Lesser space heroes around this time included **Rocky Jones Space Ranger** (1953) and **Rod Brown of the Rocket Rangers** (1953), and the not surprisingly short-lived **Captain Tootsie and his Interplanetary Space Ship** (1950), – hardly a moniker that would strike fear into the hearts of creepy aliens and robotic enemies.

The first show, *Captain Video and his Video Ranger* sparked a surprising number of toy and collectible spin-offs including electronic goggles, a ray gun, decoder, twelve spacemen, a spaceship and a flying saucer ring. This show was the first TV series to feature a robot. As mentioned earlier, the first companies to mass-produce plastic dime-store space toys were **Lido** and **Archer Plastics** from the USA and a scarce **Captain Video** spaceship by **Lido** is pictured. Variations of these toys were also issued as breakfast cereal premiums and are now eagerly sought as collectibles. A scarce early plastic survivor is the green and white hard plastic **Space Ranger Z1010 spaceship,** also pictured here. Made by **Moldex Plastics** of Australia, it has metal wheels and measures 11 inches long (28 centimetres). **Pyro Plastics** from the USA originally produced this toy with plastic wheels, the Australian version however is very rare (refer Early Plastics Chapter).

Space Patrol (1950–1955) ran over 1100 shows during its five-year period, proving extremely popular as the show developed. Interestingly, food and chocolate giant Nestle were one of the main sponsors. In an unusual twist of fate, they are mentioned

Captain Video Spaceship, Lido Toys c. 1950s, USA, 4 ¼ in (11 cm).

Space Ranger Z1010 spaceship, plastic, c. 1950, Moldex Plastics, Australia, 11 in long (28 cm).

later in this chapter when they demoted New Zealand iconic and long-serving hero character **Sergeant Dan** from his role in promoting a New Zealand breakfast cereal.

Tom Corbett, Space Cadet (1950–1955) left a legacy of wonderful illustrations including books and comics. Based on the book *Space Cadet* by Robert A Heinlein (1948) and further developed by Joseph Greene, there were eventually nine **Tom Corbett** books published including *Tom Corbett: A Trip to the Moon* in 1953. Dell

Tom Corbett, Space Cadet, Dell Comics, USA, 1952.

Tom Corbett, Space Cadet coloring book, 1950s, 15 x 10¾ (38 x 27 cm).

comics produced at least thirteen **Tom Corbett** comics between 1952 and 1954, which are also highly prized by collectors for the wonderful cover illustrations such as the 1952 *Space Cadet* comic issue pictured.[61] The illustrations, including the cover, are signed by A McWilliams. In the stories these early space pioneers train to become members of the Solar Guard and journey on the rocket ship *Polaris* to the outer reaches of space in the solar system. They take an oath: 'Upon entering space and the space academy…to pledge [his] life and

career to the services of mankind.' In the *Space Cadet* story space pirates attempt to hijack a space rocket to pick up a cargo of 'mercurium' from planet Mercury. They took a lead in health and safety prevention by taking gloves. A reasonable array of **Tom Corbett** merchandise was offered over this time, including books, comics, costumes, lunchboxes, a space academy playset and space guns by **Louis Marx,** a **View-Master** reel and a pocket watch. Similarly to the **View-Master** and pocket watch, **Tom Corbett** prose became somewhat dated, cluttered with ancient seafaring phrases and terminology. Corbett eventually disappeared into a black hole, not reappearing until 1990 and 2009, cast in a new series of comics.

Another interesting board game mentioned earlier, produced at about the same time was **Space Pilot** made by **Cadaco Ellis** of Chicago in 1951. There were no trips to the Moon for the young space pilots playing this game however, the object being to occupy Mercury, Venus, Mars, Jupiter and Saturn by spinning the diecut space rocket. On landing, the pilot claims mineral rights worth between $10 billion and $50 billion, perhaps one of the few toys or games that betrayed a fundamental motive behind the actual space race. Similar to Coggins and Pratt's *By Spaceship to the Moon* book, this game could be viewed with some disquiet in that Planet Mercury was loaded with hills of gold valued at $10 billion, while Saturn possessed the mother lode of riches with a vein of plutonium valued at $50 billion. Skipping apocalyptic undertones and suggestions for now we can nevertheless gain comfort from the paradoxically uplifting and colorful graphics displayed on both the playing board and game box of **Space Pilot**, illustrated here. The fresh, postwar graphics are reflective of

Space Pilot game by Cadaco Ellis, Chicago, USA, 1951, 24 x 10½ in (61 x 27 cm).

Tom Corbett Space Cadet, Space Pistol, tin plate by Rockhill Products, Louis Marx, USA, 1950s, photo courtesy Bertoia Auctions, USA.

manufacturing from toys to television, which ushered in an unprecedented flood of consumer items borne from space-age design, materials and technology.

The baby boomer era had commenced in earnest during this time and with it a new dimension and era of toy production also began. To assist in the rebuilding of war-

Space graphics domino set, Bakelite, 1950s, made in Russia, 6 x 2 in (15 x 5 cm) approx.

torn occupied Japan and West Germany, light industry was quickly established, toy production becoming a significant part of the restructure. As British rule was restored following the Japanese surrender in 1945, Hong Kong soon began to mass produce toys on behalf of many countries, particularly Britain and America, and as far away as New Zealand. The Japanese battery-operated robots, pictured, are fine examples of the ingenious tin plate and plastic space toys produced by countries such as Japan, that literally rose Phoenix-like from the ashes of nuclear destruction.

The space race by now was well underway, fueled at first by President Eisenhower, and then his successor John F Kennedy's burning desire to beat Russia to the moon. Russia had taken the lead with the successful launch of their satellite *Sputnik 1* in 1957, and in 1961 Yuri Gagarin became the first human to head into outer space and successfully return. Russian-made space-related toys were relatively hard to find in the Western world until ecommerce sites such as eBay became established in the market. Now many turn up, such as the rare 1950s Bakelite/early plastic **domino space-race set,** illustrated here. Housed in a pastel-green container, it is decorated in relief with a Russian space rocket launch pad scene. Three planets, including Jupiter, are depicted in the background. Primitive type robots come to the market occasionally from this era, notable for their unusual pastel shades.

America continued the race with Alan Shepard aboard *Freedom 7* in 1961 and John Glenn orbited the earth three times in the spacecraft *Mercury* in 1962. The two-person NASA space capsule *Gemini* successfully orbited the earth in 1963. A plethora of space toys soon flooded planet Earth, and it was not long before children growing up in this era began discovering them in their morning breakfast cereal. All the space ships, satellites and spacemen were produced as cereal premiums, even turning up in bubblegum packets made in Germany (see pictures). The walk to school on a frosty day eased considerably with a plastic *Gemini* space capsule tucked into your pocket, discovered in the breakfast cereal box that morning.

There are parallels here between the remarkable influence the Egyptian tomb discoveries in the early twentieth century exerted on fashion, culture and design, and the influence of the space race some thirty years later. In the 1950s motor vehicles were designed and named referencing space rockets and spacecraft, one General Motors vehicle rolling out in 1958 as an Oldsmobile Rocket. Ford produced a Mercury, Chevrolet a Nova, DeSoto a Fireflite and Packard a Constellation. Kitchenware and appliances were touted

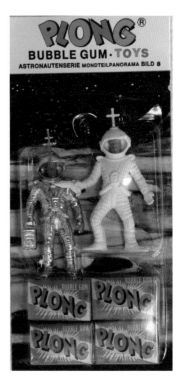

Plong plastic spacemen with Plong bubble gum, Germany, 1960s, 7½ x 3½ in (19 x 9 cm).

Spacecraft figurines, breakfast cereal premiums, plastic, 1950s, approx. 2–2¼ in (5–6 cm).

TT2 spaceship jigsaw puzzle, Tip Top, New Zealand, icecream premium, 1950s, Walt Disney Productions, 8 ¼ x 6 ¼ in (21 x 16 cm).

Television Spaceman robot, tin plate and plastic, battery operated, made in Japan, 1960s, 15 in high (38 cm).

Video Robot, tin plate and plastic, battery operated, SH, Japan, 1960s, 9½ in high (24 cm).

as encompassing space-age design down to eggcups molded as space capsules and salt and pepper shakers as Sputniks. Popular songs soon hit the charts inspired by the space race such as David Bowie's ballad 'Space Oddity', featuring a doomed astronaut and Elton John's uplifting song starring a 'Rocketman'.

Space toys flooded the market including the first Chinese toys of significance, being largely copies of Japanese toy space ships, flying saucers and space rockets. Once regarded as undesirable by collectors, these early Chinese toys are now highly sought by collectors from a rejuvenated and affluent superpower.

Many variations of toys, games, books, cards and puzzles appeared on the market as well, often in association with other consumer products. A space race **Donald Duck jigsaw puzzle** with a New Zealand connection (pictured) is a **TT2 iceblock advertising premium** for **Tip Top New Zealand** icecream and ices. Commissioned by Tip Top in the 1950s, the mini jigsaw puzzle (7½ x 6 inches/20 x 15 centimetres) depicts a stylized space ship TT2 iceblock with an integral game on the jigsaw. It states: 'Message from space – to find where we are going copy the letters on the stars and planets in their numerical order' (spoiler alert – it's Mercury). Ironically, another New Zealand icecream company (**Westland Snowflake Icecream Ltd**) named their icecreams Uranium. Sounds like an interesting flavor. **Apex Ice Cream Ltd** joined the party producing icecream Bombs and Choc Bombs in keeping with contemporary space-age marketing trends.

TT2s were a New Zealand invention and registered as a trademark in 1957. As Hoover, Xerox and other

'Rockets, Missiles and Outerspace', Sergeant Dan's collector's card album, Flemming Company, New Zealand, 1965, 6¼ x 9½ in (16.5 x 24 cm). Illustration by Alister Simpson.

Invaders

The Invaders collector's card, 1967. Roy Thinnes starred as David Vincent in the Larry Cohen, Quinn Martin sci-fi television series which ran for forty-three episodes in 1967 and 1968.

colloquialisms entered the modern vernacular, **TT2 (Tip Top 2)** became known as the word for any iceblock in New Zealand. The number '2' referred to a second line product not being an icecream confection. In line with the ongoing space race, Tip Top soon produced TT2s such as Moon Raider, Meteor, Moggy Man, Star Strobe, Red Rocket, Astro Flash and Zero X.

In 1965, **Fleming's of New Zealand**, who manufactured **Creamoata** breakfast cereals, produced a full-gloss, color, space-race collectible card set together with a **Sergeant Dan's Space Flight Album** (see illustration). The twelve-page album included supporting illustrations and detailed explanatory text for the twenty-five card set. The back page of the album sends 'a message to all space-age children', encouraging the collector to 'read everything you can about astronomy and inter-planetary travel, to keep abreast of the latest rockets and satellites in the space-race'. Apparently, 'before each manned space-probe the astronaut enjoys a hearty hot breakfast which keeps him alert and energetic before each flight'. This now fifty-two year old space album, produced in New Zealand, is extremely rare. **Sergeant Dan the Creamoata Man** was given an honorable discharge from the breakfast cereal ranks following a takeover by Nestle in 2006. The irrepressible soldier began promoting Fleming's oatmeal porridge in 1920 and appeared in promotions during the Second World War, lasted beyond the space race, survived *Star Wars,* but finally succumbed to a force more powerful in the ruthless, take-no-prisoners corporate and financial rationalization army. **Sergeant Dan,** although severely wounded, survived to market horse feed products (Sergeant Dan's Stockfoods Ltd) in his area of birth (Gore) in the South Island of New Zealand, albeit a rather ignominious drop from the heights and ranks of outer space.

It is notable that at this time the production of tin-plate toys, a dynastic period of toy making, gradually began to phase out due to advancements in manufacturing methods and plastic molding resins. Tin-plate robots, for example, were originally made with mainly tin plate, then a combination of tin plate and plastic, and eventually such as the *Lost in Space* robot and *Man from Mars* spaceman,

virtually solely from plastic. The wonder of plastic toys is highlighted in Chapter 6.

The **Sergeant Dan** album card set, although seemingly insignificant as opposed to a classic toy, is however a reflection of toys from this period, which were based on real events and real spacecraft. Ironically, although toy makers from countries such as Japan, Russia, and now China, produced tin plate and plastic toys based on reality, such as landing craft, lunar modules, satellites, astronauts and space stations, before long science-fiction toys once again enveloped the market, spurred on by advancements in television and movie making. Serials and movies such as *Lost in Space, Star Trek, Dr Who, The Invaders, The Jetsons, Thunderbirds* and others soon established a new, exciting and comprehensive collectible toy supply base for collectors worldwide.

Thunderbirds and *Captain Scarlet*, British hit sci-fi television and movie shows premiered in 1965 and 1966 respectively, **Thunderbirds** becoming one of the first series to morph into a significant franchise. Produced by the brilliant British husband and wife team, Sylvia and Gerry Anderson, it seems improbable that puppets and science fiction would in any way be compatible. So compatible, they proved to be, the Andersons became the uncrowned King and Queen of innovative children's television. They produced two further successful puppet/ marionette sci-fi series with *Captain Scarlet* and *Joe 90* along with several other children's television serials. On reflection, the **Thunderbirds** success must be considered rather surprising, with a cast of quintessential English 'upper crust' characters forming the family of super-rescue heroes portrayed by stilted puppets. The Tracy family of six, headed by ex-astronaut Jeff Tracy, saw his sons, Alan, John and Scott, pilot a spacecraft in *Thunderbirds 3* and Alan and John man a space station in *Thunderbirds 5*. While some may have expressed misgivings regarding the show's credibility, it was actually inspired by a real-life tragedy. Sylvia and Gerry Anderson were greatly moved by a 1963 German mining disaster where twenty-nine miners perished and a further twenty-one were trapped. Recognizing the need for an international rescue initiative due to delays in major or complex rescue logistics, the Andersons conceived imaginary supersonic vehicles that could travel immediately to assist at disasters worldwide.

There is a surprising link here to our 'Westerns' chapter, as the creators credited the success of the television series *Bonanza* in influencing their decision to cast the Thunderbirds as a tightly bonded family group. The main protagonist in the *Thunderbirds*, Jeff Tracy, was also a widow, similarly to patriarchal father figure, Ben Cartwright, in *Bonanza*. If *Bonanza* was as American as apple pie, the **Thunderbirds** were as British as strawberries and cream, with Lady Penelope's clipped, haughty instructions (just like the Queen), always delivered in no uncertain terms to her Rolls Royce driving chauffeur/butler Parker. Despite the show's image as

Dinky Toys brochure, *Captain Scarlet* and *Thunderbirds*, die-cast toys, c. 1968.

Thunderbirds jigsaw puzzle, Waddington/Holdson Products, New Zealand, 1965, 9 x 6½ in (23 x 17 cm).

Thunderbirds action figures, Carlton Toys, Vivid Imagination, approx. 12 in high (30 cm).

Thunderbirds movie poster from Japan, 2004.

distinctly upper class, it became a smash hit, with merchandise sales reputedly exceeding *Star Wars* in 1992. Over 3000 **Thunderbirds** products have been released on the market since 1965, including vehicles and playsets by the die-cast toy behemoth **Matchbox** and **Vivid Imaginations**.[62] Lady Penelope's pink Rolls Royce is surely one of the most enduring and classic toy vehicles of all time, which most collectors worldwide either have or would like to own. The **Tracy Island Secret Base playset,** made by various manufacturers including **Matchbox** over time, is a neat toy, with figures, vehicles and other accessories. Full-length movies were released in 1966, 1968 and the 1990s and the figures, pictured, produced by **Carlton**

Toys are extremely realistic, being fully dressed, 12 inches high (30 centimetres), and very comparable to the actual puppets. The **Thunderbirds** were also very much 'Go' worldwide, including Japan. A dramatically illustrated movie poster from Japan dated 2004 is included here.

Following on from the success of **Thunderbirds** in 1967, the Andersons immediately released a further sci-fi super hero with **Captain Scarlet and the Mysterons.** Although the characters were once again portrayed by puppets, this show projected more gravity with a hero who was '…leading the fight against the Mysterons…who were sworn enemies of earth.'[63] Although the thirty-two episode series ran for less than a year, it gradually gained traction and has been reinvented, re-run and reproduced, including re-animation, in a computer reboot in 2005 and 2006. The nicely illustrated jigsaw puzzle boxes (pictured) were produced in a series with a scene from various shows. These period examples were produced by Holdson Products in New Zealand (1967). The New Zealand versions are quite rare, while more well known **Captain Scarlet** toys include die-cast versions of the **Spectrum Patrol Car** and **Spectrum Pursuit vehicle** by **Dinky Toys.**

Captain Scarlet was followed by

Space Family Robinson, Lost in Space, Gold Key Comics, August 1967, December 1967, Western Publishing, USA.

another puppet with geek-type hero **Joe 90** who ultimately transpired to be the final Anderson puppet hero. Jigsaw puzzles were also produced similar to the Scarlet puzzles in New Zealand in 1968, the one pictured here showing **Joe 90** at his expansive control center.

The classic television series *Lost in Space* created by Irwin Allen was launched by CBS in 1965 and ran until 1968. While *Bonanza* must be considered an unlikely influence for *Thunderbirds*, it is not surprising to discover *Lost in Space* was based on a novel re-counting the adventures of a family marooned on an island in 1812. Johann

Captain Scarlet and the Mysterons jigsaw puzzle, Waddington/Holdson Products (NZ) Limited, 1967, 9 x 6½ in (23 x 17 cm).

Captain Scarlet and the Mysterons Spectrum Pursuit vehicle, die-cast, Dinky Toys, 6¼ in long (16 cm).

Wyss's classic novel, *The Swiss Family Robinson*, published in 1812, was the story Allen used to base his *Lost in Space* family upon. This time a family were marooned on a planet, rather than an island, in the first instance the planet Priplanus. A film released in 1998 revived the franchise and new merchandise was released, including the plastic, battery operated robot M3B9 (pictured). It was designed by Robert Kinoshita who designed the iconic **Robby** the **Robot** from the early classic sci-fi movie *Forbidden Planet* mentioned earlier. This was a precursor to other classic 'personality' robots of this era which soon followed, such as **3CPO, R2D2, Johnny 5** and **Buzz Lightyear.** The **B9** robot toy is a traveling, talking robot with fun actions such as a lighted, flashing, revolving, telescopic, talking head – 'Danger Will Robinson – Danger!' He's not just a good toy but a good friend. This robot has been reproduced by various makers over the years, as has the Robinsons' spaceship, *Jupiter 2*. Every toy collector should have a **B9** robot. Mine is a version which only cost $30, made in 1997 by Trendmasters USA (manufactured in China). The original Remco Toys B9 robot is quite rare and currently sells for over $1000, depending on condition. Other toys produced by this franchise include action figures, comics, playsets, card games, space ships, die-cast vehicles by **Johnny Lightning,** model kitsets, lunch boxes, a laser pistol and trading cards.

Star Trek, which debuted in 1966 starring William Shatner, has grown to become a mega franchise where merchandise sales reputedly exceeded over US$4 billion in 1999, taking a leaf from its mission statement: 'to boldly go where no man has gone before'.

Gerry Anderson's *Joe 90* jigsaw puzzle, Waddington/Holdson Products, New Zealand, 1968, 10 x 8 ¼ in (25 x 21 cm).

Lost in Space robot, plastic, battery operated by Space Productions/Trendmasters 1997, 10 in high (25 cm).

Star Trek Annual, World Publishing, England, 1960s.

As a television series, *Star Trek* claims a social history landmark being the first show to present a multiracial cast, with Scotty, Mr Sulu, Uhura, Chekov, and other characters. Again, there is also an unusual link to our 'Westerns' genre when the creator, Gene Roddenberry, originally proposed a 'Western' space theme, namely 'Wagon Train to the Stars', owing to the overwhelming and continuing popularity of TV Westerns. Fortunately, this idea became merely a spaghetti western flash in the pan when Roddenberry satisfied his wish in episode 'Spectre of the Gun' where, after landing on an alien planet, Kirk and his men find themselves in a Western setting facing Wyatt Earp and Doc Holiday in a gun duel.

The toys produced over time have been numerous; from action figures and space craft to puzzles, dress sets, card sets, books, comics and kitsets. The kitset, pictured, is a rare **USS Enterprise spaceship model,** which was made in New Zealand under license by **Tonka Toys (NZ) Ltd.** The box is dated 1966 and states, 'Box made and lithoed in NZ'. The toy remains new in the box, unassembled. Like many kitsets, they became unfashionable with children during a period where they preferred a toy already assembled and set to go, hot out of the Christmas stocking.

The whole franchise had earned over US$10 billion by 2016. William Shatner became synonymous with the show, eventually producing his own sci-fi magazine *Tek-World* with Marvel Comics in 1992. In the children's *Star Trek* annuals, such as the one pictured, Captain Kirk (William Shatner) and Dr Spock (Leonard Nimoy) featured on most covers, or end papers.[64] Cool as a cucumber, yet luridly green blooded like the skin, Spock gained a tremendous cult following, eventually earning Nimoy a fortune himself from royalties.

A rare set of **Star Trek Topps Chewing Gum Inc.** collectible cards is pictured here, which depict thumbnail scenes from various TV episodes.[65] Explanations of the scenes are on the reverse. These cards were released in association with publicity release merchandise for the first *Star Trek* movie in 1979. The reverse of the card number 1 states: '…*Star Trek* Lives again…Gene Roddenberry has delighted fans the world over when he announced plans to make a full length movie based on *Star Trek*'. Eventually, thirteen full-length *Star Trek* movies were released, the third and fourth were directed by Dr Spock himself, Leonard Nimoy. *Star Trek* went on to become one of the great sci-fi classics of the twentieth century. A new TV series was slated for the future and hopefully more new toys.

One man however elevated science fiction emphatically above reality when he launched a movie named *Star Wars* in 1977. There are complete novels published on *Star Wars* movies and collectibles (and deservedly so) so subsequently this book will only briefly pay homage to the impact and influence these blockbuster movies cast on the future of space and sci-fi toys and other movies such as *Independence Day*, *Battlestar Gallactica* and some yet to screen.

Star Wars toys, similarly to *Star Trek*, are of course a complete collecting field and it must also be noted that toys from this period were produced almost completely in plastic, signaling the end of significant toy-making history, which ran for close to 100 years. Tin plate toys, in the main reproductions, are still made today but these remain very much in the minority. The

Star Trek USS *Enterprise* space ship, model kit (unassembled), plastic, marked 'A.M.T. made under license in New Zealand by Tonka Manufacturing, Star Trek created by Gene Roddenberry', c. 1960s.

Star Trek Topps Gum collectors cards, 1979, 2½ x 3¾ in (9 x 7 cm).

C3PO *Star Wars* plastic figurine, marked 'General Mills Fun Group', made in Hong Kong, 1978, 12 in high (30 cm).

blockbuster *Star Wars* movies broke virtually every record in film making, including the record for the most successful film merchandising franchise ever at an estimated US$42 billion. To date, eight *Star Wars* movies have been produced, with others scheduled, and while original *Star Wars* characters and spacecraft have endured, new characters have been introduced throughout the series. George Lucas optimized all the possibilities in relation to licensing and the creation of a comprehensive movie/toy/collectible package deal that led the way for other franchises to follow such as JK Rowling's *Harry Potter* and Peter Jackson's/ Tolkein's *Lord of the Rings*. Not since Walt Disney's Mickey Mouse and Friends, William Boyd's/Clarence Mulford's *Hopalong Cassidy* and Roddenberrys *Star Trek* had a product proved such a runaway success, providing a mother lode of riches to the creator. Such was the success, Walt Disney inserted a finger in the huge pie, purchasing distribution rights to some *Star Wars* movies in 2012. In December 2017 *Star Wars* movie *The Last Jedi* was released. By April 2018 the movie had grossed over US$1.3 billion worldwide. Followers of each movie wait with great anticipation to see exciting and quirky characters such as **Chewbacca, R2D2, C-3PO, Han Solo** and perhaps the return of the inimitable **Darth Vader** and his **Storm Troopers.** The figurines (such as **C-3PO** illustrated here), became a huge part of the collectible genre of the late twentieth century. The articulated and plastic chromed **C-3PO** robot here is 12 inches tall (30 centimetres) and arguably a sculptural work of art. Surprisingly, these robots have no mechanism similar to other myriad figurative toys produced from the *Star Wars* era. Other robots such as **R2D2** did come with a battery-operated option but despite this, many *Star*

Star Wars card back figurines, Ben (Obi-Wan) Kenobi and Luke Skywalker, 1970s.

In November 2017, these action figurines sold for $76,700 and $50,622 respectively at Hakes Americana and Collectibles Auction, photos courtesy Hakes Americana, USA.

Wars figures are now extremely valuable. A **Boba Fett** figure sold for £18,000 at auction in 2015 and a mechanical droid fetched £7000. Vectis' Star Wars expert, Kathy Taylor, said 'It isn't anything that is just a toy – it's actually a way of life and a cultural thing – people look at these card backs (Star Wars figurines new in the packet) we sell as a work of art.'[66] In 2017, as discussed in the introduction, a *Star Wars* figure **Obi-Wan Kenobi** sold for over US$70,000. Fortunately, most *Star Wars* collectibles are plentiful and still very accessible to entry-level collectors. The choice is comprehensive with items as diverse as children's **Darth Vader** cake molds. Apart from spacemen, cereal premiums and early dime-store figures such as those illustrated here, small-scale sci-fi figurine toys designed with such creativity and character had never entered the market en masse before.

George Lucas wrote the original *Star Wars* scripts with assistance from various writers including sci-fi writer, the late Leigh Brackett. It is interesting to note the two covers of *Analog* (illustrated here), the science fiction/science fact magazine (published by Condé Nast in New York) dated November 1973 and July 1975, both look remarkably similar to *Star Wars* characters who appear in the series. The 1973 issue is illustrated with an instrument-playing alien who looks very like **Tedn D'hai,** who plays a flute-like instrument in the Figrin D'an band in the cantina at Mos Eisley Spaceport.[67] The scene where **Luke Skywalker** and **Ben (Obi-Wan Kenobi)** visit the cantina and apprehensively merge with a menagerie of incredible creatures and spacemen from other planets, is surely one of the most enduring from the *Star Wars* genre of movies. The gun toting hairy creature depicted on the cover of the July 1975 issue of *Analog* looks most certainly related to **Chewbacca** – perhaps his brother?

It was not long before a further blockbuster television and movie series

Two sci-fi figures depicted in *Science Fiction Science Fact Analog* magazine published by Condé Nast, USA. The Tedn D'hai-type musician was drawn by notable illustrator Frank Kelly Freas (1922–2005) for the Stanley Schmidt sci-fi short story The Sins of the Father, where Beldan plays an 'Intricately shaped instrument of Black Metal'. Published November 1973. The Wookie-type figure was designed by legendary illustrator John Schoenherr (1935–2010), illustrator of Dune. The illustration here relates to a George Martin sci-fi story And Seven Times Never Kill Man, published November 1975 appeared in *Battlestar Gallactica*, created by Glen A Larsen. Several toys and games have spawned from this franchise, the most common being the eponymous board game Battlestar Gallactica, produced by Parker Brothers USA in 1978. One actor who also made the transition from Westerns to sci-fi was iconic Westerns actor, Lorne Greene from *Bonanza*. He starred as Commander Adama in *Battlestar Gallactica*, which aired for one year in 1978 and 1979 (17 September 1978–4 August 1979).

There are other lesser known sci-fi and space heroes who materialized during this momentous period of sophisticated toy making. The ones mentioned or discussed in this chapter are either the most significant or, in some cases, the most obscure, but they are referenced in collectibles that are represented in my forty-year collection. There are complete books written about most of these, such as *Captain Scarlet*, for example, so further reading material is available for readers seeking more history and information to the background of the shows and toys involved.

While this chapter does not question the originality of sci-fi movies, television and radio shows or the classic toys from mega sci-fi franchises and sci-fi heroes, it does attempt to clarify the backstory and unravel the origins of this wonderful

era of toy invention and production. It is remarkable and significant the influence early science-fiction writers had on movie, radio and television serials, and ultimately the brilliant toys that are collected, still made and played with today.

Star Wars Tedn D'Hai figurine (Cantina band), plastic *Star Wars* collector series, Kenner/Hasbro, 1997.

CHAPTER 6

EARLY PERIOD–LATE PERIOD PLASTIC TOYS

It is quite remarkable that a firm link exists between ivory and toys, early plastics and toys and toys and art. Ivory was coveted for centuries as a highly desirable material for detailed artworks, particularly carvings, statues, wall panels, plaques and other ornamental objects. Carved ivory objets d'art are among our earliest museum pieces and are held in major museums and private collections throughout the world. The pieces are now categorized and labeled into complex historic periods, dynasties and styles that are often critiqued, debated and cataloged in international auctions. Cataloging ivory items in auctions may also soon become part of ancient history. This practice has been banned in the United Kingdom and government plans outlined

Early plastic/Bakelite marbles 1930s.

in 2017 look set to ban the sale of ivory items completely, including exports. Long established auction house, Leonard Joel of Melbourne, Australia, recently announced they would no longer auction ivory items. The war against abhorrent ivory poaching and the ivory trade continues to this day so it may be surprising to read of the

Bakelite color chips, 1930s.

Pool balls, cast phenolic resin/ Bakelite, c. 1900, Permac, England.

Ivory chess set, nineteenth century, 1½ to 3½ in (4–9 cm).

notable link between the history of the ivory trade and the invention of plastics and toys.

As discussed in Chapter 1, ivory was used for carving exquisite game pieces, often for the aristocracy or those of high rank. A chess piece dating from the twelfth century AD held in a French museum, depicting a king mounted on an elephant, is of the highest quality, even signed by an Arab craftsman Yusut al Bahili. [68] An ivory games box discovered in Ekomi in Cyprus dating from the fourteenth century, is highly decorated in low relief with hunting scenes, while as far back as 200 BC, Meng Ch'ang-Chan (d. 279 BC) is on record as commissioning a bed made completely from ivory[69] after which he surely suffered many sleepless nights. Chou rulers from this period even rode in chariots made from ivory. Not surprisingly, a shortage of elephant tusks and ivory soon became apparent in China.

Such was the extent of trade in ivory by the fifteenth and sixteenth centuries, the French named part of West Africa Côte d Ivoire (Ivory Coast) and the Portuguese named it Costa do Marfim, again translated as Ivory Coast. The first consignment of African elephant tusks arrived in China via Arabian traders and complete shiploads of elephant tusks departed from the African coast bound for England and Europe in the eighteenth century. In 1445 a Portuguese trader/explorer acting for Prince Henry of Portugal is recorded as sailing from Africa with gold and elephant tusks and in 1555 the English vessels the *Hart* and the *Hind* took on tusks in exchange for gold. The value of ivory in the middle of the sixteenth century was reputedly £50 sterling for one cwt (100-pound weight) of ivory, a considerable sum. By

1680 the second Manchu explorer K'ang-Hsi had established twenty-seven imperial ivory workshops. Shanghai, once a small fishing village, became an international port in the nineteenth century and soon became known for its extensive ivory industry, mass producing items for export including ivory and bamboo mahjong sets. The collection and use of ivory for manufacture remained unchecked well into the nineteenth century. It is somewhat sobering, if not tragic, to reflect upon the mass destruction of wildlife, sacrificed to produce items such as holy water buckets, sculptures, dagger handles, fan handles, walking sticks, parasol handles, card cases, games pieces, teetotums and playing dice.

Ivory king and queen chess pieces, c. 1890, 3½ in (9 cm).

Aetdorf a seventeenth century German toy maker produced toys made from wood and ivory and early ivory toys were made by Inuit tribes, including birds and dolls.[70] The invention of plastics in the middle of the nineteenth century may well have saved many animals, perhaps even elephants, from virtual extinction. By the nineteenth century elephants were in danger of being wiped out, particularly in Africa.

Pictured is an ivory chess set dating from the early nineteenth century where the castles and rooks have been carved directly from cylindrical shaped ivory pieces. It is unsurprising that the invention of plastics, which dates back to the middle of the nineteenth century was motivated by the urgent desire to discover or invent an alternative material to ivory. Early inventors such as Christian Schönbein (Swiss, 1799–1868), Alexander Parkes (English, inventor of Parkesine, 1813–1890), Daniel Spill (English 1832–1887) and John Wesley Hyatt (American, inventor of celluloid, 1837–1920) came up with groundbreaking alternatives. Here the game of billiards, or more specifically, billiard balls, takes center stage. The American Hyatt was motivated by a competition to discover an alternative to ivory for the manufacture of billiard

Bakelite draughtsmen, Chad Valley, England, c. 1930s, 1¼ in (3 cm) diameter approx.

Pai gow dominoes, green and butterscotch, cast phenolic resin, c. 1900, 2½ in long (7 cm).

problems. Some balls reputedly exploded after several hits with the cue. One saloon proprietor in Colorado reported when it happened, 'Instantly every man in the room pulled a gun'. Legal battles ensued between Spill and Hyatt but eventually Parkes was declared the actual inventor of celluloid. Subsequently, all issues were resolved and Spill and Hyatt were free to continue with the development of celluloid and the first plastics. Hyatt formed the **American Celluloid Company** in 1871 and Spill the **Xylonite Company** in 1869 ,which re-emerged as the **British Xylonite Company** in 1877.

Celluloid soon became a worldwide phenomenon and while it was used to make dolls by Hyatt and others, it was used initially sparingly for toys. The celluloid racehorses c. 1900 mentioned in Chapter 3 are some of the earliest game pieces made from celluloid. This innovative plastic product involved curing homogenized casein in formaldehyde. **Kewpie** dolls, inspired by Rose O'Neill's comic strip characters in 1909, were originally made from bisque in Germany. Soon they were produced from celluloid and **Elfanbee Company** (a doll maker est. 1912) mass-produced **Kewpies** in celluloid and later, in 1949, hard plastic (see picture). Celluloid was used extensively in Germany and

balls, after a company offered a prize of $10,000 to anyone who could invent a new product. Hyatt entered a gum, shellac, pulp and cellulose nitrate ball which did not actually win the competition. It did however become the basis for celluloid products such as billiard balls, pool balls, piano keys and false teeth by 1870. Hyatt's billiard balls were not without their

Japan for toy making, including festive decorations until the Second World War, as we shall see, and few toys were made from Bakelite at all. Celluloid however was fragile, subject to implosion, and although mass-produced, the toy survival rate has been limited. There are nevertheless many wonderful survivors, particularly dolls and licensed or unlicensed **Disney character toys** produced in the 1920s and 1930s.

These trail blazing products such as **casein, celluloid, Parkensine, Catalin**, phenolics and **Bakelite**-type materials were ideal substances to replace ivory and bone, which required laborious hand cutting, shaping and carving, particularly for items such as game pieces. Game playing pieces, traditionally made from bone, ivory or wood – such as dominoes, backgammon, chess, mahjong and checkers – soon graced the shelves of department stores and toy shops, made from these new materials. Counters that had traditionally been made from bone or ivory were also now made from Bakelite or similar materials.

Pictured also is a scarce set of Chinese **pai gow** gambling dominoes made from cast phenolic resin. These have an interesting history and were purchased from a New Zealand bric-a-brac auction for a few dollars over thirty years ago. The Chinese were early immigrants to New

Kewpie Doll, cellulose acetate plastic, c 1950, 'Fethalite' plastics, Australia, 10½ in high (27 cm).

Zealand (similarly to the west coast of North America), working to establish mines in the South Island and market gardens in the North Island. Stories of Chinese gambling dens are legendary, often portrayed as seedy or rambunctious backdrops to a movie act, and in early New Zealand mining towns in particular, it seems this was no exception. A book published revealing the history of New Zealand gambling describes early Chinese immigrant miners as '…frugal at work and exuberant at play…bringing their own games of **fantan** and **pakapoo**.'[71] Historical records from early mining settlements in the 1860s, such as Tuapeka in the South Island of New Zealand, mention Chinese gambling games such as **pai gow** (dominoes), **fantan** (played with stones), **pakapoo**, ('pak ah pu', a type of **lotto** game) and **mahjong.** By 1859, gambling had been outlawed but this did not seem to curtail the gambling activities. In 1869 an *Otago Witness* journalist reported '…astonishment at his ease of entry into a Chinese gambling den in Tuapeka, Central Otago, and the openness with which **fantan** was played, considering it was against the law.' He further stated, 'considering the uproar and confusion that prevails it is a remarkable fact that open rupture seldom or never takes place'.[72] Was this set pictured here similar to the one used at Tuapeka? The playing pieces are quite exquisite, molded from butterscotch and green phenolic resin with hand painted recessed dots. The set is contained in the original decorated tin with bone dice. Despite **pai gow's** rather checkered career, the game has endured throughout the centuries and as recently as 1992 a fine set of pai gow betting dominoes was seized by the police during a sting on the Canton Social Club in Wellington. Perhaps one of the boys in blue is a toy or game collector.[73] Only a year later **pai gow** enlivened the headlines again, when an armed raid took place among forty or so gamblers in the Four Seas China Society clubrooms in Symonds Street, Auckland. As they made their escape, one of the perpetrators fired a round into the good luck shrine. This bravado seemed to tempt fate somewhat as when they arrived back at their robber's lair, it was discovered they had indeed forgotten the rare set of **pai gow** dominoes.

The inventor of **Bakelite,** Dr Leo Baekeland (Belgian, 1863–1944) has been described as the father or inventor of plastics. There are many excellent publications documenting the complex history of plastics manufacturing with Dr Baekeland together with several of his contemporaries. Suffice to say, Baekeland was posthumously inducted into the National Inventors Hall of Fame in 1978, such was his influence on the history of manufacturing. Soon after the revolutionary material **Bakelite** was invented in 1907, among a myriad of uses that included game pieces, it was widely used in industrial and domestic applications, for the manufacture of electrical components, phones, radio cabinetry, household items, cameras, jewelery and motor vehicle componentry. Complete car dashboards were made from **Bakelite** for Morris Series E and early Ford Prefect cars in the 1940s. The Ford V8 Pilot cars made in England between 1947 and 1951 sported a dashboard and interior panels completely of Bakelite. If Bakelite was good enough for cameras, radios, phones and car dashboards, it was certainly good enough for toys. Nevertheless, there was an obvious reluctance by toy makers to invest in expensive compression molds to manufacture relatively low-priced and essentially short-lived items. At this time materials such as tin plate, cast-iron, lead, slush metal, celluloid and pressed steel remained the most common materials for toys. Die-cast toys and even vehicles made from rubber began their significant manufacturing history in the late 1920s with companies such as **Tootsietoy** and **Sun Rubber** from the USA, and **Meccano's Dinky** toys in 1934. As we shall see later in this chapter, new plastics and injection molding processes eventually changed the direction of toy manufacturing history.

It seems the first significant series of Bakelite plastic toys were produced by an English company **Automobiles Geographical Limited (AGL)** in 1931.

'Ranlite' toy cars advertised in *Meccano Magazine* 1931. Possibly the first advertisement for Bakelite toys it promises 'There are good times coming' despite an unprecedented current global economic depression following the Wall Street crash in 1929. These outstanding toys have survived almost 100 years of good and bad times, a credit to the makers, Automobiles Geographical Ltd of England, and the enduring qualities of Bakelite plastics.

A maroon and black model of a 'Ranlite' 1930 Austin 16/6 Burnham saloon, 10½ in (27 cm) long approx.

Early plastic, pressed steel and tin-plate cranes by Gama, West Germany, c. 1950s, 16½ tall (42 cm).

AGL manufactured three relatively large-scale vehicles which even today are not only rare, but outstanding toys of the highest quality. This company were minnows in the context of toy production but the legacy they have left places them at the forefront of early Bakelite/plastic toy making history. The cars produced under the **Ranlite** brand were scale models 10 inches (25 centimetres) long of a 1930 **Austin 16/6 Burnham saloon** and a 1930 **Singer Six saloon.** The real Singer Six was advertised as 'Maintaining British Leadership', and 'Reflecting tomorrow's vogue!'[74] This car was the top of line Singer model, priced at £350. Singer started out as a bicycle manufacturer in 1874, moving into motor vehicle production in 1901. The

company was initially taken over by Rootes Group in 1956 and ended its days after the takeover by Chrysler Corporation in 1970.

These impressive toy cars are fitted with powerful clockwork motors, telescopic steering and removable wheels and tires. The **Austin** parades a sliding sunshine roof while the **Singer** has a folding rear carrier and a side mounted spare wheel. The chassis and guards are pressed steel; the only criticism could be the lack of headlights – no night-time driving in these vehicles! There were a number of color variations which included maroon, black, two-tone green and black, two-tone black and tan and 'mottled' (see picture). These toys have survived well but originally priced at 35 shillings each, it is unlikely there was a large production run. The survivors are often found in good condition with their original boxes, sometimes with the odd crack to the Bakelite due to an accident. The most common failures are the rubber tires and die-cast steering linkage, which is often broken due to metal fatigue.

The third Bakelite toy made by **AGL** was a model of the spectacular **streamline Golden Arrow** land-speed racer, which set a new flying mile record of 231.45 miles per hour (372.46 kilometres per hour) in 1929 at Daytona Beach in the USA, driven by Major Henry Seagrave

(1896–1930). Unusually, the vehicle was cooled by ice chests rather than a radiator. Seagrave died in 1931 after setting a water speed record. The vehicle never ran again, having covered fewer than 50 miles, and now sits in the National Motor Museum in Beaulieu, England. Several toy makers produced period versions of the famous racer including Gunthermann of Germany and **Kingsbury Toys** of the USA. These classic, antique Bakelite toys have stood the test of time and are now almost ninety years old. As we shall see in this chapter, Bakelite toys have outlasted many plastic toys produced since the pioneering days of **Ranlite.**

Another toy maker who utilized Bakelite for toys early on was well-known German toy maker **GAMA** (1882), acronym for the founder Georg Adam Mangold. **Gama** is known for its production of quality tin-plate toys such as the mobile and fixed pylon crane pictured. These cranes are somewhat transitional toys, featuring strong plastic cabs mounted on pressed steel frames, made in the 1950s. Also pictured is a very rare two-tone green **Bakelite 1934 Graham saloon** with a clockwork motor and tin-plate grille. Originally listed as toy 'automobile number 550' it measures only 4 inches (10 centimetres) long and is a rare survivor from what was soon to be a war

1934 Graham sedan, Bakelite and tin plate, clockwork by GAMA, Germany, 1930s, 4 in long (10 cm).

Cord style sports coupe, Codeg, England, 1930s, Bakelite, 13¼ in long (34 cm).

Maker's stamp on base of Bakelite truck.

Two Singer and one Austin clockwork 'Ranlite' sedans, Bakelite and pressed steel, c. 1930, by Automobiles Geographical Ltd (AGL), England.

torn and broken empire.

While relatively few toys were made from Bakelite, there is no better evidence of toys imitating art than the Bakelite automobiles made by **Codeg** (Cowen de Groot) of Clerkenwell, London, in the 1930s. The toys included here are spectacular, large in scale, 13½ inches long (34 centimetres) and quite sculptural. **Codeg** was founded by SD Cowan and A de Groot in 1919 and operated mainly as an importer and wholesaler of a variety of goods including toys. The maroon-speckled Bakelite open coupe is based on a 1936 **Cord 810/812,** a Gordon Buerig (1904–1990) designed automobile which has a reputation as one of the most classic automobiles ever designed, but was a lemon

on the road due to continual problems with the semi-automatic transmission. The toy, and likewise the real car, sit in museums and collections, coveted and much admired but rarely leaving the safety of captivity. The other **Codeg** vehicle pictured seems in unplayed with condition. This vehicle is a toy which actually delivers on the promise of the illustration on the box cover. Produced with electrically operated lights and steering, the blue color is captivating. The sports car was also available in pastel green, red, blue and cream.

Various countries experimented with Bakelite toy production. Two Bakelite trucks, pictured, are at the opposite ends of the spectrum in terms of sophistication but that does not lower their collectibility.

The speckled brown, Bakelite. flat-deck truck was made in Australia sometime in the 1940s. It is a large-scale toy measuring 12 inches (30 centimetres) but could be considered almost an example of folk art. There is a minimal amount of detailing on the molding, although the truck has telescopic steering and is stamped in relief 'J.H.' on the underside of the tray. The other truck is a superb scale model of a **1946 Ford Jailbar tip-truck.** This clockwork toy measures 12½ inches (32 centimetres) and features an opening bonnet (hood) which reveals a black, Bakelite, V8 engine. Made by Jelba of Madrid, Spain around 1947, it was purchased with the original instruction brochure from the maker, **Creaciones Mecanicas Jelba. Jelba SL** raised the bar further by producing an even more impressive truck and trailer unit. The trailer unit sports a covered wagon type canvas looped top. These are beautifully made toys of a classic Ford truck, commonly called the 'Jailbar' due to the grille design.

From Spain we head across to Czechoslavakia (Czech Republic) where one of the first streamline airstream cars was designed. **Tatra** first manufactured cars in 1897 and manufacture trucks to this day. The green, Bakelite, streamline toy, is also large in scale at 9 inches long

Codeg sports car, electric lights, clockwork, Bakelite plastic, Codeg, England, c. 1930s, 13½ in long (34 cm).

Tatra T77 sedan, green Bakelite, 1930s–1950s, made in Czechoslovakia, 9 in long (32 cm) long.

(32 centimetres) and is a replica of the aerodynamic **Tatra T77,** which was first produced in 1933. It is well made with brown Bakelite wheels, black rubber tires and a black Bakelite base. Czechoslovakia can lay claim to a number of locally produced Bakelite composite toys made by toy company **Sery.** Also pictured here is a very rare 1940s/1950s **Skoda Tudor 1101** saloon car made from a Bakelite-type composition. Skoda produced this car from 1946 until approximately 1952. This toy

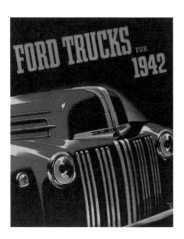

Unusual flat deck truck, speckled brown Bakelite body and wheels, marked J.H. on base, possibly James Holden, Melbourne, Australia, 1930s, 12 in long (30 cm).

Ford Jailbar tip truck, Bakelite by Jelba, Spain, c. 1947, 12½ in long (32 cm).

FORD TRUCKS FOR **1942**

Advertisement 'Ford Trucks for 1942', 1942 'Jailbar' V8 pick-up. The Ford Jailbar and Ford Bonus pick-up trucks are considered two of the most iconic pick-up trucks ever made.

was recently found unplayed with in an original plain brown cardboard box. Labeled 'Sery' on the Bakelite base plate, the toy was made around 1950. Accented with gold leaf brightwork and black rubber tires, the box label states 'Auticko Tudor' – a rare and stylish toy in any condition. This particular Skoda model was imported into Australia in 1950 and reviewed in the *Australian Monthly Motor Manual*, in July 1950. Headlined as a 'newcomer to Australia', the review was generally very positive, stating, 'The body design is conventional in every respect, modern and well streamlined.' An advertisement earlier in the magazine states 'Here it is – the outstanding car of the year.' With a 'gravity feed' fuel tank, fitted under the bonnet, I would have some doubts about that claim. The toys that remain however are safe and highly prized by eccentric collectors such as the writer.

Moving back to Germany, we see the classic Bakelite **Car Ju sportsmodell** vehicles, which came in a range of colors including cream, red, black, maroon and tan and Bakelite brown. There may be other colors but if so I have not seen them. These clockwork toys have several operating parts, including steering, horn, opening boot and doors. The number plate reads MC50, the initials of the maker, **Max Carl Judenbach** of Germany. The vehicle is possibly based on a BMW and comes in the original box; another quality Bakelite plastic toy.

A rare example of transitional manufacturing from New Zealand is the large-scale **Packard 'Sloper' sedan** made by **Plastic Products NZ Limited.** This car was made from a formulation of sawdust, casein and formaldehyde, similar to the established compositions developed by Hausser (Elastolin, est. 1904) and Lineol of Germany (est. 1903), which were early doll and toy figurine makers. Casein was invented in 1897 by Adolf Spitteler (1846–1940) and Wilhelm Krische. The formulation for Elastolin and Lineol figurines was reputedly invented by an Austrian company, Pfeiffer, in Vienna in 1898. Not long after, complete armies of extremely detailed figures emerged, which are highly collectible today. **Lineol's** figurines and animals were designed by notable German sculptor and artist Albert Caasmann (1886–1968). Cassmann also designed for famous porcelain makers Rosenthal AG and Volkstedt and his designs and toy soldiers are housed in several museums. Similar compositions were employed to make dolls prior to the 1940s by dollmakers such as the **Ideal Toy Company** from the USA. From their recipe, **Plastic Products NZ Limited** began making dolls' heads in the 1940s, which they also exported during the Second World War. Their toy car seems to be based on a late 1940s **Packard,** possibly cast from an American plastic or pressed-steel model. Somewhat unusually, I have a rough, cast-iron version of this toy, possibly made experimentally, by **Plastic Products.** An aluminum version, exactly the same, stamped 'PP NZ', is held in a private collection in New Zealand. Materials at this time were in short supply and manufacturing processes were at the threshold of groundbreaking changes and developments. **Plastic Products NZ Limited** progressed to become a major early New Zealand plastics manufacturer until their sale to glass, plastics and steel maker, **Alex Harvey Industries** in 1963.

Classic building sets that must be included in this chapter are **Bayko** building sets manufactured by

Skoda Tudor 1101 saloon, maroon, Bakelite-type composition, made by Sery, Czechoslovakia, 1950, 8 in (20 cm).

Skoda 1101 saloon, advertisement, *Australian Monthly Motor Manual*, July 1950.

Packard 'Sloper', composition, marked PPNZ, c. 1940s, 10 in (26 cm) long.

Car Ju sportsmodell, red Bakelite/plastic by Max Carl Judenbach, Germany, c. 1950, 8 in long (20 cm).

German Second World War soldiers, Lineol, Berlin, c. 1930s, composition 3 in (8 cm) high.

Plimpton Engineering Co Ltd from Liverpool, England. **Bayko,** made from **Bakelite,** was invented by Charles Bird Plimpton (1894–1948) in 1933 and the first sets were actually named **Bayko Light Construction Sets**. Plimpton, who had served on minesweepers in World War I, developed tuberculosis shortly after, in the 1920s. While recovering in a sanatorium, Plimpton designed his **Bayko** sets based on **Mobaco** wooden building sets that had been made in Holland. He applied for a patent in 1933 and by 1935 the sets were advertised in *Meccano Magazine*. The building sets were a success and eventually exported around the world, mainly to countries in the Commonwealth, including New Zealand. Plimpton sadly died of tuberculosis in 1948 but the company, carried on by his wife Margaret Plimpton,

soon saw production peak at 155,000 sets in 1950. By 1958, the sets were produced in polystyrene plastic instead of Bakelite but production by then had fallen to 50,000 sets. The company was sold to **Meccano** in 1959 but by 1967 **Bayko** had lost the building set market to opposition such as **LEGO.** The set, pictured, is essentially new in the box, hardly played with, if at all. **Bayko** building sets are superb examples of toys made from **Bakelite** and early plastics and this set is a favorite in my collection. My early experiences with Bayko however always carried the thought it was surely quicker to build a real house than a Bayko one – then again, perhaps that is why I am not a builder.

Another early British plastics toy maker was **International Model Aircraft Ltd** who manufactured **Frog** model aircraft and ships from 1936. Their toys are mentioned and illustrated in Chapter 8.

To round off this section relating to early plastic toy making, while considering the history of billiard balls and their contribution to the discovery of early plastics, we see a Bakelite billiard/pool set illustrated here titled **Permac.** Proudly labeled 'British Made', these balls were manufactured in the early twentieth century. **Permac, Crystalate** and **Duperite** are some of the many trade names coined by manufacturers of Bakelite-type products during this period. A **Crystalate** product from this period is a combination draught and chess set labeled 'St George Series – made in England' (**Chad Valley**). These sets were supplied to POW soldiers in the Second World War. **FJ Hayter** (England) and **Chad Valley** also made draughts sets in Bakelite in the 1930s.

A degree of overlap obviously exists where compression molded toys were superseded by those that were injection molded. Bakelite toys were still made by some companies after the Second World War such as **Bayko** and **Tedsco Plastics** in the USA, which made a series of streamline compression-molded coupes in the 1950s (see picture). These toys are quite sculptural, echoing the final throes of Art Deco design, which began in the 1930s. Some Bakelite products are still made today, proving the durability and longevity of this innovative product.

LATE PERIOD PLASTICS

Although the 1950s signaled the beginning of the golden age of plastic toy production, or as the title of this chapter suggests, the arrival of late period plastic, manufacturing toys by injection molding processes advanced to an extent

Bayko building set, plastic and Bakelite, c. 1950.

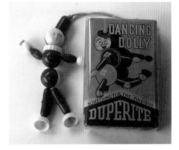

Smaller dolls were made in the form of crib toys. An unusual 'Dancing Dolly' crib toy is pictured here in white and maroon Bakelite plastic 'Duperite', Modern Plastics (New Zealand), c. 1950, 6½ in (17 cm) long.

An earlier pair of crib toys by Little Tikes, USA, cast phenolic resin, 1930s, 3½ in (9 cm) long.

Playmate Toys rare block set, catalog page showing early interlocking blocks and other plastic toys.

Playmate plastic blocks, Moulded Products Australasia Ltd.

Crystalate combination draughts and chess set, Bakelite, c. 1940, 6 in (15 cm) long .

by trial and error. **AGL** (Ranlite Toys), pioneer plastics toy maker in the early 1930s, proved that precision quality toys could be manufactured successfully in Bakelite plastic – similarly with Plimpton's **Bayko.** New thermoplastics, polyethylene and bright color ranges available from molding resins in the 1950s witnessed a phenomenon – an explosion of bright and attractive toys produced in their millions. A common problem associated with early plastic toys and those made from polyethylene and polystyrene was warping due to exposure to heat. This was not necessarily a problem with early Bakelite toys, which have proved to be much hardier. Manufacturing toys with plastic was to some extent viewed with suspicion by toy designers. In 1939 Hilary Page (1904–1957 England) designed the **Kiddicraft** interlocking blockset cubes (see picture). These four-stud half-brick cubes and eight-stud full-brick cubes designed to interlock, were precursors to plastic **LEGO** and similar sets developed after World War II. Such was Page's apprehension towards producing a traditionally robust toy in plastic, he and his co-directors set up a separate company, **Kiddicraft Limited,** to mitigate any business failure.

At this point, we should acknowledge the forerunners of the plastic block and construction sets, which of course were largely made from wood, although there were others made of stone or brick. **Crandells** of USA (est. 1860s) were arguably the finest maker of interlocking wooden block sets in the nineteenth century (refer chapter 9). Germany created a legacy of fine wooden and stone building sets, boxed in precise wooden cases, and much later **LEGO** produced fine wooden boxed blocksets in the 1940s. These early **LEGO** blocksets are very collectible and likewise valuable, a 'good condition' set in the original box selling for over $1000. They are not, however interlocking sets. A nice early folk-art block set is illustrated here, made in New Zealand from native kauri timber in the nineteenth century, one of many types that have endured and are still manufactured today. It is interesting to note **LEGO** did not move to plastic for their blocks until 1947 when they reputedly copied the **Kiddicraft** self-locking building blocks after purchasing a plastic injection-molding machine. The plastic interlocking blocks Hilary Page designed were 1¼ inch (4 centimetre) half bricks and 2½ inch (6 centimetre) whole bricks. Page's daughter is on record as stating she was glad her father never lived to see LEGO's success.

The early plastic blocks, pictured, marketed as **Protex** plastic play blocks, are probably based on Page's original interlocking cube blocks and appear to be the first plastic construction blocks manufactured in New Zealand. **Custom Moulders (NZ) Ltd,** who manufactured **Protex** toys were the innovative plastics division of the National Brush Company from Auckland, New Zealand. Many companies who moved to plastics for their manufacturing during this time often made toys with a mixture of various colored

LEGO building set #112, 1977, Denmark, 13 ¾ x 9 ½ in (35 x 24 cm). This is one of the first LEGO sets to feature human figures.

Doll, composition head, torso and hands, Plastic Products New Zealand, c. 1940, marked PPNZ, 23 in (58 cm) long.

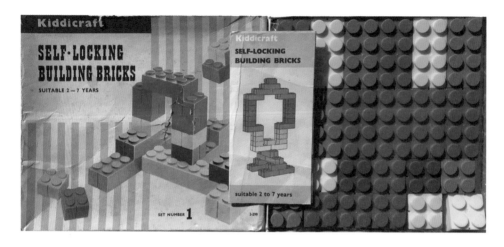

Kiddicraft blockset, Hilary Page, England, plastic, c. 1950. Precursors to LEGO blocks. These blocks were originally marketed by Page as 'Bri-Plax' building blocks in England in the 1930s.

Streamline coupes, Bakelite, Tedsco Plastics, USA, c. 1950, 6 in (15 cm) long .

molding resins left over at the end of the day's production runs – their 'end of day' plastics. These items, which were not just restricted to toys, are variously described as 'variegated' or 'mottled' plastic. Many of these early **Protex** blocks were made from a mixture of colored molding resins and as such have become collector's items. Other toys with this effect, pictured here, include a brown **American coupe,** an

Australian **Winna streamline coupe,** a blue plastic **pick-up truck,** and a green **Ford pick-up** made by **Luxor** in Holland.

The mottled hard plastic locomotive came from Australia and seems to originate from an English plastics toy company **Kleeware** mold, which produced a very similar locomotive. This toy was made by **Mouldex** of Melbourne, Australia who also made the impressive green and white spacecraft mentioned in Chapter 5. Unlike the **Kleeware** toy, it has tin-plate wheels. Several variegated plastic toys are illustrated throughout this chapter. The

Protex plastic cube blockset, Bakelite and plastic, Custom Moulders (NZ) Ltd, c. 1950, 1½ x 1½ in (3.5 x 3.5 cm) approx.

Wooden block set, Kauri wood, New Zealand, c. 1890, 7 x 7 in (18 x 18 cm).

marbled look creates an abstract art effect similar to some marble Murano glass or, in the case of the **Protex** speckled Bakelite blocks, a Jackson Pollock (1912–1956) miniature. The hard plastic polystyrene **Protex** blocks are relatively brittle, although the box cover claims the toys are 'unbreakable, colorfast, washable and educational'. While **Protex** could justify most claims on the box, 'unbreakable' was stretching a point. Some of the first **Protex** blocks, which are stronger, appear to be manufactured from Bakelite, the variegated and speckled blocks, while collectible, are considerably cheaper than a Pollock painting. In fact, I just bought twenty from the New Zealand Trademe website for $10. Good art or vintage toys for that matter do not have to be expensive.

A similar plastic blockset was produced by **Playmate Toys of Australia.**

Locomotives in variegated plastic. Large size locomotive by Mouldex, Melbourne, Australia and plastic locomotive whistle by Kleeware Plastics, England, c. 1940s. Large locomotive 11 in long (28 cm), whistle 3¾ in (10 cm) approx.

Three variegated plastic vehicles, 1950s, 4½–5 in long (11–14 cm).

Three Bakelite streamline roadsters made by Winna Toys, Australia, c. 1940, 7 in long (18 cm).

Playmate was a brand name of **Moulded Products Australasia Ltd,** which claimed to be Australia's largest plastics organisation.[75] They manufactured a fine example of a **Renwal** (USA) speed racer, a set of cylindrical stacking blocks and plastic dolls, among other toys (see pictures). **Playmate Toys** also made a notable early interlocking blockset called **Bilda-brix.** This is another building set designed with interlocking studs, similar to many toys produced that copied **Minibrix, Kiddicraft** or **LEGO. Bilda-brix** plastic brick sets were also made in New Zealand by **Downs Poole Limited** of Wellington, probably under license to **Playmate Toys.** Plastic brick sets such as **LEGO** could not in effect be imported during this postwar era of import license and tariff protection that was afforded to local manufacturers in New Zealand. These brick sets are remarkably similar to **LEGO,** but it seems at this stage of proceedings all bets were off in the plastic toy brick and block construction world. Most of the real world after all was experiencing an unprecedented period of construction or reconstruction and these brick and building sets are ostensibly a reflection of this monumental era of building and rebuilding.

Another designer of an iconic construction set that was produced in plastic, although only for a short time, was John Lloyd Wright (1892–1972), son of famous architect Frank Lloyd Wright. John Wright designed and patented **Lincoln Logs** interlocking wooden building sets in 1916, which were initially made from Redwood (see picture). In the 1970s

Bilda Brix construction set, plastic, Playmate Toys, Australia, c. 1950.

production was changed to plastic but before long the decision was made to revert to genuine wood logs – one of the few toys to buck the trend of manufacturing with plastic. **Lincoln Logs** are still made today by **K'nex** in Maine, USA, again going against the grain by transferring production back to the USA from China.

Despite a few anomalies, the precision of injection-molded thermoplastics changed the face of toy making. Toy construction blocks and other toy building set manufacturers soon mined a rich vein of the market producing thousands of sets, many based on designs originally produced in wood or rubber. In the 1940s **Halsam** from Chicago in the USA produced

Lincoln Logs may have been named with reference to the famous nineteenth century American President. One of the first Lincoln Logs sets involved a design for the President's famous log cabin.

American Bricks, plastic, Halsam Products Co. Inc., USA, 1940s.

Town and Country Building Set, plastic interlocking brickset by Greyshaw, Atlanta, USA, c. 1950, cylinder 6½ in long (16 cm).

studded bricks which predate LEGO. They later produced similar bricks in plastic as **American Plastic Bricks** (see picture). **Greyshaw** from Atlanta Georgia made **Town and Country** plastic interlocking bricks in the early 1950s, as did **Elgo** (see picture).

The first plastic (as opposed to Bakelite) toys made in the late 1930s and 1940s were less detailed, generally small in scale and pitched at a dime-store level. Examples of these from my toy collection include the pale blue sedan, pictured, made by **Kilgore** of the USA, previously a significant cast-iron toy maker. This toy was one of the first plastic, injection-molded toys produced in the USA, advertised in *Playthings* magazine in April 1938.[76] Made from cellulose acetate, the advert states, among other claims, 'The trend is definitely towards plastic'. Another early, prewar plastic injection toy maker was **Lapin Products Inc** from the USA who made a similar range of toy vehicles that were advertised in *Modern Plastics* magazine in 1939.[77]

Molds and dies were soon hired by other companies internationally enabling them to produce locally for their domestic market or near neighbors. **Playmate Toys,** mentioned earlier as a pioneer Australian plastic toy maker, produced their streamline racing car from a **Renwal mold** produced in 1950. Similarly, the plastic fire truck, pictured, was made in New Zealand by **Custom Moulders (NZ) Limited** under their **Protex** brand. The molds originated from **Banner Plastics** in the USA and these toys still retain the **Banner** logo underneath the toys, with 'USA' removed from the mold.

A rare find while trekking through bric-a-brac stores and collectible fairs in Australia thirty years ago was a

Plastic sedan by Kilgore, USA, 1930s, 4 in (10 cm) long approx.

'Plastic' fire truck, Protex Plastics (NZ) Ltd, 1950s, from Banner Plastics USA mold 1948, 4 ¼ in (10 cm) long.

complete box of new streamline coupes, petrol tankers and pick-up trucks from the 1940s marked **Marquis Toys.** The old store-stock box is labeled '3 doz Assorted Toys, Marquis Plastics, Commonwealth Moulding Pty Ltd, Princes Highway, Arncliffe, NSW, Australia'. These toys were originally made by **Kilgore Manufacturing** of the USA and it is likely the molds were purchased from them. The petrol or gas tankers are molded with a 'Power Chief' name in relief on the tank. While a few budding collectors have begged for one or two examples, I think it would be a shame to split the contents having survived intact for over seventy years. While they remain in sparkling new condition, despite a few warping in the Aussie heat, they are now safe and sound in New Zealand. Other toys **Marquis** produced include plastic ducks, a train set, a garage for their vehicles, children's tea sets, and a real must have – 'midge', the

Assorted toy vehicles, as new, old store stock, three dozen toys by Marquis Plastics Commonwealth Moulding Pty Ltd, Australia, 1940s, each 4½ in long (10 cm) approx.

Bakelite Plastics, Monsanto Plastics, General American advertisement, By 1939 Monsanto offered a wide range of plastics including cellulose acetate, cellulose nitrate, cast phenolic resin, vinyl acetate and polystyrene. *Fortune* magazine August 1939.

plastic mouse.[78] The cats must have got them all as I have yet to find one.

From small beginnings in the 1930s, following the Second World War, American manufacturers embraced plastic toy making with renewed vigor. The raw materials and plastic products were promoted widely by monolithic chemical companies such as **Monsanto, Don Corning** and **Du Pont** (see pictures).[79] Cast-iron, a perennial staple material for many toy makers in the USA became almost obsolete overnight, no longer fit for purpose. Grand toy makers like **Arcade, Hubley, AC Williams, Kenton** and **Kilgore** either ceased toy making or reverted to plastics. **Louis Marx** moved from tin plate to plastics while **Hubley** embraced both plastics and die-cast metal. A few manufacturers (referred to in Chapter 4) tried aluminum. While **Lapin** and **Kilgore** produced plastic toys prior to peace in 1945, it was companies such as **Renwal, Thomas, Louis Marx, Ideal, Banner, Irwin** and **AMT** who dominated the market with a stunning array of inventive and colorful plastic toys. A fine example is the impressive, large-scale, red and blue convertible produced by **Renwal Manufacturing Co** in 1950, pictured. Problems associated with early plastic toy making are evident here however, where the roof has warped and the bodywork alignment is no longer true. Made from cellulose aretate plastic, this handsome, 9 inches (23 **centimetres**) long toy boasts a 'long life motor', including the claim the car will 'scoot away when stroked on the floor'. Sadly, this is no longer the case, although this car is basically new in the box, as shiny as the day it was made, as the rear wheels are jammed to the wheel arches. Advertised in 1950 as 'shatterproof, durable and safe, built with **lumarith** acetate plastic'[80] it seemed a good deal at 79 cents. The toy still displays well, a much-admired keeper in the display cabinet.

The early plastic **Ford V8** made by **Palitoy** of England has fared better. **Palitoy**, a trademark of a British company, **British Pylonite,** began injection molding with plastics in 1941 for their range of toys. **Palitoy's** origins lie with their pioneering founder AE Pallet and his company **Cascelloid Ltd,** which made celluloid toys and dolls from 1919. Pallet purchased the right to **plastex** in the early 1930s, which was touted as 'unbreakable' due to its secret ingredient – glue made from rabbit bones. **Palitoy's** first plastic vehicles were apparently made in 1946, which is about when the toy illustrated here was made. The toy is clockwork and appears new in the box, unplayed with. The box also serves as a garage, thus the toy has 'always been garaged', adding a premium to the value. The original packing label remains inside the box, stamped 'Number 613 – in case of complaint, please quote number – do not overwind'. Sky blue with red wheels – just so right!

Other significant early toy makers from England utilising plastic were **Victory Industries Toys,** of Guilford, Surrey (1945–1965) and **Lines Brothers** with

Convertible sedan, Renwal Plastics, USA, 1950, 9 in long (23 cm).

Ford V8, plastic, Palitoy, England, 1946, 4 in long (10 cm).

their **Triang Minic** range of clockwork miniatures. They are illustrated here along with a selection of other early plastic toys including three **Fethalite** streamline sedans from Australia and a small, yellow American sedan, ironically made by **All Metal Products Co** of America. It seems

Dime-store soldier advertisement, '100 Toy Soldiers for $1.25', Lucky Products, New York, USA, advertisement *Gold Key Comics* February 1974.

most manufacturers by this time were looking to plastic and cost was a large factor in their decision. Economies of scale were easier to achieve with injection molding and not only was the end result appealing, colorful and well-priced, shipping costs were reduced dramatically. Some cast-iron toys weighed over 4 pounds (2 kilograms) alone.

Victory Industries were another of the first British toy makers to resort to plastic injection molding for toy-vehicle manufacture. This company produced the most sophisticated scale model vehicles since the days of **AGL** (Ranlite Toy Vehicles) when they gained a contract from **Nuffield** to manufacture promotional models of the new **Morris Minor** in 1950. This car was set to become an iconic classic of the British motor industry and a precursor to the **Morris Mini,** designed by Sir Alec Issigonis, which became a true icon. **Victory Industries** (VIP) began production of the **Morris Minor** after obtaining injection molds and produced a well-detailed and most successful result. From there **VIP** expanded the range, producing exact scale models of British-made vehicles powered by electric motors, which they also manufactured. The models included an **Austin A40 Somerset,** a **Triumph TR2,** a **MGTF,** a **Vauxhall Velox** and several other locally made vehicles. Unfortunately, they have not lasted all that well, suffering from severe warping. I have owned most of these vehicles at one time or another, and sadly all had suffered the same fate.

VIP and **Lines Bros** soldiered on to trail blaze the slot car set market in the 1960s, but once that phase petered out, so unfortunately did **Victory Industries,** closing in 1969. Victory can still be classed as winners in the game, however, as they have left a fine legacy of early plastic toy making, notwithstanding the spirit of these classic 1950s vehicles, which are rarely, if ever, seen on the roads today. It does seem however that the Bakelite models of 1931 have outlasted the plastic Victory models made twenty years later – such was the experimental history of manufacturing with plastics.

Likewise, scaled down plastic promotional toys by American makers like **AMT** (est. 1948) experienced problems with plastic cellulose acetate warping. In 1960 **AMT** switched to plastic styrene, which effectively solved the problem. By the early 1960s most plastic toy makers had changed to other molding resins. It is perhaps an oxymoron that **AMT** retained their name for their range of plastic toys. The acronym **AMT** stands for Aluminum Model Toys. Their first model, a 1948 promotional for **Ford Motor Company,** was made from aluminum but plastic was the material they used for the rest of their illustrious sixty-year career.

As a fact, it was cheaper to build with plastic, which made plastic toys available for all. Dime-store soldier sets were advertised in the 1960s and 1970s at 100 for US$1. One box of 100 soldiers advertised in 1974 for US$ 1.25 came with a decorated 'pasteboard footlocker'[81] (see picture). **Archer Plastics** from the USA were one of the early leaders in plastic dime-store figures in the 1950s, along with **Lido** and **Ajax.** Substantial makers in England included **Britains, Crescent, Herald, Timpo, Cherilea** and **Tudor Rose** and I still have most of my **Crescent** and **Herald** plastic soldiers and cowboy sets from the 1950s. Available as cereal premiums as well, every child from that era could join in the fun for free. Injection molding enhanced the detail and the fact many, like the **Herald** toys **Scottish Regiment Band,** were supplied hand painted increased their desirability twofold. Plastic space figures were advertised for around $3 for ten in the early 1950s. By the 1960s, a large proportion of plastic manufacturing had been out-sourced to Asia, mainly Hong Kong, and as children we were astonished at the number of toy soldiers a paper run could buy.

Despite current rumblings the age of plastic toys has certainly not ended, with millions of fast-food franchise toy giveaways and **LEGO** bricks virtually paving the world. An ever-changing cliché is the number of **LEGO** bricks

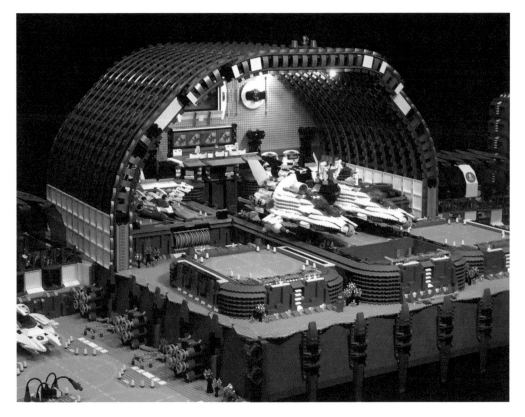

Enceladus Moon of Saturn LEGO space station build at New Zealand LEGO Show 2017, by Mark Lusty, New Zealand.

reputedly prevailing for every person on Earth – around seventy apparently in 2017. I recently attended a huge **LEGO** exposition where thousands of children and adults paid $10 each to view the displays. Most of the impressive displays had been built by adults. One **LEGO** builder, Mark Lusty, informed me he had invested over NZ$35,000 on components to fabricate a stunning space station, enhanced with appropriate audio effects, named **Enceladus – Moon of Saturn** (see picture).[82] One viewer's comment was 'the trip there was worth every cent' and likewise the cost of **Enceladus. LEGO** actually did go into space aboard the space shuttle *Endeavour* in 2011. LEGO space station in Auckland, next, **LEGO** space station on the Moon. Plastic toys really are out of this world!

CHAPTER 7

TWO WHEELS, FOUR WHEELS, HOT WHEELS

If anyone can lay claim to re-inventing the wheel, it could be those who invented and developed bicycles in the nineteenth century. Motorcycles and automobiles miraculously appeared soon after, even in the Wild West, with toys and games following quickly in their tire tracks. Readers, if they are old enough, will remember their first motor car, but if not, they will just as soon remember their first bike. Cycling soon took the world by storm with the first cycling clubs established in the 1870s. Women also took to cycling with gusto, with one intrepid cyclist – Annie Kopchovsky (1870–1947) – cycling around the world successfully in 1894–1895. She deservedly won $10,000 for her epic feat. Annie was named 'Annie Londonderry'

Wheeling, a cycling game by J Jacques & Son, England, also probably inspired by Londonderry, c. 1900, board measures 30 x 15 in (66 x 38 cm).

Cycling, a fascinating game, by JAP and JW Spears c. 1900. An early cycling game based on American pioneer cyclist, Annie Londonderry.

'Cycling', John Player cigarette cards, 1939.

after she carried a placard advertising her sponsor's spring water (Londonderry) for $100 and agreed to change her name accordingly. The early 1900 **Cycling** game by **JAP** and **JW Spears,** pictured here, features a female cyclist on the box modeled after Londonderry, although it is clear cycling at this time was not necessarily for the faint hearted. Apart from the pumps, bells, spanners, repair kits, oil cans and lamps, it seems a revolver was also required. 'If you meet the "footpad" (thief) without the revolver – the player must return to obtain a "revolver" card.' Londonderry had carried a pearl handled revolver during her incredible journey.

The other cycling game **Wheeling,** illustrated here, was published by **J Jacques & Son** of London at a similar time. This game also includes obstacles reflective of the period including a watercart, tacks and the worst obstruction – 'running into an old lady'. Similar tools and accessories are required here such as oil cans, pumps and bells, but this trip, which ends at the Anchor and Ripley Hotel, must be a safe one – no revolver required or supplied. This game comes with an impressive four-panel playing board which measures 30 x 15 inches (66 x 38 centimetres).

There were no espressos, cappuccinos or performance enhancing drugs for these early cyclists, despite the sport being thirsty work. Instead, in the **Cycling** game the cyclists began at the Red Dragon Hotel for a starter and finished at the Oriental Tavern for further refreshments. While these games reflect the very beginnings of recreational cycling, cycling races and clubs began before the twentieth century.

Recreational and commuter cycling in the twenty-first century has come a long way since the days of Annie

Londonderry. With many countries building cycleways and cycle paths in moves to reduce congestion and pollution, bike sharing suppliers are ironically threatening to pollute the world with cycles. Invented over 150 years ago, bicycles it seems are here to stay.

Not long after the bicycle was invented, a motor was added to the frame. As early as 1867, Sylvester Howard (1823–1896, USA) fitted a steam-powered, two-cylinder engine to a velocipede. Various steam-powered cycles materialized in the late nineteenth century but Gottlieb Daimler is widely acknowledged as creating the first gasoline-powered cycle. Similar to the rapid development of motor vehicle production, motorcycles followed suit. By 1914 Indian motorcycles from the USA had produced a powerful 1000cc motorbike. In 1905 Indian had developed the V twin-engine racer and in 1911 achieved the trifecta at the TT Isle of Man, finishing first, second and third. Vermillion red, introduced to the color range in 1902, became known as their enduring 'Indian red' and it is this color the two fine **Hubley** motorbikes have been finished in here. If there is any doubt placing **Hubley Toys** at the forefront of American toy making between the wars, we need only observe the two large-scale 9½ inch long (23 centimetres) cast-iron **Indian** motorbikes pictured here. There is careful attention to detail with a nickel-plated four-cylinder engine on the police bike and a twin V engine highlighted in gold leaf on the US Mail version. This mail van features opening double doors, while both bikes are fitted with spoke wheels with black rubber tires. If proportion, scale, authenticity, quality casting and patina are indications of fine sculpture, then these toys are indeed examples of fine art. Similar to other

By the 1950s all forms of motor vehicles had become an accepted part of the landscape – even in ancient Rome! Here, pedestrians mingle with cyclists, moped rider, motorcyclists and various motorcars, including a Streamline Ford V8 and a woodie station wagon. Postcard, Imperos Street, Roma, c. 1956.

Advertisement for Rugby Streamline bicycle, 1935. By the 1930s even cycles were marked with 'streamline' designs, together with all other forms of transport – far removed from the Penny Farthings and boneshakers in the nineteenth century. Shapleigh Hardware Co, St Louis, brochure/catalog for 1935.

Single cylinder green moped, die-cast and pressed steel, 1930s, 2¼ in long (6 cm) approx.

'Indian' four-cylinder motorcycle with policeman, cast-iron, by Hubley Toys, USA, c. 1930, 9½ in long (23 cm).

'Indian' twin V engine US Mail Bike, cast-iron, by Hubley Toys, USA, c. 1930, 9¼ in long (23 cm) approx.

large-scale cast-iron toys we will see later in this chapter, these toys display immense presence. Although the Indian Motorcycle Company went bankrupt in 1970, the famous name and motorcycles were reborn in 2003. Despite a few ownership changes, a new, modernized Indian motorcycle, sympathetic and in spirit with the original classic bikes, can be purchased today.

WC Fields, the early twentieth century actor and circus performer, once said, 'I spent my money on unreliable cars and less reliable women, the rest I just wasted.' When motor vehicles were first invented before the turn of the twentieth century, there was no doubt unreliability was a feature of their performance. Even today, over 150 years later, racing drivers will curse vehicles upon which millions of dollars have been spent when they fail to go the distance or perform to expectations. One aspect of motor vehicles that has remained consistent and reliable has been the output of toys concurrent to the production of motor vehicles. Toys resembling tiller-steered horseless carriages were out in toy shops not long after they were scaring horses and in many cases the toys have outlasted the real motor vehicles. The early American cast-iron toy pictured here, made by **Kenton Toys,** is modeled after an early tiller-steered **Rambler** or **Chrysler.**

Panhard built cars as early as 1898 with steering wheels but some motorcars were still fitted with tiller steering some fourteen years later. Somewhat poignantly, many toy vehicles have proved far more successful than the real automobile. The **Chrysler Airflow, Cord,** streamline **Grahams** and **Kaiser** cars are examples where the toys have proved to be more plentiful and, in some cases, cars such as the **Cords, Airflows**, streamline **Studebakers**, sharknosed **Grahams** and **Fords** have become classics nevertheless, designed, after all, by famous designers such as **Loewy, Buerig, Tremalis** and **Gregory.**

Advert for 1937 Ford Lincoln Zephyr.

As early as 1951 MOMA (Museum of Modern Art, New York) recognized the artistic qualities of automobiles when they staged an exhibition titled *8 Automobiles.* The introduction to the printed catalog stated: 'The eight automobiles in this exhibition were chosen primarily for their excellence as works of art…automobiles are hollow rolling sculpture.'[83] Several of the eight classic cars that featured in this momentous exhibition are represented through toys in this chapter, including the famous **Cord,** the **Ford Lincoln Zephyr** and the **Lincoln Continental.** A more unusual vehicle in the exhibition was the **Willy's Jeep,** which we mentioned in Chapter 4.

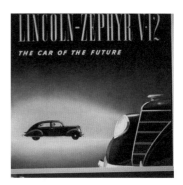

Tiller steered car, c. 1900, cast-iron, by Kenton Toys USA, 5½ in long (14 cm).

As we have seen in earlier chapters, the history of materials used in manufacturing are of course reflected in toy-vehicle making: wood, celluloid, rubber, paper, Bakelite, tin plate, pressed steel, cast-iron, aluminum, lead, die-cast, plastics and even a combination of glue, flour and sawdust. We shall see toys made in many of these materials in this chapter.

Original catalog photo of exhibit number 6, a 1937 Cord in the Museum of Modern Art exhibition, 1951 titled *8 Automobiles.*

Raymond Loewy (1893–1986) became one of the most famous designers of all and is credited with establishing

1910 'Benz' limousine, Matchbox toy, Model of Yesteryear, die-cast, 1960s. Lesney's Models of Yesteryear were beautiful and extremely popular Matchbox toys. All were carefully based on real veteran and vintage cars with a short history of the vehicle printed on the toy box.

'streamline' design. The demand for his industrial and transport designs was such that his list of achievements in the area are probably unsurpassed. Most notable of his designs include the 1930s S1 streamline locomotive, interiors for ocean liners, Greyhound buses, a Boeing 307 for Howard Hughes in the 1930s, cars from Studebakers to Hillman Minxs, the Airforce One aircraft, the Concorde interior, and last but not least, the interior for NASA's Skylab Space Station. Loewy enjoyed a long association with Studebaker cars, designing their leading-edge vehicles from the 1930s until the 1960s. The cast-iron 1934 **Studebaker Landcruiser** pictured here is made by **Hubley Toys** of the USA who were one of the most dominant makers of automotive toys in America between the wars, during a golden age of cast-iron toy making. Postwar they continued to set a new standard for manufacturing with die-cast metal and plastic automotive toy kits. The green **Studebaker** toy here is not in pristine condition by any means but retains all the attributes of a played-with antique toy, which I appreciate. This toy is one of the first cast-iron toys I discovered in New Zealand, purchased, sight unseen, from a printed listing in a Dunedin bric-a-brac auction in 1980. It had been over-painted in black high-gloss paint many years before, which I painstakingly removed. This toy, purchased together with an **Arcade Chrysler Airflow**, around the same time, set me on a journey of constant search and discovery, which for me has been never-ending. There are several versions of this model but the closed coupe, I think, is the cleanest design. **Hubley,** in their final throes of cast-iron toy making, produced a large scale 1939 **Studebaker President yellow cab** taxi. While not **Hubley's** finest work and somewhat clunky, it does have a separate nickel-plated grille which, like the **Landcruiser,** is attached to the cast-iron chassis (see picture). The blue **Studebaker** toy sedan pictured here is a 1949 model **by Fun Ho!** which measures 7½ inches (19 centimetres) long. Unlike the designer Raymond Loewy, **Fun Ho! Toys** never upgraded this model, producing the same toy until 1965.

1934 Studebaker Landcruiser, cast-iron, by Hubley Toys USA, 6½ in long (17 cm).

1939 Studebaker President yellow cab, cast-iron, Hubley Toys USA, 8 in long (20 cm).

Blue Studebaker Sedan by Fun Ho!

1938 Packard, tin plate, clockwork sedan, Toys Nomura, Japan, 10 in long (25 cm).

Packard, tin plate, clockwork, Toys Nomura, Japan, c. 1938, 8 in long (20 cm).

1940s Packard Clipper, aluminum, FunHo! Toys (New Zealand), c. 1948, 4¼ in long (11 cm).

Packard limousine advertisement for the 1940 model, *Fortune* magazine, USA, November, 1939.

Limited numbers were produced, during the 1950s, and this toy is quite scarce.

As we shall see, toy manufacturers were not the only industries affected by the Second World War, material shortages and the ascendance of large conglomerates. **Studebaker** was taken over by **Packard** in 1953, although the **Studebaker** name outlasted the **Packard** marque. **Packard,** based in Detroit, was a luxury car maker, competing with **Cadillac, Rolls Royce** and **Mercedes Benz.** The tin-plate **Packards,** pictured, are two fine clockwork models made by **Toys Nomura** of Japan in the 1930s. The 12-inch (30 centimetre), two-tone red model is a 'barn find' 1937 sedan, while the smaller scale blue 'sloper' sedan is possibly a later version with fender-mounted headlamps – perhaps artistic license. The small orange **Packard** is a 1940s **Packard Clipper** cast in aluminum by **Fun Ho!,** which shows very sleek styling. **Packard** tried a **Clipper** line of models in the 1940s and the 1950s, referring again to earlier transportation adoptions of this title. In 1956, they pushed the boat out further, introducing **Clipper** as a separate make. **Packard** also produced Dream and Concept cars, the earliest the **Pan American** in 1952. It is surprising one of the **Packard** marketing gurus at the name-storming meeting didn't chime in with the question, 'Say, haven't I heard that name before?' Perhaps he had but all those around the table replied, 'No, no, I don't think so – no, definitely not – never heard that name before – let's go with it!' The small independents struggled in the 1950s despite takeovers, mergers and planned mergers that never came to fruition. By 1958, **Packard**, together with their **Packard Clippers** and

Pan Americans, had disappeared into the Bermuda Triangle of the automotive world.

A fabulous cast-iron toy, pictured here, is a 1934–35 **Hupmobile** made by **Kenton Toys** of the USA. Founded by Robert Craig Hupp (1877–1931) Hupmobile were active from 1909 to 1941. This model was also designed by Raymond Loewy and is the **Hupmobile Aerodynamic** model. The toy is impressive at 7½ inches long (19 centimetres), finely cast, finished in two-tone purple and black, featuring a nickel-plated grille with oversize white rubber 'donut' tires. This is a very rare cast-iron toy. The **Hupmobile Motor Car Company** became embroiled in a definitive conclusion to the production of the classic **Cord** motor car mentioned earlier when, in a questionable decision in 1938, they purchased the production dies and tooling for the **Cord 810** for a massive US$900,000. At the same time, **Hupmobile** merged with the **Graham Paige Motor Car Company** to manufacture new versions of the car. Named the **Skylark** and the **Hollywood,** only 319 **Skylarks** were produced and even fewer **Hollywoods. Hupmobile** ceased production in 1940.

Several toys in my collection introduce us to another famous automotive designer, Amos Northup (1889–1937, USA) who designed several significant cars including the 1931–1932 **Reo Royale,** the 1932 **Blue Streak Graham** and the 1938 **Spirit of Motion** sedan. An outstanding large-scale model of the **1931 Reo Royale** was made by **Arcade Toys** (Illinois, USA) in cast-iron. The 9¾-inch-long (25-centimetres) toy features a separate nickel-plated grille, white rubber tires and twin side mounts. The **Reo Royale** was one of the first

Hupmobile, 1934–35, cast-iron by Kenton Toys, USA, 7½ in long (19 cm).

Wooden motor vehicle puzzles. Motor vehicles also appear in many versions of toys and games for young ages. The two wooden screen-printed puzzles here are both classed as 'easy' puzzles for pre-schoolers. The eight-piece puzzle depicts what appears to be a 1948 Dodge and is marked at the lower right, 'Arnold Leech no. 107'. The other is a thirty-two piece puzzle that depicts a 1950s Alvis or Armstrong Siddeley saloon cruising through a picturesque rural English village. This 'Happy Hour' puzzle is made by Philip and Tacey Ltd of Fulham in England and titled 'Motor Car'. The Arnold Leech puzzle measures 7¾ x 9¾ in (20 x 25 cm) while the one from England is larger at 11 in x 11 in (28 x 28 cm), 1950s.

Reo Royale 1931–1932, cast-iron, by Arcade Toys, USA. This Reo is currently in the shop for a full service. Slush-cast figures by Barclay USA, 1930s.

Blue Streak Graham sedan by Tootsietoys, USA, 1930s, 3½ in long (9 cm).

Tootsietoys of the USA were probably the first die-cast model maker. Two early die-cast toys are pictured here. The C Cab van was actually made by Tootsietoys in England in the 1920s, while the other is a Buick made around the same time by Tootsietoys in the USA, 3 in long (8 cm) approx.

American cars to feature curves to the roofline, a slightly slanted windshield and a V-shaped grille. The styling was also very narrow, the widest part of the car at the front seat region. Northup apparently said he worked on the Reo design at night under candlelight for added inspiration.[84] Despite winning a first prize for design at the 'Concours d'elegance' in Rome, the new slimline Reo did not sell well with only 2736 sales in the 1931 year end to September. Regrettably, by 1937 Reo were reduced to making only trucks.

The **Blue Streak Graham** designed by Northup in 1932 is also famed for advancements in aerodynamic design, featuring a slanted windscreen and grille, a curved roofline and skirted, curved fenders. These features were soon adopted by other carmakers and it is Northup who is credited with these quite radical designs for the time. **Tootsietoy** were also impressed, making millions of die-cast versions of the **Blue Streak Graham** such as the yellow and black twin side-mount version, pictured. Although play-worn, at 3¾ inches long (10 centimetres), it is a quality casting, fitted with a separate grille with white rubber donut tires fixed to separate wooden hubs. **Tootsietoys'** origins date back to the late nineteenth century and they possibly produced the first die-cast toy car before the

1936 Graham sedan by Kuramochi & Co. (CK) of Japan, tin plate, clockwork, 11 in long (28 cm).

First World War, heading off other die-cast makers such as **Solido, LEGO, Meccano** and **Lesney. Tootsietoys,** however, sold more toy **Grahams** than the real car. The economic depression proved too much of a hurdle, despite groundbreaking styling and design for the **Graham Car Company.** Ray Graham took his own life in 1932, although the two remaining brothers persevered with the volatile automotive industry.

Pictured is an outstanding c. 1936 tin plate, clockwork toy **Graham sedan** by **CK (Kuramochi & Co)** of Japan. At 11 inches long (28 centimetres) the toy is impressive, featuring chromed split fenders, headlamps, grille and side-mount bracket. Possibly based on the sleek 1936 **Cavalier Graham model,** took the design one step further, positioning the headlamps on the fenders. Some toys look better than the real cars. Two years later a quite spectacular Northup design appeared with the **1938 Spirit of Motion Graham-Paige.** The toy pictured is made by French die-cast maker **Solido,** a quality die-cast toy maker that began making die-cast toys in 1932, two years before Meccano's **Dinky**

'Shark nose', Graham-Paige, die-cast, Solido Toys, France, 5 in long (12.5 cm).

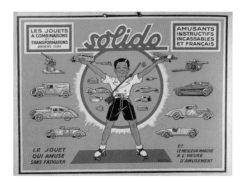

Solido, 1930s advertisement for their die-cast toys.

Toys. Their early die-cast toys were fitted with interchangeable parts and advertised as 'indestructible' (see picture of poster). Despite winning design awards in Paris, the car, which to many prospective buyers looked like a shark, soon became known as the 'shark nose' and failed to sell. Production ceased in 1941. Tragically, the innovative designer died following a fall on an icy sidewalk while in the throes of designing an updated model. The **Solido** model is one of my favorite die-cast toys.

One of the best toys of the famous **Cord 810** cars is the large scale pressed-steel model, pictured, made by **Wyandotte Toys** of the USA. **Wyandotte** (All Metal Products Co., Michigan, USA, 1921–1957) began in the 1920s making toy guns. When their line of BB guns threatened the dominance of the opposition's **Daisy rifles, Daisy** bought out the toy rifle division of **Wyandotte. Daisy** promptly collected all the stock and dies and the trucks crept to a remote part of the Detroit river and dumped the lot – no more pesky **Wyandotte** rifles.[85] **Wyandotte** toys, marketed as 'good and safe' were also extremely strong, the toy cars pressed from scrap motor vehicle gauge steel. In

Cord car and trailer, pressed steel, by Wyandotte Toys, USA, 1930s (restored), 24 in long (60 cm).

Cord coupe (fire chief version), pressed steel, by Wyandotte Toys, USA, c. 1936, 12½ in long (32 cm), photo courtesy Bertoia Auctions, USA.

Cord 810/812, stamped, 'Front drive, Auburn Rubber Co, USA,' c. 1936, 6 ½ in long (15 cm).

general terms though, and in comparison to other toy makers in America and around the world, **Wyandotte's** early efforts slot more into the category of folk art, similarly to New Zealand's **Fun Ho! Toys.** Despite this, during a thirty-six year stretch of toy making, the **Cord car and trailer** is surely **Wyandotte's** pièce de résistance. The car and trailer measure 24 inches long (60 centimetres) and were found in New Zealand in extremely poor condition (sans base plates, wheels and brightwork). The car was originally an unusual fire or police department version with a hole in the hood (bonnet) where a bell once sat. I restored it, painting it in my favorite automotive color – a rich cream. The company exported to New Zealand in the 1930s and it is possible this toy is one of the original exports. **Wyandotte's** toys became more sophisticated in the 1950s but with increasing costs and competition from mega toy makers such as **Louis Marx, Wyandotte** toys went bankrupt in 1956.

Another fine model of the **Cord 810/812** was produced by the **Auburn Rubber Company** of Indiana in the USA in 1936. Hard rubber toys were made by several American toy makers in the 1930s such as **Rainbow Rubber, Sun Rubber** and **Auburn Rubber (Arco).** The toy car pictured here is a well-designed toy and other rubber models by these companies will appear throughout this chapter. Most

life begins with **Airstream**

A whole world of new interests, relaxed easy living is yours in an Airstream. This is travel!...care-free, exciting, economical. Enjoy the sea, the woods, the mountains with all the comforts of home. **Write for interesting free booklet "World At Your Doorstep."**

AIRSTREAM TRAILERS Dept. AG
11 CHURCH ST JACKSON CENTER OHIO • 12804 E FIRESTONE NORWALK CALIF

Airstream trailers advertisement, c. 1958.

China Clipper, USA, Pan American, cruising speed 150 mph. Players cigarette card, 1930s, 'International Airlines', number 44 of 50.

of these companies, apart from **Auburn,** ceased production during the war due to restrictions on the supply of rubber. These toys appeal to me also for their sculptural qualities. Many, however, have warped or deteriorated over time but a number of great survivors remain.

The classic streamline trailers, pictured here, deserve a special mention. **Airstream trailers (caravans),** which were built in aluminum, were born from a fusion of designs by trailer builders Wally Byam (1896–1962, USA) and Hawley Bolus (1896–1967, USA). Bolus was an expert glider builder who had also overseen the construction of Charles Lindberg's *Spirit of St Louis* aircraft. He built the first riveted aluminum trailer in 1934 but as his company labored under the economic depression, Byam, who had started building trailers from masonite in the late 1920s, took control in 1936. Together they produced the first aluminum trailers built from aluminum coachwork in 1936 that have now become iconic streamline vehicles, referencing a seminal period of design and aerodynamics.

The first **Airstream trailer** was rather ambiguously and unimaginatively named the **Clipper,** the same moniker as the trans-Atlantic seaplane built from aluminum (see picture). They were also expensive at around US$1200 each, the price of a 1936 **Nash** car. Despite this, the trailers sold well and have featured in several period antique toys such as the **Hubley** and the **Wyandotte car and trailer sets,** pictured. A large **La Salle saloon** also manufactured by **Wyandotte** toys was released with an **Airstream trailer** as well. Restrictions in the supply and use of aluminum during wartime curtailed the production of **Airstream**

trailers but by 1948, with an economic boom on the horizon, trailer-making was soon underway again. In the 1970s **Airstream** morphed into producing motorhomes, including a classic version in polished aluminum referencing the seminal streamline trailers. Taking a leaf from the defunct American car company **REO** (1905–1967), **Airstream** named one of their new models The Flying Cloud after **REO's** 1927 Flying Cloud motor car.

The **Hubley cast iron toy trailers** were produced in different scales and **Kenton** toys of the USA released a fine cast-iron version, which was usually coupled with a very nice 6-inch (15 centimetre) model of a **1935–36 Nash 400 sedan** (see picture). In 1935 **Nash** offered 'super hydraulic brakes, aero form design, all steel one-piece bodies and flying power developed from twin ignition.'[86]

Nash was an innovative company that introduced features such as a form of air conditioning following the merger with Kelvinator in 1937. Their advert showed a cozy interior with lightly clad passengers in their **Ambassador 6** model, while the snow and ice on a winter's evening is kept at bay (see picture). **Nash** claimed it was

Advertisement for Nash Ambassador 6 model, 1937–38. Nash claimed it was the world's first air-conditioned car.

1935–36 Nash 400, cast-iron, Kenton Toys, USA, 6¾ in long (17 cm).

1949 Nash Airflyte, slush cast, National Products, USA, 6½ in long (17 cm).

Nash Metropolitan, 1950s, Shell Petrol collector's card, 1960s.

the world's first air-conditioned car. **Nash** also introduced 'unitised body and frame construction' from 1942.[87] Having owned six **Nash** models dating from 1938 to 1955, I can attest they were built to last. A brass plaque fitted to the dashboard of my 1938 **Nash La Fayette** stated, 'Precision built made by Nash', and it was – unlike many cars today. The other toy **Nash,** pictured, is a 1949 **Airflyte** made by **National Products,** a division of **Banthrico,** in pot metal. The words 'authentic scale model' are impressed on the base of the toy. **Banthrico** of Chicago made promotional models of most American makes and along with AMT models, these toys constitute a complete collecting field. While few of the real cars have survived, the toys leave accurate and fond (and not so fond) memories of cars we owned, grew up with, or wish we owned. I bought this model

because I used to own a **Nash Airflyte** – I still have the spare hubcaps.

Aerodynamics were on the minds of many designers in the 1950s with cars such as the Nash named with references to aircraft. The **1949 Nash Airflyte** boasted 'airliner styled interiors', 'cockpit control' and 'uniscope'. In 1950 **Nash** claimed to be the only automotive company that built cars on the fuselage principle.[88] In 1949 **Nash** developed their aerodynamic designs with the help of wind tunnels, claiming the 1950 Airflyte had '20.7% less drag than other cars – true streamlining'.[89] Other innovations **Nash** developed and introduced during this era were the first American cars fitted with seatbelts (1950), Italian influenced styling (Pininfarina, 1951),[90] an association with English sports car makers (Healy and Austin)[91] and the introduction of the first true compact and

Streamline sedan with rear fin, 1930s, cast-iron, A C Williams, USA, 8½ in long (21 cm).

economy passenger cars (1950). At this time **Nash** introduced a smaller six-cylinder passenger car engine that they cheekily named The Flying Scotsman 600. With Scottish ancestry and wearing my green and black tartan scarf, I guess I should be highly offended. While the engine may have been economical, it proved sadly underpowered for the heavily bodied **Nash.** A twin-carburettor version was fraught with problems – I know, because I owned three. Changing rear flatties with fixed fender skirts was no fun either.

In 1950 an independent designer for **Nash,** William J Flajole, walked out of his studio late one night and exclaimed to his wife, 'Honey, I've shrunk the Nash!' Born out of a Nash concept vehicle with a nod

to Pininfarina styling, the compact Nash Metropolitan was eventually launched in 1953, specifically targeting the female market for use as a shopping basket or as a commuter car. Somewhat ironically, it was the police in southern California and Canada who also purchased the vehicle as a handy, easy to park runabout. The cars were assembled in England by Austin Motors and powered by their A40 and A50 engines. Right-hand drive versions were also exported around the world from England, including to New Zealand, and a few beautifully restored models remain. The **Nash Metropolitan** model has been produced by several die-cast toy makers in recent years and was included in a collectible card set issued by Shell Oil NZ in 1960

Chrysler Airflow, tin plate, Kuramochi, Japan, 1930s, 11½ in long (28 cm).

1935–1936 Toyota AA Sedan, made in Japan, tin plate, clockwork, 6½ in long (16 cm).

1934 Chrysler Airflow and 1939 De Soto, Kingsbury Toys, USA, 14 in long (36 cm).

that is pictured. With smaller independents struggling to compete with the big three (GM, Ford, Chrysler), many merged or simply disappeared. **American Motors Corporation** was formed in 1954, a friendly merger with **Nash** and **Hudson.** By the 1960s, similarly with **Packard,** the classic **Hudson** and **Nash** marques had, like many cowboys of the same era, faded into the sunset. **American Motors** carried on with their **Rambler** cars and purchased **Kaiser-Jeep** in 1970. The final curtain eventually fell for **AMC,** concurrent with the share market turmoil of 1987 and **AMC** were taken over by **Chrysler Corporation. Nash** toy vehicles are unfortunately few and far between.

If you haven't already guessed, streamline toy autos are a favorite collectible. Several of the **Chrysler Airflow** toys are featured in this chapter but one streamline toy that is a favorite is a red, 8½ inches long (21 centimetres), 1930s cast-iron concept sedan (see previous page), which was made by **AC Williams** of the USA. The epitome of streamline elegance and design, with a lowered roofline, closed fender skirts and an aerodynamic rear fin, the car is a precursor to vehicles of the 1940s, and even later cars of the early 1950s. This quality casting is essentially a sculptural object. The other toys pictured here are all based on real streamline cars, **Chrysler** or **De Soto Airflows** from the 1930s, and made by a variety of manufacturers from various materials including rubber, die-cast metal, cast-iron, pressed steel and tin plate. A wonderfully detailed period **Chrysler Airflow** made from celluloid from Japan also exists but I have never found this toy. A toy I did find, however, in the same bric-a-brac shop as the red **Arcade Chrysler Airflow** (a year later) is the royal blue 6¼ inches long (16 centimetres) Japanese tin-plate **Airflow,** pictured. This toy is actually a model of the first **Toyota**, a 1935–36 AA sedan that is based largely on the design of the **Chrysler Airflow.** In what was to be a template for much Japanese motor vehicle design for the future, **Toyota** copied a six-cylinder **Chevrolet** engine and, among other components, a **Ford** chassis. Similar to the Christchurch bric-a-brac shop that failed to survive the Christchurch earthquakes, very few real **Toyota Airflows** survived hostilities after production ceased in 1943. This toy, sans mascot, is a great survivor.

1939 Chrysler Imperial, Dinky Toys, England, 4 ¼ in long (36 cm).

The Airflows in my collection were made by famous makers such as **Hubley** (USA), **Kingsbury** (USA), **Triang Minic** (England), **CK** (Japan) and **Arcade Toys** (USA). Accompanying the small blue Japanese tin-plate Airflow is a finely restored Japanese tin plate **1935 Chrysler Airflow by CK** (**Kuramochi**) of Japan, 11½ inches long (28 centimetres), one of

1934 Chrysler Airflow, cast-iron, Hubley Toys, USA, 8 in long (20 cm).

many superb, large-scale clockwork tin toy autos made in Japan prior to hostilities and nuclear apocalypses. Several other fine examples from Japan will appear late in the chapter.

The **Kingsbury** pressed steel toys, by virtue of their size (14 inches/35 centimetres), are just as impressive. These are strong, well-made toys that feature nickel-plated brightwork and came fitted with a quality, in-house designed clockwork motor. Some models were upgraded with electric lights. A classic 1930s trailer (caravan) was also available to combine with the car. Pictured are the first and final streamline cars by **Kingsbury,** the **1934**

Brochure for the 1939 Chrysler Imperial.

'Be Modern, Buy Chrysler', brochure for Chrysler range of cars.

Chrysler Airflow and the **1939 De Soto Sloper** (slant back). **Chrysler** also produced the quite beautiful **Royal** and **Imperial** model with the 'waterfall' grille in 1939. These cars incorporated streamline designs as well but by 1939 **Airflow** was not a word **Chrysler Corporation** were using. A die-cast **Dinky** toy was made of the 1939 **Chrysler Imperial** or **Royal** and one is pictured. The advertising for the **Chrysler Royal** and **Imperial,** illustrated here, shows extremely sleek, svelte, flowing lines, illustrations perhaps more in keeping with the red, cast-iron, futuristic car illustrated earlier.[92] The cars though were wonderful. I owned a 1939 **Chrysler Royal** with the waterfall grille. It now resides in a museum. I miss it a lot.

Several **Chrysler Airflows** were made by American cast-iron toy makers in the 1930s. One of the best is the **Hubley 1934 Chrysler Airflow** (see previous page). This model is finished in an unusual lavender color, a nice variation from the standard primary colors of toys from the period. At 8 inches (20 centimetres) this toy is a quality **Hubley** toy with separate nickel-plated bumpers, grille, electric lights and white rubber tires. A spare tire is fitted to the slant back body. This two-piece casting epitomizes the intrinsic design and appeal of American cast-iron toys – in my opinion, worthy of a place in any museum. Some models were not as sophisticated such as the red, 6 inches long (15 centimetres) **Arcade toys Airflow,** also pictured. For sentimental reasons, it remains in my collection, representing an early discovery in the Christchurch, New Zealand bric-a-brac shop in 1981, mentioned earlier. **Arcade** produced two smaller scale 4-inch-long (10 centimetres) **Airflows,** which were

more successful. Along with the matching 4-inch **1936 Pontiac,** these made great little pocket toys for lucky boys in the 1930s. A miniature **Airflow** toy in my collection is a tiny 1 inch long (2 centimetres) tin plate clockwork toy by **Triang Minic** of England. Minic toys, produced by **Lines Brothers,** were clockwork or friction-drive vehicles of mainly English origin. The **Chrysler Airflow** is an exception and was also produced in a larger 5-inch (13 centimetres) size. Another fine **Triang Minic Vauxhall cabriolet saloon** is pictured here, which survives mint in the box. We will see more **Triang Minic** toys shortly.

A 1934 Airflow, 5 in long (14 cm) and a selection of 1930s rubber vehicles, 5–9 in (14–23 cm)

An unusual rubber version of a **Chrysler Airflow** is also pictured. Made of solid rubber, the toy appears to be a **1934 Airflow coupe.** There is no maker identified but underneath it is stamped 'All Rubber – harmless to furniture and woodwork'. Although it measures only 5 inches long (14 centimetres), it is the heaviest rubber toy in my collection. Other **Chrysler** toy cars were manufactured in rubber, including a **1939 Plymouth** by **Auburn** and a **1940 Dodge** by **Sun Rubber** (see pictures). Rubber toy vehicles are unique, most beautifully molded and well detailed, such as the 1940 Dodge, finished in two-tone red and gray. Pictured here is

1940 Dodge by Sun Rubber, USA.

Vauxhall Cabriolet, tin plate, clockwork, Triang Toys, England, 1930s, 5 in long (13 cm) approx.

1936 Pontiac, cast-iron, Arcade Toys, USA, 4 in long (10 cm).

1953 Pontiac, tin plate, friction drive, Ichiko, Japan, restored by New Era Toys, USA, 13¾ in long (35 cm).

Three 1936 Pontiacs with an Arcade cast-iron version, Japanese tin plate, clockwork, 1936, CK Kosuge, Japan, 14 in long (35 cm).

1954 Pontiac, plastic, friction drive, by Louis Marx Toys, USA, 9½ in long (24 cm) approx.

a fine example of a **1935 Oldsmobile** by **Rainbow Rubber Company** of Butler, Pennsylvania. I also have a smaller **1938 Oldsmobile** by **Auburn Rubber.** The larger **1935 Oldsmobile** is, like the red rubber **Airflow,** very solid and heavy, but finished with more attention to detail and scale. Rubber toys, however, can be a mixed bag with some versions somewhat crude in both detail and scale, some surviving better than others. These flaws and issues though must be forgiven

as they were precursors to the production of rubber and vinyl figurative toys, which gave pleasure to millions of children in the following decades. Rubber toy vehicles from the 1930s and 1940s are a refreshing and novel collectible, indicative of an era when alternative materials were used in the manufacture of toys for imaginative play. While not plentiful, many fine survivors remain, more of which we shall see shortly.

General Motors (GM) vehicles are well represented in my collection with

Pontiacs. They hold a special place in my heart as my first cast-iron toy discovery was the 4-inch (10 centimetres) **1936 Arcade Pontiac** in the late 1970s, mentioned in the book's introduction. This toy (see picture) was much the worse for wear but the aged patina, for me, held enormous appeal. At the time I had no idea who had made it, or where it had originated. I found it in a bric-a-brac shop in Auckland, purchasing the toy more as a miniature sculpture. Eventually I was able to purchase the large scale **1936 Arcade Pontiac** from noted toy collector, the late Bill Weart, which is also illustrated here. Special features of my **Pontiac** collection are the Japanese tin plate, clockwork, 1936 sedans. Similar to the **Packard** featured earlier, these are beautifully made toys and at 14 inches long (35 centimetres) would stand up proudly in any antique toy collection.

Another favorite in my collection is the 1953 tin plate **Pontiac** sedan by **Ichiko** of Japan. This toy I found in 'wreckers yard' condition in Melbourne, Australia. I sent it to New ERA Toys in the USA who restored it beautifully, finishing the bodywork in rich cream. These toys feature the suited, bow-tie wearing, businessman driver, a whimsical touch, which adds greatly to the appeal of this toy. Sometimes called a 'fat car', I call it a brilliant toy –

and enormously underrated. The yellow, plastic, 1954 friction-drive **Pontiac** by **Louis Marx** is a nice example of a plastic toy from the period. This toy came from the Louis Marx Museum stock disposal auctions, which were held in England in the 1980s (see picture).

No automotive toy collection would be complete without a **Ford** and many are scattered throughout my collection. As we have seen, a feature and attraction of the automotive world is styling and design and **Ford** remain leaders in this field, displaying remarkable longevity in an industry laced with failures and subsequent disappearances from the marketplace. One of the first stand-out designs represented by a toy in my collection is the **1936–1937 Lincoln Zephyr** with matching streamline trailer (caravan) by **Hubley Toys** (see next page). Copied by **Fun Ho! Toys** in the 1940s, their less detailed version is so rare it is now a higher price than the original **Hubley** version (currently **Fun Ho!** car and caravan is valued at NZ$1000). The **Lincoln Zephyr** is a classic design by Eugene Gregorie (1908–2002) who became a famous **Ford** motor-car designer. Edsel Ford hired Gregorie in 1931 when he was only twenty-two years old, but within four years he rose to be head of Ford design. While Edsel Ford dreamed

1936–37 Lincoln Zephyr with trailer, cast-iron, Hubley Toys, USA, and Lincoln Zephyr with trailer, aluminum, FunHo! Toys (New Zealand), 1940s.

Mark I Zephyr, Monte Carlo Rally card game featuring the winning English Ford Mark I Zephyr, Pepys, England, 1954.

Mark II Zephyr Zodiac, Shell Oil collector's card, c. 1960.

up the idea of the **Lincoln Zephyr** (based on the Greek name *Zephyrus* – God of the West Wind), it was Gregorie who designed the legendary **Ford.** Advertising in 1936 stated, '…beautiful and authentic aerodynamic design with a low roof line,' while another brochure boasted that the speedometer went to 100 mph, a speed which was possible with the V12 110HP engine.[93] The problem was the cars diced with mechanical brakes until 1939 and this combination was not always a happy union. Gregorie went on to design the first **Lincoln Continental** and the 1939 and 1949 **Ford Mercury** cars, which later became perennial favorites with custom rodders. The 1949 **Mercury** was in fact the last car Gregorie designed for Ford. He retired from automotive designing to continue his original design preference – yachts.

The **Ford Zephyr** name did not end with Gregorie however. A **Ford Zephyr** series was introduced to England in 1950 with a powerful six-cylinder engine and variations and upgrades of the car continued until 1972. The **Mark I** and **Mark II Zephyrs** and **Zodiacs** have become classics in their own right, the convertibles designed with a nod to American cruisers are now collectible and valuable classic cars, particularly in

England, Australia and New Zealand. A **Mark I Zephyr** won the 1953 Monte Carlo Rally, which elevated the car's status considerably. Toy makers were quick to follow the car's success. **Dinky Toys** (England), **Micro Models** (England and New Zealand), **Lincoln Toys** (England and New Zealand), produced fine, die-cast models while **Victory Toys** (England) and **Triang Minic** (England) released scale models in plastic and die cast. The 1954 **Pepys** card game **Monte Carlo Rally,** is typically superbly illustrated, with the box cover showing Stirling Moss in his **Sunbeam Talbot,** while the card illustrated here shows the winning **Mark I Ford Zephyr** racing through the mountainous coastal landscape. According to Rex Pitts in his booklet on the history of **Pepys** games, the illustrator for this card set was Mr Lane, the *Motor* magazine artist. Another classic car pictured in this card game is the first GM **Holden** car from Australia, the **1948 FX Holden. Micro** models issued a model of this car also and a rare 'taxi' version of the classic **Holden** car is pictured. The small, blue die-cast car is a **Fun Ho!** model of the last English **Zephyr Ford** produced, the 1972 **Zephyr Zodiac.**

The white tin-plate car, pictured, is a 1958 **Mark III Ford Lincoln Continental** two-door convertible. A classic American motor car, it features rear fins, triple rear lights, twin headlights, a criss-cross chromed grille and rocket-shaped chromed additions to the bumpers. **Lincoln Continental** suffered a bad experience in 1963 when a stretched 1961 model carried the famous American President JF Kennedy to his untimely death. The car was eventually upgraded and repainted from midnight blue to black and kept in service by the White

FX Holden sedan, Australia, taxi version, die-cast metal, Micro Models Australia, 1950s, 4 in long (10 cm).

1958 Mark III Ford Lincoln Continental, tin plate, Bandai, Japan, c. 1958, 11¾ in long (30 cm).

1947–48 Ford coupe convertible, chromed tin plate, Marchesini, Italy, c. 1950, 10 in long (25 cm).

1949 Fiat 1100 SS coupe, chromed tin plate, INGAP Toys Italy, c. 1950, 9½ in long (24 cm) approx.

House for many years. The car now resides in the Henry Ford Museum.

Two quite unique toys in my collection were made by two fine Italian toy makers, **INGAP** (Industries Nationale Giocattroli Automatic Padova) (1919–1972) and **Marchesini – MLB** (Marchesini Luigi Bologna). These beautiful tin-plate toys are both chromed with copper-flashed grilles and bumpers. The American styled two-door chromed convertible by **Marchesini** appears to be based on a 1946–47 **Ford coupe.** The 10-inch-long (25 centimetres) toy is superbly crafted and assembled, devoid of metal tabs with all components and bodywork screwed together. The detailed dashboard includes a speedometer and a clock, in keeping with the real car. A nice detail is the two gas cans in the trunk (boot) with working screw caps. Another version of this toy featured working headlights and music box. From reading an illustrated article by Steve Butler in *Antique Toy World* magazine in 2015, it seems possible my car could also be supplied with a clear plastic roof. The toy retains its original box which shows a green car with the label 'Chromato, Auto Spyder – America'.[94] The Hollywood movie classic *Back to the Future* featured a **1946 Ford convertible,** although the car was reputedly a converted sedan.

1929 Ford woodie station wagon, Hubley Toys, die-cast kitset, 1950s–1960s, 8 in long (20 cm).

Ford woodie, unassembled.

The **INGAP** toy is a model of the classic **1949 Fiat 1100SS** which raced in the famous Mille Miglia 1000 mile endurance race in Italy. Labeled 'SS Auto Sport' on the box, the toy features chromed bodywork with copper-flashed brightwork, including the headlamp fairings, door handles and windscreen frame. The base plate is also chromed. This toy is fitted with a music box, which plays, appropriately, an Italian classic, 'O Sole Mio' (It's Now or Never). Wind the toy, lift the aerial and you can serenade your date for the afternoon as you cruise along the Italian coastline. 'O Sole Mio' is one of the most well known Italian songs and, like the Fiat car, a classic. **INGAP,** founded by Tullio Anselmi, was a quality toy maker employing over 600 employees before the Second World War. Apart from outstanding tin plate toy vehicles, the company produced train sets, remote controlled cars and a wide variety of toys. **INGAP** released an unusual **Topolino Mouse** series of toys in the 1930s, which were in effect plagiarisms of **Mickey Mouse,** designed by Giove Toppi. Toppi had based his graphics on an original **Mickey Mouse** cartoon, but after some negotiation, Disney approved Toppi's imagery. So, we can appreciate the Italians not only made beautiful cars (**Alfa Romeo, Ferrari, Fiat, Lancia, Lamborghini**) and beautiful music, but just as importantly, beautiful toys – *grazie mille* Italy!

For most collectors classic cars and classic toys go hand in hand. 'Woodie' station wagon toys are very collectible, as are the real cars. The first real woodie station wagon was made by **Ford** in 1929, and a fine die-cast model by **Hubley Toys** of the USA is pictured. This vehicle is part of a sophisticated series of kitsets produced by **Hubley Toys** in the 1950s and 1960s. **Hubley** was one of the few automotive toy companies who successfully transitioned from manufacturing with cast-iron prior to World War II to toy making in die-cast metal and plastics from the 1940s. The **1939 La Salle** is a transitional toy for **Hubley,** made in die-cast metal with nickel-plated cast-iron headlamps. Although this toy is a fine, scale, period model of the real car, the developments in manufacturing with plastics and die-cast metals twenty years later are significant. The **Model A Woodie** is pictured, both unassembled

and assembled, and the build required a definite degree of skill despite a claim on some brochures the kits were suitable for '8 years to adult'. The **Duesenberg** brochure stated, 'A kit for car-lovers under 100 years old' which seemed a little optimistic. The small print later on admits, 'Hubley kits are for master car builders who want the best in model car kits', and this statement is quite accurate. These kit sets were arguably the best of their type in the market and, once successfully assembled, the result was a stunning toy replica of a classic vintage vehicle. The best one of the series is possibly the large-scale 12 inches long (30 centimetres) **1930s supercharged SJ Model Duesenberg town car,** pictured. The brochure states, '…the engine – it has 34 parts – is accurately scaled to the last nut and bolt'. Models in this series included a full range of **Model A Fords, Packards, Chevrolets, Cadillacs** and **Pontiacs.** Fittingly, it was **Hubley Toys** that produced the first cast-iron station wagon with their **1934 Pierce Arrow woodie.** A two-piece casting at 4¾ inches long (12 centimetres), **Hubley** also issued a larger 6½-inch-long version (17 centimetres) with a higher roof line (see picture). Finished in two-tone colors with twin side mounts, these are great toys.

Hubley Toy Company were one

1939 La Salle sedan, die-cast, nickel-plated, cast-iron headlamps, tin-plate baseplate, Hubley Toys, USA, c. 1940, 6¾ in long (18.5 cm) approx.

of the foremost producers of automotive toys in the USA, particularly their cast-iron toys, during the 1920s and 1930s. Their **1928 Packard** is one of the most valuable and rare cast-iron toys, highly sought by collectors, some selling in excess of US$30,000. **Hubley** continued their reputation for quality right up until production of their die-cast kits faded away after a change in market forces and takeovers between 1960 and 1980.

SJ Supercharged 1930s Dusenberg, die-cast and plastic kitset, Hubley Toys, 1960s, USA, 12 in long (30 cm).

Similar to the toy market, the market for woodie bodied and woodie styled vehicles ebbed and flowed over the decades. The early **Ford woodie** was also replicated

1934 Pierce Arrow woodie station wagons, cast-iron, Hubley Toys, USA, 4½ in and 6½ in long (11 cm and 17 cm), photo courtesy Bertoia Auctions, USA.

Town and Country station wagon, plastic,clockwork, Irwin Toys, USA, 1950s, 12 in long (30 cm).

by **Kingsbury Toys** in pressed steel in 1930 and other makers produced versions of woodie sedans and station wagons over the next three decades. If there was a golden age of woodie production, it was the 1940s when **General Motors, Ford, Chrysler, Willy's, Packard** and **Nash** produced classic versions of woodie coupes, sedans or station wagons. The toys that followed included the **Irwin** large-scale clockwork plastic town and country sedan and the green plastic station wagon. The scale of the red **Irwin woodie sedan,** at 12 inches long (30 centimetres), is impressive, and with an opening trunk with luggage, it is a fun toy. I added a 1970s, New Zealand native wood Piha Beach souvenir surfboard on the roof for effect. The woodie look was cleverly stenciled on the sedan model that **Irwin Toys** liberally named a 'station wagon'.

Surfing, The Beach Boys, SoCal, woodies and long hair were synonymous with 1960s 'flower power' and an escalating hippie counterculture movement. The hippie movement spread throughout Europe in the 1950s and 1960s, where an actual hippie trail was established from major cities in Europe to India and beyond. Old **Bedford** buses, **VW Kombis** and even vintage hearses were popular conversions to what we now call campervans or motorhomes. As this 'return to nature', 'make peace not war' crusade spread, to some extent the revolutionary culture influenced European motor vehicle and toy manufacturers. **The British Motor Corporation (BMC)** had previously manufactured a woodie **Morris Traveller** in the 1950s and they extended this theme to their new Alec Issigonis designed **Mini** in the 1960s. Rootes Group of England produced their American

BMC Mini Countryman, die-cast, Corgi Toys, 1960s, 3 in long (8 cm).

'Now – a Mini Wagon', *Modern Motor* magazine, 1960 Mini Countryman Woodie, November 1960, p. 25.

Die-cast toy catalogs, 1950s–1970s.

Queen of Spades 3 window Ford coupe, diecast,Hot Wheels Toys ,USA, 1990s, 3" long [8cm] approx.

Mack trucks, cast-iron, c. 1930, Arcade Toys, USA, 11½–13 in long (29–33 cm).

inspired **Hillman Californian** in the 1950s and even **Bentley** and **Rolls Royce** produced woodie-bodied versions in the 1950s, surely a paradox in the history of automotive design. In fact, *Modern Motor* magazine, in their review of the 1960 **Mini Countryman** woodie, were not impressed at all, stating 'There is one criticism – that silly perishable woodwork outside – hope BMC Australia will have the sense to whip it off if they decide to offer them down under.'[95] The cheeky Aussie went on to say, if BMC didn't like his suggestion, they could send a telegram to their PO Box number!

Dinky Toys issued a **1950 Plymouth woodie station wagon** and later a **1960s woodie Mini Countryman.** It was **Corgi Toys,** however, who embraced the times emphatically when they made an excellent 'surfing' **Mini Countryman** that came with two surfboards, a roof rack and a surfer boy thrown in for good measure. The box for this toy is nicely illustrated with the surfer boy 'hanging ten', coming out of a barrel wave.

American Motors (AMC) embraced the era in 1969, advertising a 'Mod Top Plymouth Barracuda'. Bizarrely advertised as 'The Car You Wear', the sports coupe was aimed squarely at the female market. 'Why did we do it?' (do tell). 'To win you over to Plymouth naturally – we've been designing cars with women in mind for years.'[96] To feel 'real cool' or 'hip', the buyer could choose between a paisley or flower design for the roof and interior. I can feel nostalgia coming on…I want one! I may have to be satisfied with a toy. **Toys Nomura** from Japan issued a 12-inch (30 centimetres) flower powered 1968 **Chevy Camaro,** a 'flower power' **E-type Jaguar** and **VW Kombis,** VW sedans and

'White' removal van, cast-iron, Arcade Toys, USA, 1930s, 13 in long (33 cm).

other vehicles were produced with similar finishes during this watershed era. More recently, **Corgi** and other toy makers have produced retro, flower-power decorated vehicles for nostalgic toy collectors who have kept their paisley shirts and ties.

Quite apart from social upheavals and space exploration, this era bore witness to the glory days of die-cast toy making and collecting. Mega toy makers such as **Dowst (Tootsietoys), Meccano (Dinky), Lesney (Matchbox), Mettoy (Corgi), Solido** (France), **Tekno** (Denmark) and **Hot Wheels** (USA) produced millions of die-cast toy vehicles which met with unprecedented success worldwide (see pictures of toys and toy catalog from this period). As they say, all good things must come to an end, and indeed companies, such as **Lesney** and **Meccano,** succumbed to changes in the rapidly evolving toy market in the late twentieth century.

Despite the demise of many of these companies, die-cast toys remain a huge part of the toy market and collectibles field. There are simply too many die-cast toy makers to mention in this book, although examples of other makers are scattered throughout the chapters. Many of the iconic names or companies have been revived over the past decades (eg **Matchbox**) and new die-cast toy makers have also entered the market. The most

1938 International van, slush-cast metal, National Products USA, 12 in long (30 cm).

Mack truck, Wrigley's Gum, die-cast, 1930s, Tootsietoys, USA, 4 in long (10 cm).

Guy vans, die-cast, clockwork Weekins range, 1950s, Chad Valley, England, 4¼ in long (11 cm) approx.

significant of these is **Hot Wheels** (Mattel, USA), which entered the market in 1968. **Hot Wheels** toys established a distinct point of difference producing, in general, exciting customized classic vehicles (with speedy, customized wheels). Most were designed by specialist **Mattel** automotive designers such as Larry Wood and Harry Bentley and the inventive customized paint finishes are a collecting field in themselves. One of my favorites is the Queen of Spades graphics on the 1980s released 1934, three-window **Ford coupe,** pictured. **Hot Wheels** produced their two billionth car in 1998 and have certainly carried the baton representing the affordable and collectible die-cast market since. Some **Hot Wheels** vehicles are not so affordable now with many earlier models selling on the secondary market for thousands of dollars. A **VW Beach Bomb** (with surfboards) sold for $72,000 in 2015 and many are now valued at several hundred dollars. As for the classic woodies, there were no toys as 'SoCal' as **Hot Wheels** and their many customized cars, vans and pick-up trucks featured woodies, several with surfboards included. The choice was comprehensive with customized models based on a 1931, 1937, 1939, 1940, 1948, 1949 and a 1950 **Ford.** The 2003 **Ford Switchback** utility included two surfboards on the rear tray.[97]

Vans, trucks and buses are interesting collecting categories, as the toys are often finished with trade names, various liveries or a title related to a particular industry. The two early 1920s large-scale cast-iron **Mack trucks,** pictured, are made by **Arcade** toys. The small, cast-iron removal van pictured beside the **White**

Mack 6 bus, cast-iron, Arcade Toys, USA, 1928, 13 in long (33 cm).

blue removal truck gives an idea of the wide range of scales in which these cast-iron toys were made. The **White** removal truck is 13 inches long (33 centimetres). Likewise, the **1938 International** panel van, pictured, is one of National Products' large-scale, slush-cast, pot-metal promotional vehicles measuring 12 inches long (30 centimetres). Most of **National Products'** promotionals were around 6 inches long (15 centimetres) but they produced several spectacular large-scale vehicles, including a 1935 **Studebaker trunk-back sedan,** a **Diamond T** and two **International vans.** There is considerable paint loss to my 1938 van but, after all, it is the toy's eightieth birthday this year. The fabulous detail on

the casting is commendable, right down to the **International** logo on the hubcap on the side-mounted spare wheel.

Excellent examples of early die-cast trucks and vans are pictured: a **Tootsietoys Mack Railway Express Agency truck** and three **Chad Valley (England)** removal vans. The **Tootsietoy truck** sports an attractive Wrigleys Spearmint Chewing Gum livery while the **Guy** removal vans are equally appealing. These clockwork **Weekins** range of **Guy** vans are superb; in my opinion, they are equal, if not superior, to other die-cast toys such as **Dinky** and **Solido** of the same era. **Chad Valley** also produced a small range of English **Weekins** sedans.

My collecting friend from New Zealand,

in his lyrical English Cornish accent, said to me once when I showed him one of my buses, 'People collect buses' and indeed they do. I for one – but I only have a few. One of them happens to be a toy I feel is a key piece of my collection. It is the **Arcade Toys Mack '6' bus** with a separate cast grille and a single, side-mounted spare wheel. It is true some novice collectors, for some reason, have remarkable luck and this 'find' is a case in point. During one of my first toy hunting excursions to Australia in 1982, I had heard a story that a cast-iron bus was in an upmarket antique shop in Woollahra in Sydney. The story was confirmed when I attended an antique toy fair not far from the city. My only thought was, why was it still there? I soon tracked the shop down later that day and, as I walked in, an experienced and long-term collector from New Zealand was walking out – but surprisingly he had no bus in his hand. 'Is the bus still there?' I asked. He replied it was, but the 'snobby' owner wanted $300 for it, which he thought was far too expensive. I hurried in and sure enough the bus was there. I had never seen such a toy. By now I had a few cast-iron toys, but nothing this size (13 inches/33 centimetres long). I enquired about the price. With a large plum in his mouth he replied, '$300'. Obviously realizing I was a visitor to

Australia from the 'Shaky Isles', and unlikely to have $300, he returned to polishing his silverware. I asked if he would consider an offer. 'Absolutely not,' he snapped as he continued polishing faster and with more intent, not bothering to make eye contact with this 'nuisance'. I walked out of the shop, aware that my wallet contained about $300 perhaps, but that was designated for hotel accommodation, taxis and food. I stopped 50 yards up the road and counted $310. I walked back and placed $300 on the desk of the shocked antiques dealer. I cut my trip short and flew back to New Zealand that night. I was offered several thousand dollars for the rare toy many years later by a serious American collector, but it is not for sale. It is a wonderful cast-iron American toy.

It is appropriate this chapter concludes discussing several of my favorite toys and evidence that novice collectors do seem to fluke a rare toy, but as the champion golfer, Gary Player, said, 'The harder I work, the luckier I get.' I am sure there is an analogy there for collectors.

CHAPTER 8

TRAINS AND BOATS AND PLANES

TRAINS

The title of this chapter was inspired by a classic song written by famous composers Burt Bacharach and Hal David in 1965 titled 'Trains and Boats and Planes'. Popular singer, Gene Pitney, surprisingly turned the song down, so presumably he was not a toy collector – or the judge of a great song for that matter. The ballad rose to number four in the United Kingdom pop charts, while Dionne Warwick's cover enjoyed seven weeks on the USA Billboard Hot 100. Just as the song remains a classic, likewise hundreds of toys from these categories can also now be classed as classics. The categories are expansive, but I trust the scope of toys discussed, although limited in the main to those in my collection, will outline and showcase not only wonderful toys, but absorbing history.

Over a few hundred years civilization progressed from living in the medieval

The small, plastic locomotive toy whistles were made by Kleeware of England in the 1950s.

Not all toy trains were large. Train sets and other transport vehicles were produced as cereal premiums in the 1950s and 1960s.

Trains and locomotives also featured in card sets, posters and puzzles. A tin-plate blockset from the 1950s features a steam train resting at a railway fettler's hut (Chad Valley, England).

A great 1960s Japanese, tin-plate bullet train over 36 in long (91 cm). Japanese bullet trains were launched in 1964 carrying over 150 million passengers per year. They have reached a top speed of 374.68 mi/h (603 km/h) and the commuter trips run at over 198.83 mi/h (320 kph). Photo courtesy Bertoia Auctions.

middle ages without a toothbrush to flying in outer space. The toys, games, books and magazines inspired by these life changing forms of transport not only record the historical development of trains, boats (ships) and planes but also the very foundations of international travel. While many are ingenious, comprehensive and made to last, others were made from experimental or fragile materials but, remarkably, many of these items have survived well into the twenty-first century. Did anyone actually throw away their **Hornby** or **Lionel** train set? This chapter incorporates a selection of these toys from my collection, and while they encompass interesting history, most have been well played with and enjoyed at some point in their career.

It seems almost incredible now that the first locomotives were built over 200 years ago (Pen-y-darren locomotive 1804, *Catch Me Who Can* 1809) by Richard Trevithick (1771–1833). George Stephenson built his *Rocket* steam train in 1829 and by 1830 he had engineered the first commercial railway line. While only 32 miles long

A fine 'O' gauge size cast-iron locomotive and tender produced in America – typical of the trains which traveled across America after the opening of the West by rail in the nineteenth century. This is a classic 4–4–0 four band locomotive which features the typical cow catcher and bell, 14 in long (36 cm).

(51 kilometres), the track entailed the construction of bridges, viaducts and tunnels. Although the world was in theory coming to the end of the industrial revolution, there may be a case for claiming it began with the steam engine and steam train. Steam trains were invented before the sewing machine (1845), the typewriter (1867) and barbed wire (1873). London's underground railway, the Metropolitan, opened in 1863. The 'New World' was in its infancy, California only becoming a US territory in 1847, colonies of Britain in the South Pacific, such as Australia and New Zealand, were yet to be firmly established and the Treaty of Waitangi signed with indigenous Maori did not occur until 1840. The development and opening of

America by linking east with west can largely be attributed to the invention of the locomotive, or 'iron horse'. Although railroads on the east coast of America were operating as far back as the 1830s (South Carolina Railroad), the completion of the Transcontinental Railroad in 1869, finally connecting east with west, changed the course of history and the future of America. The establishment of the railroad through mountains, deserts, snow and ice was a monumental task, one American senator stating in 1845, 'What do we want with the region of savages, and wild beasts, of deserts of shifting sands and whirlwinds of dust, of cactus and prairie dogs'.[98]

Once the cow catchers had clinked together, signifying the joining of the railroad, Going west (see Chapter 3) was no longer the comparatively arduous and dangerous journey on horseback or by stagecoach for adventurous travelers or gold diggers. Business boomed as mail, livestock and goods deliveries improved dramatically. Only five days following the joining of the rails, the Transcontinental Railway announced a regular passenger service. Post offices and eventually new towns expeditiously appeared.

The legendary Pony Express mail service, often the subject of dime-store novels, paintings, Western short stories, plays and movies, in reality only existed for nineteen months following the launch of their daring and fearless service in 1860. The completion of the transcontinental telegraph line proved to be the last hurrah for the Pony Express and two days later, on 26 October 1861, the company folded. Six riders were recorded as having perished while riding 'to always get through' but like many legends of the West, stories and reputations have become taller or embellished with time.

As we have seen earlier, no sooner had new modes of transport been invented than toys followed soon after. The cast-iron American locomotive and tender (pictured) is one example of the many toy train sets that were made by various toy makers in the nineteenth century. Cast-iron toy train sets are not only sublime classic toys but have become collectible as antiques and decorator's pieces, similarly to tin-plate battleships mentioned later in this chapter. Cast-iron train sets and money banks arguably canonized American toy making, underscored later by formidable automotive cast-iron toy makers such as **Hubley Manufacturing Company** and **Arcade Manufacturing Ltd** (refer Chapter 7). Trains

Hornby Train catalog advertisement 1950s and *Meccano Magazine* cover 1954.

Mallard streamlined train, steam powered train designed by Sir Nigel Gresley of England in 1938. Plastic model, c. 1990, 10 in long (25.4 cm).

not only 'won the West', but opened up Europe. In 1863, 38,000 people rode the first underground railway in London – 3.7 miles (6 kilometres) in gas-lit wooden carriages. That was further than many had ever traveled.[99]

The cast-iron locomotive here is a pull-along set, which many early sets were, although Ives (1868–1932) of Connecticut, soon became the leading producer of clockwork cast-iron train sets in the USA. Ives chose not to produce electric train sets until 1910, unlike other companies, as they claimed many American households had no electricity. Following increasing competition from opposition American toy-train maker **Lionel, Ives** went into bankruptcy in 1928. The same year, Ives was purchased by **Lionel** (1900–1995). **Lionel Corporation** arguably made the best train sets in America,

their finest sets, in my opinion, being their electric, three-rail die-cast and tin-plate-bodied sets from the 1930s (see picture). **Lionel** produced electric train sets from the get-go – a standard gauge (wide gauge) with two rail tracks. By 1915, along with most toy train makers, **Lionel** moved to 'O' gauge. The O gauge train sets illustrated here are quite accurate models of classic streamlined locomotives, Union Pacific's *City of Portland* and *City of Salina*. As the locomotives were die-cast, more detailing was achievable compared to tin-plate alternatives. **Lionel** also produced toys of Robert Loewy's famous streamlined Pennsylvania locomotives, which were designed in 1937 and 1938. We mentioned Loewy's diversity and status in Chapter 7 and this is evident here also, where he designed not only the passenger cars' interiors, but their stations as well.

The famous Lionel Lines Blue Comet 'O' gauge train set, pressed steel and tin plate, USA 1930s. Value: $8000–12,000. Photo courtesy Bertoia Auctions.

An equally famous designer of streamlined trains was Sir Nigel Gresley from England (1887–1941). Gresley not only designed the locomotives, carriages and interiors, but also the engines. His greatest achievement was possibly the design of the *Mallard* streamline locomotive (1938) pictured here which broke the world speed record for a steam locomotive in 1938 reaching 126 miles per hour (203 kilometres per hour) during a decent of the Stoke Bank area in England. Unusually, Gresley's locomotives were steam powered when many toy train sets had been electrically operated thirty years earlier. The rare **2130 locomotive** made by **Voltamp** of the USA (pictured), for example, was made around 1907 and is electrically operated. Diesel and electrically powered locomotives could not match the power of steam-driven trains until the 1950s. There remains a large degree

Lionel Lines 1930s catalog page for Union Pacific streamliner.

The 1936 Raymond Loewy designed Torpedo streamliner. Lionel Lines catalog, c. 1930s.

An unusual electric locomotive in pressed steel and cast-iron by Voltamp (1907–1923) of Maryland, USA, c. 1908, 10½ in long (27 cm). Voltamp made some of the first electric train sets, which are now extremely rare and valuable. Value: $4000–6000. Photo courtesy Bertoia Auctions.

of elegance and *je ne sais quoi* surrounding a steam locomotive or early cruise liner pulling out from a railway station or noisy dockside.

Although somewhat of a departure, modernist design is evident in a rare 1930s **Bakelite locomotive** made by **Chad Valley** of England. There are distinct elements of modernist Bauhaus design where the overall effect is quite architectural. The **Bahaus School of Design** in Weimar, Germany, began

in 1919 with a goal of successfully fusing architecture and design into manufacturing and buildings. This rare toy train is not only an iconic example of famous design aspects reflected in a toy, but is also representative of the early use of plastics for toy making. This locomotive was produced with Bakelite bogies, which hook neatly into male and female dovetailed lugs to join the locomotive. The bogies, which were produced in various colors, are extremely hard to find. These toys, if they can be found, are often cracked or damaged. The red wooden locomotive pictured here is also made by **Chad Valley,** but in a more conventional design. I believe the Bakelite locomotive possibly pre-dates the wooden locomotive, although they have the same wheels and dovetail lugs. The wooden locomotive was probably made in the 1940s when materials were in short supply and German-inspired design was hardly flavour of the month.

An early European company that still makes real trains is **Skoda** from the Czech Republic (est. 1859). This is the same company that made the **1940s Tudor saloon car** which was featured in chapter 7. The old postcard (pictured) shows the **Skoda** works built *Mikado*-type steam locomotive, which operated between Dresden and Prague between 1926 and 1937. Apart from locomotives, **Skoda** manufactured heavy machinery, artillery and other equipment. This quite historic company began as an arms manufacturer in 1859, eventually supplying heavy artillery and Panzer tanks to Germany during World War II. **Skoda** was nationalized after the war, continuing to build locomotives, buses and various vehicles, with the odd nuclear reactor thrown in (quite diversified then). In

A superb Art Deco style Lionel Lines tin plate power station #840, c. 1930s, 19 x 26 in (50 x 66 cm).

Pull along Bakelite trainset and red wooden locomotive, 1930s, Chad Valley, England, with variegated plastic locomotive by Moldex Plastics, Australia. Locomotives measure approx. 11 in long (28 cm).

A wonderful American Flyer Lines wide gauge electric train set, c. 1930s. Photo courtesy Bertoia Auctions.

A 1930s Lionel Lines streamlined Union Pacific Railroad set, die-cast and tin plate. Each carriage 16 in long (40 cm) approx. Photo courtesy Bertoia Auctions.

Skoda Mikado locomotive, which was based in Prague, 1926–1937 (photo R Stettinger), Czechoslovakian postcard 1990s.

1992 **Skoda** was privatized and acquired **Tatra** vehicles, which were highlighted in Chapter 6. As well as quality motor vehicles, **Skoda** remains a significant manufacturer of trains, buses and rapid rail systems.

There are many famous toy train makers from many other countries but two of the most long-serving and prominent were **Meccano** of England with their famous **Hornby** Trains and **Marklin** of Germany. Several fine books and publications already exist regarding these toys but I would like to highlight the eponymously titled *Meccano Magazines* which ran from 1916 to 1981. Full color covers were introduced in 1924 and these superbly illustrated pages are worthy collectibles in themselves. These magazines contain well researched, informative articles regarding what was then the latest developments in railways, other forms of transport, toy trains, hobbies, toy making, industry in general and archival toy advertisements are scattered throughout each issue (see picture).

Marklin of Germany began making train sets in 1891 while **Hornby** were underway by 1920. They were prolific manufacturers and Hornby trains were exported to countries around the world. It seems few train sets were ever thrown away – many produced in the last 100 years still survive in captivity – and that is a lot of train sets. It is little wonder the price of many vintage train sets, even those from the nineteenth century has dropped considerably and storage is another issue. The magnificent **Lionel 1930s City of Denver** train set, which I paid over $1200 for twenty years ago, has decreased to a value of $700-plus depending on condition. **Hornby** train sets appear regularly on the market and can be difficult to sell. Very early **Marklin, Bing** and **Lionel** trains are quite another matter, looking at sets pictured here. A **Marklin** piece recently sold for $36,000 and a **Lionel** locomotive for $27,000.

Some train sets and locomotives produced more sparingly were pull along models made by **FunHo! Toys** almost seventy years ago (refer Chapter 4). The rarest is a model cast in aluminum of a **New Zealand Railways RM (Standard) Class diesel/mechanical rail car.**[100] These railcars were built in New Zealand at New Zealand Railways Corporation's Hutt workshops in Gracefield, Lower Hutt, Wellington in 1938 and 1939, designed to carry between forty-eight and fifty-two passengers.[101] One of their regular runs was between Wellington and New Plymouth, which is where the maker of **FunHo! Toys,** Underwood Engineering Limited, was based (see Chapter 4). The founder, Jack Underwood, would have been a regular passenger as he often visited the then Department of Trade and Industry and the New Zealand Customs Department head offices in Wellington, seeking protection from imports for his locally produced toys. The six railcars built in Lower Hutt were given Maori names, similarly to many local ships and Air New Zealand aircraft. The railcars operated between 1938 and 1972 in New Zealand. Fortunately, the *Aotea, Tokomaru, Pangatoru* and *Tainui* still exist

FE locomotive and tender 1021 by Marklin of Germany. Value: est. $6000–8000. Photo courtesy Bertoia Auctions.

A delightful train box car transporting a refreshment carriage by Bing of Germany c. 1900, sold for $12,000 November 2017. Photo courtesy Bertoia Auctions.

A beautiful Central Train Station c. 1900s, tin plate by Marklin of Germany, sold for $16,800 November 2017. Photo courtesy Bertoia Auctions.

A classic New York central passenger train set by Bing of Germany. 'O' gauge. Photo courtesy Bertoia Auctions.

Aluminum Railcar by FunHo! Toys, New Zealand #155, (1946–1952), 9 in long (23 cm).

Aluminum Locomotive by FunHo! Toys, New Zealand #163 (1947–1965), 9 in long (23 cm).

in the safe keeping of New Zealand vintage railway societies, two fully restored, the others in various stages of restoration. This **FunHo! toy railcar** is, unusually, painted yellow, as the few others I have seen were painted red, the main color of the real railcars. This toy retains its original Mervyn Taylor designed gold **FunHo!** label. **FunHo! Toys** also produced an 'O' gauge pull along train set between 1947 and 1965. These toys, designed to be enjoyed in sandpits and kindergartens, were often repainted and are now discovered with missing parts or significant paint loss, such as the red locomotive pictured here. The railcar is extremely rare in completely original condition, while the locomotive, a survivor with a certain charm, has been much enjoyed. After all, that is what toys are for!

SHIPS, BOATS AND BATTLESHIPS

While our song and title for this chapter says 'boats', we are going to raise the sea level to 'toy ships'. There are some fabulous toy ships in the world and the best and most valuable are generally those made by **Marklin** of Germany, similar to the ones pictured here. Toy ships are some of the most coveted and sought antique toys, several recently selling for record prices in excess of US$100,000. In fact,

a **Marklin** tin-plate battleship, the *Sankt Georg*, sold for US$160,000 at Bertoia Auctions in the USA in November 2017. A **Marklin** paddle steamer *Providence*, c. 1902, sold for US$215,000 in the same auction.[102] **Marklin,** mentioned earlier as a significant toy train maker, are regarded as one of the premier toy makers in the world and the auction prices recorded here reflect that honor and status. A **Marklin New York-class battleship** made around 1905 also sold at Bertoia's for US$95,000 but other wonderful toy

Red and cream tin-plate two-stack dreadnought battleship, c. 1900. Photo courtesy Bertoia Auctions.

The battleship Majestic is an impressive 34 in long (87 cm), tin plate by Marklin of Germany c. 1900, estimated value $30,000–40,000 (photo courtesy Bertoia Auctions, USA). ,

Tin plate ocean liner by Marlin of Germany, c. 1930s, 38 in long (97 cm), estimated value $15,000–20,000 (photo courtesy Bertoia Auctions, USA).

Dreadnought New York by Dent Hardware, USA, cast-iron, c. 1910, 20 in long (48 cm).

ships sail by at more reasonable prices for collectors like me with much shorter pockets. One of the most impressive is a cast-iron toy made, coincidentally, of the US dreadnought battleship the *New York*, which was built prior to World War I. It is ironic that this toy ship should be made from cast-iron, although it was designed as a pull toy – not to sail. Few real dreadnoughts have survived the ravages of war or time and, in fact, the original *New York* dreadnought this model was based on was destroyed by friendly fire while used as target practice in 1948. The term or title dreadnought originates from the British battleship *Dreadnought*, built in 1906 and powered by steam turbine. This is generally accepted as a vessel that initiated the naval 'arms race' prior to World War I. Soon every superpower longed for a dreadnought and before long America, Germany, Russia, Japan, France and Italy were able to hoist their flag from a dreadnought mast for other powers, to in theory, sit up and take notice.

This large-scale toy, made by **Dent Hardware** from the USA, measures 20 inches long (48 centimetres) and like the real ship, is imposing and surely one of the most impressive cast-iron toys ever made. The masts are made from tin plate (as were the originals) and are replacements and while a few guns may have gone over the side in battle, for a toy over 100 years old it has weathered well. **Dent,** who were based in Fullerton, Ohio made a number of cast-iron ships but this toy must surely be their pièce de résistance. I have seen a 'copper flashed' version finished in battleship grey, which is possibly a one-off. I originally came across an example of this **Dent battleship** at the London Toy Museum in

Union Steamship Company advertisement, New Zealand as a Tourist and Health Resort, Thomas Cook and Son, 1899, p. 155.

SS *Aquitania* jigsaw puzzle by Chad Valley, England, c. 1920s.

SS *Queen Mary* jigsaw puzzle by Chad Valley, England, c. 1940.

Lifeboats were built as far back as the eighteenth century (although land based) and the Lifeboat Association was founded in 1824. Few lifeboats were carried by vessels prior to the twentieth century but the Titanic disaster resulted in a rethink. 'Famous inventions' collector's card series #24, WD & HO Wills.

Old galleons lithographed, tin plate, watercolor paint box, Page of England, c. 1965, 9½ x 6½ in (24x 16.5 cm).

Thomas Cook Travel advertisement in the New Zealand Thomas Cook Travel Guide, 1899.

the 1980s (since closed). I thought it was stunning and my quest to add one to my collection ended when one turned up at an antique toy auction in the USA not long after – a most under-valued toy in my humble opinion ($2500). One real 'dreadnought' has survived for posterity, the USS *Texas*, which, quite appropriately, is now berthed at San Jacinto battleground, La Porte, Texas, USA.

CRUISE LINERS

The most romantic, impressive and luxurious of all vessels are cruise liners. Outstanding period posters, paintings, toys and other memorabilia represent the great liners such as the 'Two Queens' (Queen Mary and Queen Elizabeth) and others which appear in this chapter.

Samuel Cunard (1787–1865 ,Canadian) founder of the legendary Cunard Line of passenger vessels, initiated regular trans-Atlantic passenger voyages in 1840. To say there were problems would be an understatement. By 1860, thirteen vessels had sunk to a watery grave taking with them more than 2200 unfortunate souls. In 1863, a wary traveler observed 'a trip to the States was held to be quite a serious enterprise. You made your Will before you sailed.'[103]

Ship builder Edward K Collins from America soon entered the fray with the backing of the United States Government. In 1847 the Senate funded the building of five steamships by the tune of $385,000 per annum. Senator Asheton Bayard Jnr stated Collins 'was to proceed with the absolute conquest of this man Cunard.' Congressman Edson Baldwin Olds agreed, saying, 'We have the fastest horses, the prettiest women and the best shooting guns in the world and we must

Lithographed, tin plate, paint box set, cruise liner Queen Elizabeth by Lane, England, c. 1960, 14 x 9 ¼ in (36x 23 cm).

also have the fastest steamers.'[104] Collins' luxuriously fitted out steamers soon held the record for the fastest trans-Atlantic crossing when the *Pacific* arrived in England in less than ten days on 19 April 1852. As history records, a combination of speed and luxury does not necessarily equate to success. Two years later Collins' other luxury steamship sank after colliding with a French vessel. Not only did 322 crew members and passengers perish, but Collins' wife and two children. Bad luck and misfortune continued to plague the shipping magnate when he lost the *Pacific*

with all on board in the North Atlantic after departing from Liverpool in 1856. By 1858, Collins was bankrupt. In an ominous harbinger of what was to follow some fifty years later, it was presumed the *Pacific* had collided with an iceberg (which were prevalent at the time), never to be seen again. Despite maritime disasters, bankruptcies and experimental designs, it was eventually speed and luxury that cemented the reputation and establishment of steamers, which opened a door to the world for early travelers, tourists and émigrés.

SS *New York* jigsaw puzzle.

SS *Queen Mary* by Tinke Toys, lead, made in USA, 5½ in long (14 cm

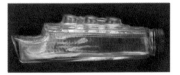

SS *Queen Mary* souvenir glass candy container, c. 1940s, 9 in long (23 cm).

Japanese Navy destroyer, plastic kitset by Tamiya, Japan.

The pioneer of world travel was probably Thomas Cook (1808–1892, British) who arranged trips to France in 1861. By 1866 he had arranged a tour party to America and by 1872 arranged a trip around the world which lasted 222 days.[105] Cook managed tours to countries as far away as New Zealand, his 1890s *Cook's Tourist Guide to New Zealand* espousing 'steamship passages to and from all parts of the world' and listing offices in the main cities in New Zealand and Australia (see pictures).[106]

As the twentieth century approached, significant gains in steam turbines were effected by Charles Parsons, who founded the Marine Steam Turbine Company in 1894. Parsons, who was born in Ireland, was a man after many readers' hearts, who reputedly 'would not eat as a child unless he had a mechanical toy or at least a building block to play with.' He built toy locomotives that were fueled by alcohol, occasionally setting fire to the carpet.[107] His radically improved steam turbine, sporting triple bladed propellers, which had been designed with the help of two biscuit tins and rubber bands, in 1895, almost ten years later, powered the launch of the pride of the **Cunard Lines** passenger liners, the *Mauretania* and the *Lusitania*. Parsons was knighted in 1926.

Despite advancements in ocean travel, disasters seemed to continue unabated. Hundreds of vessels were lost plying the Atlantic and surrounding coastal waters and the greatest disaster was yet to come.

The **Titanic,** touted as 'unsinkable' and the pride of the White Star Shipping Line on her maiden voyage in April 1912, proved no match either against a massive iceberg. Four days out of Southampton, 1503 were lost in what was to become arguably the worst disaster at sea. With every large-scale disaster there are fortunately some good-luck stories. London's famous Symphony Orchestra, founded in 1904, soon drew the attention and command of leading international conductors. In 1912 they became the first British orchestra to tour America and Canada, however they could be considered extremely lucky to have completed the groundbreaking tour at all. They were booked on the **Titanic,** bound for New York, but changed liners at the last minute. JB Priestley recalled, 'A whole London Symphony Orchestra may have been saved.'[108] The wreckage was discovered in 1985 and while salvage from the wreck was undertaken, the site has now been declared a protected area. Few period toys of the **Titanic** were made, unlike those of other passenger vessels and cruise liners which enjoyed decidedly more longevity. More recently however several kitsets have entered the market since the wreck's discovery and the release in 1997 of the blockbuster movie *Titanic* starring Leonardo DiCaprio and Kate Winslet. The movie won eleven Academy Awards.

One of the most prevalent games associated with ocean liners were jigsaw puzzles, several of which are illustrated here. A year after the **Titanic** disaster, Cunard Lines launched her new flag ship vessel, the four stacked **Aquitania.** A fine wooden and lithographed paper jigsaw puzzle is illustrated here depicting the early liner steaming from port, bound for New York. This puzzle is made by famous British toy maker **Chad Valley** who, in association with Cunard, produced several jigsaws of their ocean liners. The **Aquitania** was launched during a British/German naval race led by Winston Churchill, which in hindsight was a rehearsal for an upcoming theater of war. The vessel was the first ocean liner designed with provision for conversion to a troop and hospital ship. Lessons from the **Titanic** debacle were also taken on board, where lifeboats were provided for all passengers and crew. Before long the ship was transporting British troops to the Dardanelles during World War I, eventually transporting American troops to Europe during the last phases of the war. The Cunard Line prospered after the war, when passenger vessels suffered little competition, if any, from fledgling airlines. The **Aquitania** was soon at the behest of the armed forces again during World War II. The ship reputedly carried over 400,000 soldiers and sailed over 500,000 miles (800,000 kilometres) during military service, including transporting New Zealand and Australian soldiers to England to serve alongside the allies. In 1949 the ship was retired. The last rites for the **Aquitania** were signaled when a piano fell through the ceiling of the dining room during a corporate luncheon,[109] which no doubt provided a little more than a 'tinkling of the ivories' during the consumption of canapes and caviar. The great liner was finally sold for scrap in 1950.

Two of the most famous luxury passenger liners were the Cunard vessels **Queen Mary** and the **Queen Elizabeth.** The *Queen Elizabeth* was launched in 1934 and her sister ship, *Queen Mary,* four years later in 1938, both becoming busy troop carriers for the duration of the Second World War. The two Queens reputedly carried 1,600,000 soldiers to various locations involved in the war.[110] After the first voyage from California to Australia, while transporting GIs to the Pacific, chewing gum was banned from the *Queen Mary.* The teak deck had become paved with gum, creating an extensive clean-up.[111] At the cessation of another long and debilitating war, the two Queens were refurbished and commenced service as passenger liners. The ships, along with other liners, sailed the world, many now transporting hopeful immigrants to new beginnings from war-torn countries including England, Italy and the Balkans.

Ocean liners were the subject of many toys and games, particularly in the 1950s, such as the **tin-plate paint box sets** pictured. Tin-plate toy ocean liners continued to be a popular focus for toys from Japan, England and the newly created West Germany. Picture block sets, card sets, die-cast toys, puzzles and particularly cigarette and cereal card sets all featured liners at some stage during this baby boomer era. The popularity of passenger liners as a realistic form of transport waned considerably, however, concurrent with the 1960s jet age. Ironically, a large percentage of children who played with cruise ship toys in the 1950s are now customers of a revived twenty-first century cruise ship industry. Over 220,000 cruise ship passengers visited New Zealand in the 2016–17 season and new records are predicted for the future.[112] Passenger numbers for cruise ships worldwide have grown exponentially with numbers reaching 25.8 million at the end of 2017.[113] It is unlikely wonderful tin-plate and cast-iron ships such as these will ever be made again, although many plastic kitset companies from this era have survived, largely through adult support. Early plastic kitsets designed for children appear later in this chapter.

Passenger Liner, the *Normandie* c. 1937. 'The SS Normandie...holds the blue ribbon of the Atlantic with a record of just over four days for an Atlantic crossing...and is replete with every modern luxury and is probably the most complete single unit of transportation in existence.' 'This Mechanised Age', card No. 50, c. 1936, Godfrey Phillips Ltd.

The *Queen Mary*. The ship had not commenced her maiden voyage in 1936 at the time this cigarette card was produced. 'The promenade deck is longer than the front facade of Buckingham Palace. SS *Queen Mary* will carry some 3000 passengers.' 'This Mechanised Age', Card No. 39, Godfrey Phillips Ltd, c. 1936.

PLANES

The speculation and wonder surrounding powered flight was finally laid to rest in August 1908 when a large crowd gathered at a horse racetrack in Le Mans, France to publicly witness successful flights by Wilbur Wright (1867–1912).[114] The famous pioneers of flight, the Wright brothers (Orville Wright 1871–1948), had been experimenting with flight since 1878 when as young boys they were given a toy helicopter. It was indeed a toy helicopter that can be credited with inspiring the invention of flight and no sooner had aircraft stunned the crowds in France than 'aircraft' toys and games were rushed to the marketplace. The Wright brothers, who spent a year in France demonstrating the aircraft and its skills, soon became worldwide celebrities.

A delightful, early period biplane made in France by **Louis Mangin** is pictured, a toy that surely would have inspired its owner to eventually experience his or her first flight. The toy has been treasured over time and although more than 110 years old, remains in pristine condition in the original box. This toy recently sold at Bertoia Auctions in the USA for $5700, reflecting its rarity and condition. The early board game **Aerial Derby, The Game of the Day,** as its title suggests, was made not long after the Wright brothers' public displays in the *Flyer* and the first organized air races. The game depicts quite differing aircraft designs, including several of the earliest box-kite configurations. Box kites were invented by Laurence Hargrave (1850–1915), whose contribution to the development of flight has been somewhat undervalued internationally.[115] Although born in England, Hargrave moved to Australia in 1865, and apart from his groundbreaking inventions with gliders, he was credited with developing aerofoils and the rotary engine. Sadly, Hargrave's son died at Gallipoli in World War I in May 1915 and Laurence Hargrave himself expired from peritonitis two months later.

Aerial Derby made around 1909/1910 was probably inspired by the first air race, held in Paris in August 1909. While four aircraft entered, even less made the runway: Louis Bleriot, who had conquered the English Channel in July the same year, and an American, Glen Curtis. Bleriot was just beaten by five seconds by the American, flying a box-kite design, who not only won a magnificent Gordon Bennett trophy but 25,000 francs. His average speed for almost sixteen minutes in the air was 47.07 miles per hour (75.75 kilometres per hour). More than a dozen air races were held in Europe the same year and their popularity soon extended to America. Quite comprehensive rules and regulations were soon established for air races, based it seems, along the lines of point-to-point horseracing. Article 145, in the first rules dated 1909 states: '…the clerks of the course are empowered to affix to any machine taking part, any device… for recording of [if] the machine…shall have touched the ground in its journey around the course.'[116] Similarly, the **Aerial Derby** game states: 'if a machine hits a marker – go back and pass same in proper manner.' Might be a bit hard with only one wing.

A box-kite aircraft similar to the winning aircraft in the first race is illustrated on space number 69: 'Going strong – on to space 86'. Bleriot's monoplane is depicted on space number 85 where there is bad luck: 'Broken wing – back to 58'. This game was designed with an eye to the future where the race would go around the world. The flimsy aircraft in this game arrive at the other end of the world, in Wellington, New Zealand, the city portrayed with tall-masted ships in port, as it may have appeared around 1870. The aircraft strike many hazards before they arrive back at Windsor Castle, London including lightning strikes, colliding with skyscrapers in New York, falling into the

The Aerial Derby, The Game of the Day, by Chad Valley, England, c. 1909.

Aeroplane Biplan by Louis Maugin, France, tin plate and cloth covered wings, c. 1909, 6.5 in (15 cm) wingspan. Photo courtesy Bertoia Auctions.

Flight Around the World, board game by Chad Valley, England, c. 1920.

Playing pieces for Flight Around the World game.

'Canopus' Imperial Airways' first flying boat. '...for day travel 24 passengers can be carried, at night there is sleeping accommodation for 16 people, a smoking cabin...pilot's bridge, wireless compartment and ship's office...' Philips cigarette card No. 21 'The Mechanised Age', 1929.

Pan American China Clipper by Wyandotte Toys, USA, pressed steel, c. 1936. Photo courtesy Bertoia Auctions.

Liffey River in Dublin, leaky tanks, broken wings and tails and defective motors. The object of the later **Chad Valley** game **Flight Round the World,** pictured, is to deliver mail around the world. The mail is marked with forty cities in the world including such exotic destinations as Khartoum, Cairo, Lima, Constantinople, Petrograd, Paris, Peking, Benin, Madras, New York, Perth, Brisbane and Irkutsk, Siberia (a must see). No mail trip to New Zealand this time!

All-Fair Games (Alderman-Fairchild Co., USA) produced a board game, **The Capital Cities Air Derby,** in 1928 on the back of American Charles Lindbergh's (1902–1974) achievement of the first solo trans-Atlantic crossing in May 1927 (New York to Paris 33½ hours). He won US$25,000 in his *Spirit of St Louis* aircraft and Lindbergh's fame spread far and wide. A US stamp was issued the same year commemorating the event. As history records, however, there are risks and downsides to fame and fortune. Five years later Lindbergh's twenty-one month old son was kidnapped and murdered, despite the payment of a ransom.

Biplanes similar to those depicted in **Flight Round the World** were used in World War I and before long commercial airlines took to the skies. One of the earliest airlines was Imperial Airways, which was formed in 1924 from a conglomerate of small, independent British airlines. Imperial was the first commercial airline to offer a film on their flights from London to Paris when in 1925 they screened *The Lost World*. Based on Sir Arthur Conan Doyle's 1912 novel, the movie was a precursor to blockbusters such as *King Kong* and *Jurassic Park*. Imperial Airlines were renowned for their fleet of

'Empire Flying Boats', which were commissioned in the late 1930s. Pictured is the first of their fleet, the *Canopus*. The aircraft boasted many luxurious appointments, notably a smoking cabin sumptuously decorated in the latest Art Deco shades of green and white. The routes scheduled, suggestive of their somewhat lofty name, were largely within the British Empire, flying to colonies far and wide including South Africa, Malaya, India, North Africa, Hong Kong and Australia. Regular routes were also established between Europe and America but in the early days reaching destinations often included a transit by rail. A survey flight from England to Australia in 1926 took seventy-eight days. By 1937 the company chairman, Sir George Beharrell (1873–1959) announced a big expansion in the company's business with the impending launch of twenty-eight new flying boats. By 1939 Imperial Airways were gone, merging into British Overseas Airways Corporation (BOAC).

The American flying boats, named 'Clippers' after the famous 'tea schooner' vessels, began service in 1931. The first **Clipper** was christened by the American President Herbert Hoover's wife Lou – a bottle of water replaced champagne due to the prohibition laws. The technical advisor for the aircraft's first flight was American flying ace and pioneer Charles Lindbergh. The **Clippers** were also luxuriously appointed with wood paneled compartments and the crew dressed smartly in naval uniforms to add a sense of decorum, safety and security. There were deliberate comparisons to travel on ocean liners where even the cockpit was named a bridge, referencing a ship. Ocean travel continued to rule the waves at this time but that scenario was not destined to remain.

First parachutes. One of the first men to descend from a balloon by parachute was Andre Garnerin in 1797. Ascending in a hydrogen balloon to a height of about 1¼ miles, he cut himself adrift and descended in perfect safety. Cigarette card, WD & HO Wills, 'Famous inventions', No. 3, London, 1915.

'Frog' aeroplane models, *Meccano Magazine* May 1941. Advertisement for Frog scale-model aeroplanes, which were also used for identification purposes. Identification models for training purposes were also produced in Bakelite.

A wonderful *Meccano Magazine* cover featuring Hurricane fighter planes in action during the Second World War. The accompanying article explains the latest developments in parachute design, specifically the Irwin Air Chute designed by American Leslie L Irwin. These parachutes, also made in Great Britain and supplied to all RAF pilots, were considered the finest parachutes in the world. The cover illustration was supplied by Irving Air Chute Corporation of Great Britain (*Meccano Magazine,* May 1941).

By 1940 the world was at war again and many historians consider the **Battle of Britain,** which was fought in the skies of England and over the English Channel between July and September 1940, largely influenced the outcome of the war. Advancements in technology grew during the war years including navigation, radar and aircraft design. Although the famous **Spitfire** fighter plane has gained most accolades, **Hurricane** fighter planes were also heavily involved in the Second World War and in the victorious Battle of Britain (see picture). A wonderful illustration on the cover of a 1941 *Meccano Magazine* depicts a **Hurricane** fighter jet 'defending' a pilot baling out from his doomed aircraft. Scale model aircraft and toys were made during the Second World War on an 'essential' basis, as not only all military personnel, but the under siege population at large were encouraged to identify both friendly and enemy aircraft.

The **'Frog'** advertisement, pictured, shows a model of the **Avro 679 Manchester** bomber, the forerunner of the famous Lancaster bombers which were used extensively until 1942. Only 202 Avro Manchesters were manufactured and they were soon replaced by the upgraded twin-engined Lancasters.

'Frog' (an acronym for Flies Right Off the Ground) plastic kitsets were made before, during and after the war by **International Model Aircraft Ltd** for **Lines Brothers (Triang Toys). IMA,** founded by Charles Wilmot and Joe Mansour, were making aircraft and ship kitsets in plastic (cellulose acetate) by 1936, placing them at the forefront of early plastic toy making along with **Automobiles Geographical Ltd** and **Codeg** of England in the 1930s (refer Chapter 6, Early Period Plastic).

Rovex Plastics, established in 1950, made **Frog** kitsets after the war when they were taken over by **Lines Brothers** in 1951. **Rovex** had already manufactured an affordable 'OO' gauge train set in plastic in 1950 and **Lines Brothers,** realizing the future of toy making lay largely in plastics, incorporated **Rovex** into their factory at Margate in a move to gain further resource and expertise. By 1971 **Lines Brothers'** train sets were labeled **Rovex/Triang.** The name was also used for plastic doll's house furniture between 1965 and 1970, which was eventually rebranded **Dollies Home** (originally **Jenny's Home**) to combine with their opposition to the **Barbie** doll, **Sindy**.[117]

Airfix of England, one of the most well-known makers of plastic toy kitsets, was founded in 1939 by Hungarian Nicholas

Wright brothers biplane, c. 1903. The first flight on 17 December 1903 lasted twelve seconds and covered a distance of 100 feet (30.48 metres). Sanitarium Health Food Company cereal collector's card 'Evolution of

Bleriot's monoplane. 'On July 25th 1909 Louis Bleriot became the first man to fly the English Channel. Bleriot received the *Daily Mail* prize of £1,000.' Sanitarium Health Food Company cereal collector's card 'Evolution of Flight'.

Amphibian Flying Boat. The Seagull Mark V amphibian was especially designed to be launched by catapult in restricted areas and from naval vessels. The wings were able to be folded for ease of transport. Phillips Ltd cigarette card, #4, 1929.

Bleriot's monoplane, 'Frog' plastic kitset, c. 1965.

Kove (1891–1958) to produce inflatable rubber toys. Kove (born Miklos Klein) was also a pioneer in plastics manufacturing, establishing a plastics company in 1934 in Barcelona, Spain. He was also reputedly an indomitable and fearless character, serving in the First World War as a cavalry officer. Captured by the Russians, he eventually escaped internment and trekked his way across Siberia to his homeland, arriving four months later. Blockbuster movies have been made of lesser feats. By 1934 he had moved to Barcelona where he started his first plastics factory. Forced to then escape the brutal Spanish Civil War, he soon ended up in London where he formed the famous **Airfix** company, this time to produce his inflatable toys. By 1947, however, Kove was back into plastics manufacturing, installing a plastic injection-molding machine to diversify into hair combs. Success followed success and after producing a kitset **Ferguson TE20 tractor** promotional toy in cellulose acetate in 1949, **Airfix** decided to make a kitset of Sir Francis Drake's *Golden Hind*. Sales boomed through mega department store Woolworths. This hot seller was soon followed by a kitset of the star of the Battle of Britain, the **Spitfire fighter plane,** released in Coronation year, 1953. For some time **Airfix** didn't look back, releasing a host of plastic kitset models including the popular **Spitfire** several times in various versions. **Airfix** made kitsets of many fighter jets and war planes including the renowned German **Messerschmitt fighter plane.** It is ironic that the founder of **Airfix,** Nicholas Kove, would probably have witnessed the Messerschmitt B109 during the Spanish Civil War of 1937–1939 where they were first used. The **Airfix** company was disassembled and reassembled several times over the course of the tumultuous late twentieth century toy market. The company nevertheless remained one of the largest plastic toy kitset manufacturers in the world until forced into bankruptcy in 1981. The revived company currently operates under the wing of the **Hornby** company. Many excellent model kit makers remain including **Revell, Tamiya, Aurora, Matchbox and Italeri,** to name a few. The artworks on the boxes is fabulous too, with vintage and new sets continuing to attract collectors.

Another famous aircraft developed during the Second World War was the **Douglas DC-3,** which was used extensively as a transport plane. Pictured is a model of this aircraft made in Japan in the early 1950s. Introduced in 1936, the aircraft proved to be one of the most versatile planes ever built. A **DC-3** remains

Lockheed Electra. This early passenger aircraft starred at the end of the classic 1942 movie *Casablanca*, where in a theatrical fog setting Rick (Humphrey Bogart) persuades Lisa (Ingrid Bergman) to leave on the plane to Lisbon. 'International Airlines' player's series collectible card, c. 1936.

1950s tin plate, friction drive Douglas DC-3, 12 in long (31 cm) long, 15 in (40 cm) wingspan, Toys Nomura, Japan, photo courtesy collection of Hugh Schofield, New Zealand.

in service as a sightseeing aircraft in Auckland, New Zealand more than seventy years after production. A **DC-3** has also starred in several movies including *The Dirty Dozen* and the 2015 James Bond movie *The Quantum of Solace* starring Daniel Craig and Olga Kurylenko.

One of the most controversial and newsworthy passenger aircraft in the late twentieth century was the **Concorde**, an unlikely joint venture between England and France. By temporarily casting aside language difficulties and clichéd insults traditionally focused on cuisine, weather and bedside manners, the sleek and imposing **Concorde** was duly completed in 1973 (see picture). The engines were supplied by **Rolls Royce** and boasted a cruising speed of 1354 miles per hour (2179 kilometres per hour) or Mach 2.04 – twice

the speed of sound.[118] Regular services between Paris and New York began in 1976 and cut the travel time to around three hours, a far cry from Charles Lindbergh's 1927 33½ hour flight fifty years earlier. Commercially, however, the aircraft was a financial disaster. In 2000, after a tire burst causing a fuel line to rupture on take-off (killing all 101 on board and four on the ground), questions regarding the aircraft's integrity were posed. The aircraft were retired in 2003 and many are now housed in various museums around the world. While **Airfix** made a kitset of the **Concorde** and **Corgi Toys** a die-cast display model, the **Concorde** featured in several games and card sets. **Pepys** of England featured the **Concorde** in their 1970s **Round the World** card game where the five bonus cards depicted a **Concorde** in flight.

Atom Bomber target game. The Superfortress B-29 plane features an automatic bomb release bay while the box contains an integral cardboard battlefield. Made by Popular Plastics, England, c. 1950.

Concorde. 'The Concorde carries 128 passengers in a narrow 2.63 metres wide (8.6 feet) cabin and is known for the loud "clap" as it breaks the sound barrier.' 'Airliners of the 90s' collector's card No. 8, Sanitarium Health Food Company, New Zealand 1991.

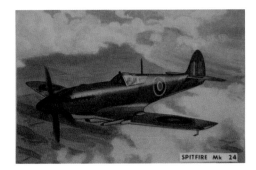

Spitfire Mk 24. A late edition of the original machine that won the Battle of Britain and gained supremacy over the Luftwaffe. 'Evolution of Flight' collector's card No. 3, Sanitarium Health Food Company, c. 1960s.

As we have seen, not all aircraft were used for establishing flight records and luxury passenger travel. Early in the twentieth century author JB Priestley lamented the fact aircraft would eventually be used in warfare to kill people. He never imagined the extent to which his prediction would come true when, in 1946 towards the end of World War II, an aircraft dropped atom bombs on Japan causing apocalyptic destruction and death. A toy pictured here appears to be based on the actual **Superfortress B-29** heavy bomber that dropped atom bombs on Hiroshima and Nagasaki in August 1945, effectively ending World War II. The bomb which fell on Hiroshima killed more than 100,000 people, with many victims dying from the effects of radiation fallout. While there are fortunately no cities illustrated on the toy target range, the title 'Atom Bomber' is contained menacingly in a mushroom cloud on the side flap of the box. This toy seems surprisingly inappropriate for this immediate postwar era considering the unsettling atmosphere of a cold war and developments in China and Korea.

Taking into consideration nuclear stand-offs in Cuba later in the 1950s, continuing grandstanding and button and keyboard rattling more recently, I would be surprised to see a toy of this nature ever re-enter the market place. That said, a similar toy presented for the edification and amusement of relevant superpower leaders to play with until their hearts and souls are content could be an option. We have already established toys can be extremely therapeutic.

Trains and boats (ships) and planes have come a long way in a relatively short time span, from box kites to spacecraft to the moon in less than 100 years (see Chapter 5). In an acknowledgment to the early pioneers of flight the Wright brothers, Neil Armstrong took mementos from the Wright brothers' 1903 aircraft in the form of a piece of wood from the left propeller and a piece of fabric from the wing on the *Apollo 11* moon mission; an appropriate touch I am sure you will agree.

CHAPTER 9

TOY MAKERS PLAY CAT AND MOUSE

Wooden toys, including pull-along toys, were some of the earliest types of toys, most depicting carved figures, anthropomorphic animals, horses or mounted soldiers. Many were handcrafted from cottage industries and fall into the category of folk art. Following the industrial revolution, these toys became more mass-produced and larger toy companies such as **Stieff** (Germany est. 1880), **McLoughlins** (USA est. 1858), **Bliss** (USA est. 1870), **Gibbs** (USA est. 1890), **Crandalls** (USA est. 1866), the **Gong Bell Co.** (est. Connecticut, USA 1866), **Schoenhut,** (USA est. 1903) and **Brio** of Sweden (est. 1884) appeared. These classic vintage toy makers were more renowned in some cases for other toys such as teddy bears (Stieff), wooden building block sets (Crandalls), doll houses (Bliss), and lithographed wooden toys (Gibbs).

Krazy Kat doll's house tea tray, tin plate, 1930s Chein, USA.

From the 1860s, **Crandalls** (Charles Martin Crandall, 1833–1905) were probably the first mass manufacturer of wooden interlocking block sets in America. By the 1870s, **Crandalls'** advertisement in the *American Agriculturist* magazine (November 1874) boasted 'the manufacturers are now making and selling 1500 boxes a day'.

Brio's 1907 catalog listed more than 170 items available to order, including the **Goinge horse,** a wooden pull toy.[119] By 1914 the company offered 6000 items for sale. This horse, known as the **Osby horse** was **Brio's** first toy as previously their main line was baskets and domestic items. A raft of other toy makers began producing wooden pull toys in the early part of the

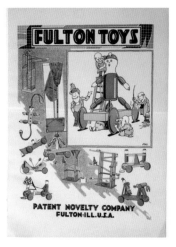

Advertisement for Fulton Wooden Toys, 1928.

Buck-a-roo horse and jockeys, Kreiger Novelty Company, California, advertisement, New York Toy Fair.

twentieth century, including **Lines Bros** of England, **LEGO, The Kreiger Novelty Toy Company** of California, **Ted Toy-lers,** Massachusetts (est. 1925), **Hustler Toy Company,** Illinois (est. 1920), **Rich Toys** (est. 1923), **Tinker Toys, Gibbs, Fulton Toys** of Chicago and **Alderman Fairchild Co.** of Rochester, New York, which made the **Tutoom** game featured in Chapter 1. **All Fair Toys** made some quality wooden pull toys in 1931 promoting them as 'kicking and quacking toys', two of the best being **Mr and Mrs Quack Duck.**

In the 1920s **Gong Bell** were making a popular wooden pull-toy named **Jingling Jim** #907 (see picture The Gong Bell News, 1928).[120] An unusual toy I purchased in Australia many years ago is a duck pull-along toy of a very similar design (see picture). Beautifully stylized in green and black Bakelite, the toy is made by **Glensunite** of Australia, probably in the 1930s. The duck's head bobs in and out and up and down, emitting a low quack as it is pulled along. The toy retains an original Wisemans Sports Stores, Auckland gold label on the body but unfortunately the duck face has gone. This material is extremely uncommon for a pull-along toy as these toys needed to be robust to tolerate friendly pets, sidewalks, furniture, feet and teeth. As we saw in Chapter 7 (Plastic Toys), plastics and Bakelite were used sparingly at this time, although it is interesting to note the **Gong Bell Company** at this time stated in their advertising 'Celluloid pin wheels are in big demand'.[121]

Although most pull-along toys were made from wood, the **Gong Bell Company** and other early American manufacturers from the nineteenth century made their toys from cast-iron and tin. In keeping with the popularity of horseracing at this time, **Krieger Novelty Co.** (Lodi, California) introduced a **Buck-a-roo horse** and **Jockies** pull toy at the New York Toy Fair (see picture) and **Globe Manufacturing** produced a cast-iron horse and jockey pull toy. By the 1930s **Gong Bell** had reverted to a combination of wood and steel with their delightful **Trix** series of pull-toys. Such was the shortage of materials following World War II, **Gong Bell** announced in 1950 they were unable to supply any further orders due to '… acute shortages of raw materials…'[122]

Pull-along ducks seemed to be a perennial favorite with toy makers, **All Fair toys,** for example, advertising Wally and Dolly duck in 1928 (see picture). [123] LEGO produced a wooden pull-along duck designed by Ole Kirk Christiansen in 1935 before they became famous for toy building bricks.

Toy makers played their own games of cat and mouse in the 1920s and 1930s. There were three cats and two mice in the toy game but by the 1930s it was one mouse who came out on top. In 1911 **Krazy Kat** and **Ignatz the Mouse** made their first appearance in George Herriman's (1880–1944) 'Dingbat Family' cartoon feature. Some fabulous toys emanated over time from these characters, notably by **J Chein & Co.** of America (est. 1903), **Jaymar's** wood jointed dolls (see picture) and soft toys by **Averil** (1916), **Knickerbocker** (1931) and the **Cameo Doll Company** (1930s). **Fisher Price** (est. 1930) produced a wooden toy very similar to Ignatz in 1934 that they named **Hop-Ear Looie.** This was an articulated toy from their pop-up critter series from the 1930s. We will read more about the **Fisher Price** company shortly. Arguably one of the most classic and

Wally and Dolly Duck wooden pull-along toys, All Fair Toys, USA, advertisement, c. 1928.

Duck pull-along toy, Glensunite, Australia, 1930s, 5 in long (13 cm).

Advertisement for Jingling Jim, 1928, Gong Bell Toys, USA.

Trix, Gong Bell Toys, wood and pressed steel, USA, c. 1930, 11½ in long (28 cm).

endearing clockwork, tin-plate toys of the twentieth century is the **Merry Makers' Ignatz band** toy by **Louis Marx** (see picture). **The Gong Bell** company also made appealing pull toys featuring **Krazy Kat, Ignatz** and **Felix** in the 1930s (see picture). **J Chein** also made an attractive tin plate **Krazy Kat** tea set but arguably their most outstanding toy was their tin-plate pull toy featuring **Krazy Kat chasing Ignatz** (see pictures). A wooden locomotive pull toy made by the same company, **Krazy Kat**

Express, is also hard to find. The **Krazy Kat** tea set is delightfully illustrated and stamped 'J Chein & Co, made in USA' on the underside of each piece. I am unsure if this was an authorized production. At the time this set was released, one of the cartoonists, Charles B Mintz, began to model **Krazy Kat** more on **Mickey and Minnie Mouse,** with **Krazy Kat** entering into a relationship and adding a pet dog to make a happy trio. This tea set is reflective of this change to the **Krazy Kat/Ignatz** dynamic and as such their sets are often erroneously advertised or sold as **Mickey and Minnie Mouse** collectibles. Either way, with the anthropomorphic cow and pig visitors sharing tea and cake with **Krazy Kat** and friends, this set is a nice example of lithographed tin plate toys from this prewar period. **Krazy Kat** and family, including his nemesis **Ignatz,** had lost appeal to another pair of mice by 1940. The toys which remain are fabulous collectibles.

In 1919 **Felix the Cat** was created by cartoonist and animator Pat Sullivan (1895–1933) and a wooden jointed toy **Felix** is pictured. Underneath, the toy displays a gold leaf label stating 'patented 1922 Pat Sullivan'. Sullivan was actually born in Australia but emigrated to America in 1910. Controversy and disputes arose over

Krazy Kat tin-plate tea set, J Chein & Co., USA, 1930s, 2–7 in (5–18 cm).

the inventor of Felix following Sullivan's death in 1933. Sullivan, a talented but flawed personality, with the assistance of an overabundance of alcohol, went to an early grave.

Another anthropomorphic cat similar to **Felix** was **Trix.** A series of Trix pull-along toys was produced by the **Gong Bell Company** and **HD Allen** later in the 1920s. This cat was also full of tricks, being able to drive, ride a bike and attend fires from his firecar, but he did look remarkably like a brother or sister to **Krazy Kat.** Another toy with similarities to these was a mouse named Michael (Mickey) designed in 1928 by Walt Disney. **Felix, Trix, Krazy Kat, Ignatz** and **Mickey Mouse** to me look quite similar and if two weren't mice and the other three cats, I would say they were related. Similarly to the **Krazy Kat** tea set, several cat and mouse character toys

Jaymar wood jointed Ignatz the Mouse, 1920s, 5 in long (13 cm).

have been incorrectly attributed over time and often the graphics are quite generic and confusing. Quite ironically, the **Gong Bell Company** announced in 1954 they had teamed up with Disney to release a new range of toys concurrent with the *Mickey Mouse Club* TV show. By the 1960s the **Gong Bell Company** could not be saved 'by the bell' and in boxing parlance were out for the count. **The Gong Bell Company** should, however, be credited with inventing television and Skype – or at least the first television and Skype toys. They launched a television play phone in 1928 stating '…a child can see the life-like picture of one called on the phone…' (see picture – don't ask!) **Ingap** of Italy also entered a cluttered stage in the 1930s with their tin plate **Topolino** mouse (refer Chapter 7).

Early cat and mouse toys were not just based on newspaper cartoon strips. **Krazy Kat** film strip serials were first produced in 1916, *Introducing Krazy Kat and Ignatz Mouse.* Some 230 movie shorts followed between 1916 and 1940. *Felix the Cat* animated film strips were first released in 1929 but struggled to make an impact against Walt Disney's *Mickey Mouse* cartoons, which screened a year earlier. Mickey and friends eventually became superstars. **Felix** did, however, enjoy several revivals over the

Ignatz band, Marx Merrymakers by Louis Marx, USA, c. 1929, photo courtesy Bertoia Auctions, USA.

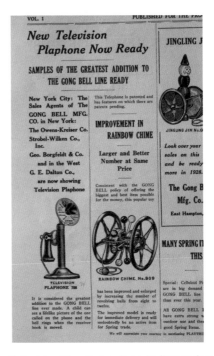

Television Playphone, Gong Bell Manufacturing Co., East Hampton Court, USA, 1928, the forerunner to Skype!

Felix Chasing Mice pull toy, tin plate, Nifty Toys, 7½ in long (19 cm) long, photo courtesy Bertoia Auctions, USA.

Felix the Cat, wood-jointed toy, Pat Sullivan, 1922, 4 in long (10 cm).

Felix on scooter, pull toy, tin plate, 7½ in (19 cm), photo courtesy Bertoia Auctions.

latter decades and now resides on the hearth and in the domain of Dreamworks Animation.

Since the trailblazing days of movie animation in the early twentieth century, well over 50 movies have screened featuring other anthropomorphic cats and mice. Character mice include **Tom and Jerry, The Great Mouse Detective** and **Stuart Little**. Cunning moggies include **Sylvester, Garfield, The Cat in the Hat** and **Puss in Boots,** who featured in Chapter 5. Immense credit must go to the early creators of these unique cartoon characters who have brought so much enduring comedy in the past 100 years.

The theme was probably set by George Herriman in one of his first **Krazy Kat** cartoons, 'Krazy Kat and Ignatz mouse discuss the letter G' (1916). Here, **Ignatz** eventually plants a strawberry pie square on **Krazy Kat's** back after frustration with the cat's display of naivety. The cat flops down gobsmacked and says…nothing, indicating that it is the tiny mouse who holds sway over the cat. The final film shorts were made in 1940.

Butterfly feather tree decoration, tin plate, c. 1890, 1 ¾ in high (4 cm).

We mentioned earlier the influence of books relating to the design and production of toys and subsequently anthropomorphic illustrations in children's books witnessed an explosion of insect toys during the twentieth century. Scarabs, ladybirds, spiders, dragonflies, grasshoppers, caterpillars, butterflies, crickets, ants, bees and, as we shall see, slater bugs, all feature in toys of this period. No insect, it seemed, was ignored. **A Bum-Bill-Bee** character appeared in **Krazy Kat** cartoons, perhaps a precursor to the several bee toys which appear later in this chapter. Little has changed. **Meccano** launched a new toy, 'Mega Spider', in 2017, with the added feature of 'spraying venom'. Conversely, a delightfully harmless butterfly, tin plate, feather tree decoration is pictured, circa 1900.

By necessity, many toy makers continued with or reverted to wood for toy making

Grasshopper, cast-iron, Hubley Toys, USA, 1930s, 3¾ in (9.5 cm), photo courtesy Bertoia Auctions, USA.

during the 1940s, however the surreal **Dippee Bug** toy is an exception. This somewhat obscure toy made by **Herbert H Schwarze** of Milwaukee, Wisconsin, is made from a composition similar to elastolin or Bakelite. It has a sweet odor, which indicates cellulose acetate (or perhaps chewing gum somewhere).

Buzzy Bee, wooden pull-along toy, Fisher Price, 1950, USA, 5½ in (14cm) with 'Buzzy Bee', wooden pull-along toy, Playcraft Products/Ramseys, NZ, c. 1950, 6½ in long (16.5cm).

Dippee Bug, pull-along toy, Composition, 1940s, Herbert H Schwarze, USA, 9 in (25 cm).

The toy, including the wooden feelers, moves up and down as it is pulled along. The illustrated box reveals the toy bug appears to be an armadillo or slater bug (woodlouse), lives in a mushroom field, and at 9 inches (23 centimetres) long is rather intimidating. The toy is essentially new in the box, rarely (if ever) having been pulled along. While it may have scared a few little sisters in its day, I doubt the toy was a big seller, being eventually consigned back to the mushroom fields.

Another mega toy maker that produced pull-along toys was **Fisher Price** of America. Pictured here is a controversial toy **Fisher Price** made in 1950 called the **Buzzy Bee.** This toy was the first toy where **Fisher Price** introduced

Buzzy Bee sculpture, wood, Matakana Country Park, NZ.

plastic (the revolving wings), however the **Buzzy Bee** toy is claimed to have been invented by a New Zealand toy maker, Maurice Schlessinger, and his **Playcraft Products,** in the late 1930s. Famous Swedish wooden toy maker, **Brio,** also made a Buzzy Bee, remarkably similar to the New Zealand toy. Whoever designed the first bee toy is now perhaps irrelevant as the New Zealand edition has, over time, cemented and enjoyed a stellar career. It is now considered an iconic New Zealand toy with the image featuring on stamps, Christmas decorations, calendars, t-shirts and famous New Zealand paintings, the most notable being *A Buzzy Bee for Siulolovao* by New Zealand artist Robin White. The toy was presented to royalty in 1983 (Prince William) and is arguably New Zealand's most famous toy, much loved and jealously protected along with other New Zealand icons such as pavlova cake, racehorse Phar Lap and rock band Split Enz. Several large sculptures of the toy have been made

The Toy Show poster, Auckland Museum exhibition, 1996. *The Toy Show* was a major and comprehensive exhibition of antique and collectible toys which toured public museums in New Zealand in 1996 and 1997.

Belle Tinker wooden crib toy, advertisement, Tinker Toys, USA, 1931.

as well as a large **LEGO** version. Because of this, to suggest the Buzzy Bee is not a New Zealand invention is comparable to skewering a sacred cow. However the toy is very similar to **Fisher Price's Buzzy Bee** and **Brio's** version as well.

New Zealand's **Buzzy Bee** came under scrutiny during a major antique toy museum touring exhibition mounted in New Zealand in 1995. The touring schedule opened at the Auckland Museum and one visitor, a Mr Vernon Davenport, advised a senior museum official that the New Zealand Buzzy Bee toy had been copied from another toy. Davenport, who had worked at the Ramsey's toy factory for forty years, claimed his work mate, George Steel's sister, had brought back a wooden Buzzy Bee toy from America. The toy he described was made of thick timber and decorated with lithographed paper instead of paint. The toy was also fitted with a clicker at the base, which is very similar to the **Fisher Price Buzzy Bee**. Davenport maintained Ramsey immediately copied the toy.[124] The toys are indeed remarkably similar and the *New Zealand Herald* soon published an article also questioning the origins of the beloved New Zealand toy. The Ramsey's well-known 'Mary Lou' wooden crib toy by **Playcraft Products** appears to be an exact copy of **Tinker Toys** USA's 1930s wooden crib doll **Belle Tinker** (see pictures). The storm in a honey pot soon passed however and the New Zealand bee has continued on her busy way to fame and fortune. A 'Buzzy Bee and Friends' website has even been established, which suggests **Fisher Price** possibly copied the New Zealand toy as their research indicates the New Zealand toy was made in the 1940s.[125] While this would be a first and the evidence seems somewhat inconclusive, Fisher Price did cease the manufacture of their Buzzy Bee toy in 1952 but later resurrected the bee as **Queen Buzzy Bee** in 1962. The smiling bee sports a plastic crown on her head. Fisher Price, which started business in 1930, had fittingly opened their innings with the launch of sixteen wooden toys at the New York Toy Fair in 1931. **Fisher Price** became one of the most significant toy companies of the twentieth century, producing toys from television series such as *Sesame Street*, *The Muppets*, *Bob the Builder* and *Spongebob Squarepants*. As their turnover spilled into the billions, **Mattel** bought out the mega company in 1993. Soon after, **Mattel** gained the franchise for *Toy Story* and their turnover in 2015 reached US$5.2 billion. It would be surprising if **Mattel** would be concerned with the success of New Zealand's Buzzy Bee. While author and historian Ronald Fritz[126] may describe New Zealand's obsession with Buzzy Bee as 'therapeutic mythology', we will claim the toy as our own, even if indelible facts to the contrary are presented at some time in the future.

Mary Lou wooden crib toy, Playcraft Products/ Ramseys Toys NZ, 1950s, 6½ in long (17 cm).

CHAPTER 10

ALL CHANGE – TENNIS, TARGET GAMES AND OTHER TOYS REFLECT SOCIAL CHANGE

There is a saying that the only thing that remains the same is change and the twentieth century has echoed this mantra more than any previous century. Suggestions of manned space flight, electric motor vehicles or a remote-controlled toy robot in Santa's sack would, 200 years ago, have been considered the hopes and dreams of an eccentric scientist, at best, or at worst the mutterings of a crackpot. These wonderful inventions have indeed come to pass but toys and games also correspond with unprecedented advancements and fundamental changes in basic human rights, including equal and gay rights, which are now endorsed by complex domestic and international legislation. The United Nations Declaration of Human Rights was sanctioned in 1948, establishing moral principles and social doctrines, largely a consequence of the horrors of World War II, and in particular the Holocaust.

These principles and doctrines have now fanned out in the twenty-first century to include the legalization of gay marriage in many countries, something which would have shocked not only game and toy makers 100 years ago. Race relations too have progressed considerably and many toys, mentioned in this chapter, reference this often controversial and topical subject. Animal rights and protection of the environment are also referenced through toys here, where threats against both have become all too real as we maneuver through the twenty-first century. Quite surprisingly, as my research developed, it became apparent that the sport of tennis and the toys and games associated with this international sport were arguably the ones which reflect many monumental changes of twentieth century social history more than any other. Changes in clothing, fashion, equipment, raw materials used in racket

Sinnet (tennis spelled backwards) board game, Chad Valley, England, c. 1930.

At the beach-Florida , original sepia photo,USA C1905.

manufacture, marketing, media, equal and gay rights, are all starkly highlighted throughout the history of this game. One player, Rene Richards (b. 1934, USA) was the first player to legally play tennis at the highest level first as a man and later in 1977, as a woman.

For better or worse, in recent years many toys and games have fallen under the spotlight and encountered the judgment of political correctness – **Barbie** dolls and **Golliwogs** are good examples, and while they are mentioned here, their trials and tribulations are well recorded elsewhere. Here I refer to other toys and games, many from my collection, which recall or record watershed or groundbreaking events that have occurred in the past 150 years.

The **Sinnet** ('tennis' spelt backwards) board game, pictured, was made by **Chad Valley** of England in the late 1920s. The gracefully illustrated box depicts two lightly clad female players dressed in ritzy short skirts and elegant sleeveless blouses. This illustration reflects the 'flapper' and Art Deco period, a time during the early twentieth century when women were breaking the shackles of Victorian and Edwardian stuffiness and entering an era of fads, sassy fashion, rebellion and social freedom. In 1925 F Scott Fitzgerald wrote *The Great Gatsby*, the charleston dance craze began and in 1928, around the date of **Sinnet,** DH Lawrence's raunchy *Lady Chatterley's Lover* was published. Is the title **Sinnet** a coincidence – bare arms and blouses – whatever sin next!

Dress code throughout this era and up until this day has arguably been the most contentious issue and many female tennis players from Gussy Moran to Maria Sharapova have been promoted as sex symbols to the same degree as movie and pop stars. Ironically, one of the first 'stars' in the tennis world was a male New Zealander and four time Wimbledon winner, Anthony (Tony) Wilding (1883–1915). While Wilding, who held a law degree, was more a gentleman than a playboy, he lived up to his 'wild colonial boy' aura while roaring around on a motorbike from tournament to tournament when motorbikes (and motor cars) were in their relative infancy. Due to marry Broadway star, actress and cougar Maxine Elliot (1868–1940, USA), Wilding was tragically killed in action in 1915 in France during World War I.

In America, before the turn of the century, pioneer women were not all outlaws and Wild West sharp shooters emulating Belle Star and Anne Oakley. In reality, many were brave colonials whose tasks included loading gunpowder into rifles and skinning game for supper. It is no surprise that the first mixed doubles grand slam events began in Forest Hills, America in 1892. Mixed doubles was not introduced to Wimbledon until 1913, and the French only relented in 1925 when a mixed tournament was introduced for the Open at Roland Garros.

Such was the growth in the popularity of tennis at schools and clubs, the clubs themselves effectively became a social hub or rendezvous for singles, families or groups to meet. The book illustrated here **Every Girl's Annual Stories of School, Adventure and Sport** features a dashing young girl on the cover sporting matching green ribboned ponytails flowing in the wind while playing a backhand volley. Published in 1922 the book features Miss Kitty McKane-Godfree (1896–1992) in the chapter 'Leaders in Sport', who won Wimbledon the following year. To provide further inspiration for girls (and no distractions) all the leaders mentioned are female.

Probably the first genuine female tennis sex symbol was 1949 Wimbledon finalist and American Indoor Tennis Champion Gussy Moran (1923–2013). Nicknamed Gorgeous Gussy after playing in revealing short skirts and frilly knickers during the Wimbledon Championships, Moran was accused of bringing vulgarity and sin [Sinnet?] into the game. She was eventually forced to wear shorts or suffer default. Not to be outdone, in later tournaments she donned even shorter shorts, some woven with gold embroidery or cut from leopard skin.[127] Moran eventually became a cover girl and respected television sportscaster.

The Pepys card game **Wimbledon,** illustrated here, was made by **Castell Bros** of England in 1960. **Pepys** illustrated card sets are quite outstanding, the games reaching their peak in the 1950s and 1960s when

Every Girl's Annual, The Pilgrim Press and Classic Color Press, England 1922.

'Leaders of Sport', Miss K McKane (1896–1992) playing in stockings, c. 1922, *Every Girls Annual.* Later McKane won the Wimbledon championship singles and again in 1924 as Kitty Godfree. Godfree was inducted into the tennis Hall of Fame in 1978.

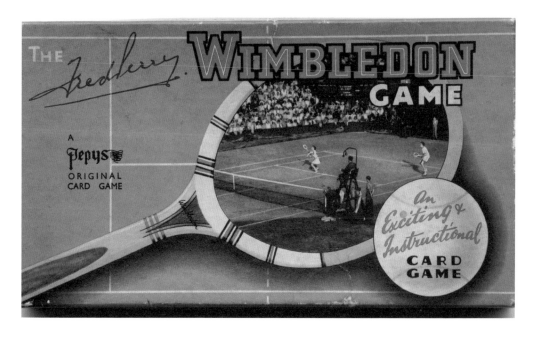

Pepys card game, 'The Fred Perry Wimbledon Game', 1960. By the 1950s most players were playing in shorts or short skirts.

color printing became more sophisticated and quality printing materials were more readily available after the Second World War. Several other collectible **Pepys** card sets appear throughout this book. This tennis card game is endorsed by three time Wimbledon winner Fred Perry (1909–1995) who, while winning a total of eight grand slam singles events between 1934 and 1936, became one of the most famous men in England. He later became well known for a clothing range of sports shirts he launched in 1952. The label was revived somewhat when worn by tennis star Andy Murray of Scotland and Great Britain some fifty-five years later. This game, similarly to many in the **Pepys** series, contains charmingly illustrated cards of tennis players, although they do appear somewhat dated. Perhaps the game was designed for an earlier production. The classic wooden tennis racket featured on the box cover was, by the 1980s, completely obsolete, superseded by rackets manufactured with aluminum and soon after, graphite, Kevlar, boron and other ceramic composites.

Long hair and the hippie look became de rigueur for trendy youths or men in the

1960s and 1970s, and the flowing blonde locks of Swedish tennis star Bjorn Borg soon saw schoolgirls shrieking with desire in scenes reminiscent of Beatlemania. After Borg's first Wimbledon match in 1973, he required a police escort to protect him from what was described as the 'gymslip army'. The Swede went on to win Wimbledon five times and acquire six French Open titles, proving he was much more than eye candy. He is featured in the **Tennis Aces** card game, pictured, described as 'Ice Cool'.

Ilie Nastase's Tennis Aces card game, featuring Arthur Ashe and Bjorn Borg, Germany, c. 1978.

Racial equality also became embroiled in sports games featured here, including tennis and Rugby football. Champion African-American tennis player Arthur Ashe (1943–1993) active in the 1960s and 1970s, won the US Open in 1968, the Australian Open in 1970 and Wimbledon in 1975. He is also featured in the 1977 card game **Ilie Nastase's Tennis Aces,** pictured here, where he is described as '… the first negro winner of Wimbledon – good temperament, fine all round player'. Ashe was also the first African-American to play Davis Cup for the USA in 1960, but he was refused entry to play in South Africa in 1969 due to the color bar in force – apartheid. In 1970 South Africa was expelled from the Davis Cup due to their segregation policy. Ashe was finally granted a visa in 1973 but he campaigned

Dusty the Tennis Champion, Denys Fisher Toys, England, vinyl doll, c. 1975, 11½ in tall (29 cm). By the 1960s the miniskirt was fashionable. Ladies' tennis dresses soon followed the trend.

The Game of Rugby, Rugby board game, c. 1950, 12 x 9 in (30 x 23 cm).

throughout his career for equal rights. Ashe also founded the Arthur Ashe Foundation for the Defeat of Aids and months before his tragic death aged forty-nine in 1993, the Arthur Ashe Institute of Urban Health'

Sports and their associated toys and games reflect the changes in social history in some countries perhaps more than others. Some issues like the South Africa/New Zealand Rugby tour of 1981 tore relationships and idealists apart while other events and protests

were more subtle in nature. The games pictured here relate to Rugby football and, while the game is not played worldwide, it is growing in stature. Two of the games are named **Rugger,** a colloquialism similar to soccer (football), or grid iron (American football). The game's origins began at Rugby School, Warwickshire, England around the 1830s, when a soccer player, apparently in true entrepreneurial and enterprising fashion, literally picked up the ball and ran with it. 'Rugger' was born, but this terminology is not recorded in use until the late nineteenth century. It may have derived from the description 'rugged' which would be no surprise as, to this day, unlike American football players, no protective equipment is worn by Rugby football players. Purchasing shares in the medical profession seems a safe and lucrative bet for the future. Growing up in New Zealand every boy was expected to play Rugby, and in many schools that was the only winter sport available apart from hockey. The game Rugger, **The National Game,** pictured, was distributed as a giveaway by Shell petrol stations during the British Lions Rugby tour to New Zealand in 1966.

An 1889 photograph illustrated here, NZ Native Football Team, indicates how relatively early indigenous people were welcomed into the bosom of the Rugby Union code in New Zealand. This team was selected as a touring team and played their first game internationally in England in 1888. Indigenous visitors were a popular fascination for royalty and apparently the population in general in the nineteenth century in England. Maori chiefs were taken back to England on long voyages (some forcibly) and an Aboriginal cricket team from Australia visited England as far back as 1847. Five non-Maori were selected to strengthen the team and

Rugger, the National Game, Shell Oil New Zealand giveaway, British Lions tour to New Zealand 1966, paper 15½ x 11 (39 cm x 28 cm). The British Lions team featured two famous players from Ireland, Mike Gibson and Willie John McBride. The top test try scorer for the Lions was a Scot, Stuart Wilson. The All Blacks made a clean sweep of the test series, winning 4–nil.

'New Zealand Native Football Team', team photo, 1889.

negative feedback from some matches included the report that 'The players did not appear as black as the promotion had promised, many appearing to be only badly sunburned.' As a response, while waiting at a railway station, several team members donned black face-masks as a wind-up. The fourteen-month tour was long and arduous, totaling 107 games, 78 of which they won.

Despite some questionable promotional antics and handling of the players, the tour was largely a success indicating, at an early stage, New Zealand's progressive social policies towards race relations and equal

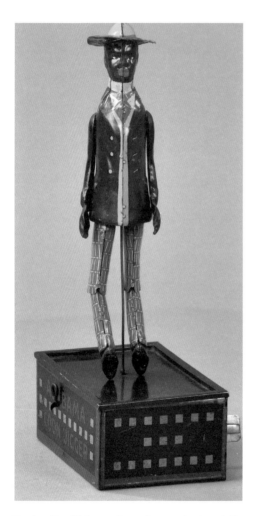

Coonie Flap, tiddlywinks target game, bone playing pieces, MOKO (Moses Kohnstam), Furth, Germany, c. 1900, 11 x 8 in (28 x 20 cm). MOKO found fame and fortune due to their association with Lesney's Matchbox toys in the 1950s as their marketing agents. Lesney, took over MOKO in 1959.

Tombo, The Alabama Coon Jigger, clockwork tin-plate toy by Ferdinand Strauss, USA, c. 1910, 10 in high (25 cm). Photo courtesy Bertoia Auctions.

Cards from The Round Game of Snap, Chad Valley Games, England c. 1900.

Cards from Bobs Yer Uncle card game, c. 1900.

rights. The first and third New Zealand All Black Rugby captains were Maori, and by 1893 Maori women could vote and receive old age pensions. Not everyone concurred with New Zealand's progressive policies regarding race relations. In 1921 when the New Zealand Maori team played the South African Springboks, a South African reporter expressed his disgust at spectators supporting 'colored' men.

Arthur Ashe's presence in South Africa was obviously not as coveted as the New Zealand All Black Rugby team. Maori All Blacks were admitted as 'honorary whites' in touring teams during this era, prior to the dismantling of apartheid. This unpleasant arrangement came to a painful and ugly end in New Zealand in 1981 when anti-apartheid and anti-Springbok rugby tour protests literally split New Zealand asunder during the South African rugby team tour to New Zealand in 1981. Family members unexpectedly appeared on either side of huge protest/supporter marches and picket lines. One protester suddenly found himself facing a baton-wielding, helmeted policeman on the front line of a protest march – his brother-in-law.

Historical racism and racial stereotyping is reflected in many toys produced over the last 120 years. The most blatant are probably toys depicting

African Americans as jolly dancers of suggested limited intelligence. Tin-plate clockwork tap dancers were produced by early German and American toy makers such as **Lehmann, Strauss, George Brown,** and others. **Alabama Coon Jigger** and **Coonie Flap,** pictured, are similar to thousands of toys produced which are now considered offensive. The game pictured is unusual in that it is a hybrid, a combination of **tiddlywinks** and a target game, the object being to flick the bone counters into the mouths of the targets. This game was made by **Moses Kohnstan** (Moko), Bavaria (Germany) around 1900, a toy maker and distribution company that fifty years later enjoyed a lucrative marketing arrangement with English die-cast maker **Lesney Co** and their **Matchbox** toys. **Happy Family** card games, produced around the same time, also included now inappropriate depictions that were considered amusing at this time.

Reclining Chinaman bank, cast-iron, JE Stevens, 1882 (photo courtesy Bertoia Auctions). This cast-iron money bank was produced around the time of anti-Chinese sentiment and the eventual passing of the Chinese Exclusion Act of 1882 restricting Chinese immigration was produced. The Reclining Chinaman bank was a comment on the perceived 'luck' of Chinese gamblers and card players. This toy bank depicts a Chinese card player holding an unbeatable hand of four aces, while holding out the other hand for his winnings. When the arm is depressed, the money is deposited. As late as 1969 Rooster Cogburn (John Wayne) in award-winning movie *True Grit* said, 'No-one ever beats a Chinese card player,' reflecting the era and sentiment.

Shy Anne Indian skater, tin plate clockwork toy, made in Japan, 1961, Line Mar Toys. Photo courtesy Bertoia Auctions. 'Shy Anne' is a corruption of the name of an indigenous North American Indian tribe, the 'Cheyenne'. This somewhat odd characterization of a surly warrior chief is a spin-off from Walt Disney's 1961 children's movie *Babes in Toyland.* The movie flopped at the box office, yet the racial stereotyping in this toy was not untypical at the time.

More common toys that have appeared under the spotlight in recent years include cast-iron African American figurative money banks and golliwog dolls. Racial stereotyping is evident in two jigsaw puzzles made in New Zealand in the 1960s by Holdson Products. The two, of a series of four, pictured, are simplistic stereotypes of a native American and a Maori couple from New Zealand. In what are now considered at best quaint descriptions and at worst casual racism, the games are titled **Red Indians** and **Maoris.** While games, toys or puzzles such as these were never intended to cause offence, they are deemed to reflect the negative stereotyping of a particular race. Even movies as recent as the *Toy Story* series cannoned into political correctness in 1999. A bandolier-toting, sombrero-wearing, mustachioed Mexican was railroaded out of a *Toy Story 2* video game, not by **Buzz Lightyear,** but accusations of racism. Hispanic people lodged fervent and impassioned protests with Disney Corporation alleging the Mexican character was portrayed as a 'degraded, dehumanized and stereotyped villain'. One protester claimed Disney had 'produced a game of genocide and accused the mega maker of being ethno specific.'[128] The mega toy maker relented and agreed to change the character.

People of the World jigsaw puzzles, Red Indian and Maoris, Holdson Products, New Zealand, c. 1960, 13½ x 19½ in (34 x 24 cm).

Mr Potato Head (Hasbro), who starred in *Toy Story,* is an enduring and classic toy invented around 1950 by George Lerner from the USA and put into production by Hasbro in 1952. The Queen of England, Queen Elizabeth II, no less, had the pleasure and honor of meeting **Mr Potato Head** at a Toy Fair in London in 1954. While Prince Phillip reputedly expressed confusion over the workings of the toy, the Queen, for once was amused

Mr Potato Head, Hasbro toys, plastic, 7 in high (18 cm). This pre-1987 version with a pipe was distributed in New Zealand by Toltoys NZ Ltd (original Toltoys NZ box).

and eruditely explained the complexities to him. They both enjoyed a joke or two and later went forth to purchase other soon to become classics such as a 'joke' rubber pencil, a space gun and a **Slinky toy** (Alex Products).[129] Who knew the Royals were also early toy collectors? **Mr Potato Head** remained largely unchanged for several decades, apart from the significant but inevitable change to plastic from a real spud in 1964.

In 1969, commensurate with events in outer space **Mr Potato Head** and his fruit and vegetable friends also went to the Moon. A Mr Potato Head on the Moon playset was produced along with several others, including, unsurprisingly, a Wild West playset. Here, **Mr Potato Head** could enter into a 'full color Western scene…to make Mr Potato Head at home on the range' (box cover text, **Hasbro**).

The ever popular but rather goofy **Mr Potato Head** was also struck by the 'PC effect' in 1987 and was forced to bow to the anti-smoking lobbyists. Amid much pomp, ceremony and shameless marketing, he handed his pipe over to the Surgeon General at the White House, signaling an end to his unhealthy habit. Paradoxically, it may not be long before our portly friend is put on a diet and summarily told to cut down on starchy potatoes and French fries. **Mr Potato Head** enjoyed a renaissance during the 1990s when he featured in the brilliant blockbuster *Toy Story* movies, voiced appropriately by the late Don Rickles. The bumptious yet lovable character was one of the stars of the series, reigniting his popularity. The toy pictured is an early boxed edition which includes a pipe, distributed in New Zealand by **Toltoys NZ Ltd**. **Mr Potato Head** was included into the **National Toy Hall of Fame** in 2000.

Subbuteo soccer, a strangely named football board game, was developed in England in the late 1940s and became so popular that it expanded into other sports such as rugby, cricket and hockey. It was invented by Peter Adolf (1916–1994) in 1946. Despite the name sounding more like a concrete flooring product, the soccer crazed nation embraced it with a passion, the game rising in popularity following England's win in the **World Cup** in 1966. By the 1970s **Subbuteo** fielded more than fifty teams, even supplying playing pieces with home and away strips (uniforms). 'By the 1980s football teams were changing kits every year and required two away strips. Subbuteo heroically strove to keep up.'[130]

Eventually ethnicity and political correctness became embroiled in team selections whereby 'three players

The Soccer Game, plastic push-button soccer game, Wanda Toys, Taiwan, c. 1966, 12 x 6 in (31 x 15 cm).

Subbuteo scoreboard, plastic, c. 1980, 9 x 6 in (23 x 15 cm).

Backgammon set, playing pieces in red and black Bakelite, by Cutler and Saleeby Inc., Springfield, Massachusetts, dated 1930, wooden shaker, ivory dice, Bakelite pieces 1 in (25 mm) diameter.

German tin plate military searchlight vehicle, by Hausser, Germany, c. 1938, 10 in long (25 cm). Photo courtesy of Bertoia Auctions, USA.

of color' were to be included in each **Subbuteo** team. Further reflections of social changes saw toy stadium sets incorporate crush barriers, crowd barriers and mounted police. How times change but not necessarily for the better. The Subbuteo scoreboard illustrated here is one of the many accessory sets which can be added to the table and board games. It is now owned by Hasbro.

Toys too have become innocent victims of sinister changes in the historical and political landscape. Many toys and games produced prior to the rise of fascism in Germany in the 1930s wore the 'good luck' insignia, or swastika, such as mahjong pieces and backgammon counters. The insignia was historically a symbol of good luck and prosperity in the subcontinent, specifically as a symbol of positive spiritual principles in Buddhism, Hinduism and Janism. By the 1940s it had become a symbol of anti-Semitism, hatred and horror. Many **mahjong** pieces with the insignia are made from bamboo, carved and painted bone, and date from the late nineteenth century, while the black and red backgammon counters (pictured) are made from Bakelite, produced by **Cutler & Saleeby,** Massachusetts in 1930. This appears to be a traveling set contained in a 6 x 3½ inch (15 x 9 centimetres)

Big Game Hunt, three-panel board game by Chad Valley, England, c. 1900, 21 x 10½ in (53 x 17 cm).

Tin plate, clockwork camouflaged troop transport vehicle with composition soldiers, Lineol Germany, c. 1938, 10 in long (25 cm).

box which includes rules, a wooden dice shaker and, to add fuel to the fire, the dice are made from ivory. Military toys produced by manufacturers on both sides of the conflict were also affected by negative sentiments towards specific toys produced prior to World War II, such as the German **Hausser** and **Lineol** toys illustrated here.

On perhaps a lighter note, the popular game of **Cluedo,** invented by Anthony Pratt and patented by John Waddington of Britain in 1947, became the subject of fans' and the clergy's ire in England when new owners, **Hasbro,** decided to make some changes in accord with a proliferating secular society, particularly in the Western world. In 2000 a decision was made to replace **Reverend Green** with **Mr Green**, as the Reverend was considered no longer relevant. The clergy in England however

doth protest, claiming they were being unfairly discriminated against. Before long the clergy gave the game its blessing again when **Reverend Green** was restored to lurk once more in the conservatory with a candlestick. The reverend was nevertheless replaced by Mr Green in the North American and Canadian versions, which were renamed **Clue.**

Many pastimes previously thought to be adventurous or sporting are no longer considered acceptable or are subject to severe restrictions or prohibited completely. These controls relate in the main to hunting wild animals, many of which have been hunted to near extinction, as their survival rate is seriously under threat. The IUCN (International Union for the Conservation of Nature) state that over 784 extinctions have been recorded between 1500 and 2004. In New Zealand alone, many native

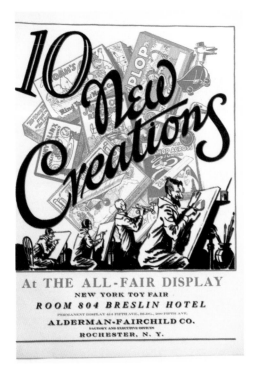

'10 New Toys for 1928', Alderman Fairchild, New York.

Pop and Plop Big Game Hunt target game by Alderman-Fairchild Co., Rochester, New York, 1928, 'All Fair' toy catalog.

birds face extinction and many like the moa and huia birds are sadly extinct.

The finely illustrated **Big Game Hunt** board game by **Chad Valley** of England, pictured, dates from the early 1900s and typically for the period shows that most wild animals were fair game, from elephants to kangaroos. As we saw in Chapter 6, elephants have been prime targets for centuries, highly prized for ivory. Ironically, in this board game, elephants are shown in the center right panel as faithful servants carrying hunters in howdahs to kill Indian tigers, while in the lower right image they are being chased by spear and gun toting hunters. One real hunter, a bloodthirsty Scot, Walter Dalrymple Maitland Bell (1880–1954) reputedly killed over 1000 elephants and wrote a book in 1923 to celebrate and record his dubious achievements titled *The Wanderings of an Elephant Hunter*. He apparently shot nineteen in one day, shooting anything that moved, as well as people. Some elephants exacted revenge against the 'great white hunters'. English soldier and adventurer, Walter Herbert Ingram, decided to add elephant hunting to his exploits following his heroic efforts fighting Mahdist rebels in Khartoum in 1885. Four years later, while elephant hunting, and desperately fleeing a huge female elephant, he fell off his horse and was trampled to death by the enraged animal. As Rudyard Kipling would colorfully describe it, 'the elephant turned Ingram into "blackcurrant jam". For days the vengeful elephant would not allow anyone to approach Ingram's mangled remains.'[131] In a curious coincidence relating to Egyptian mummies mentioned in Chapter 1, his death was blamed by some on a supposed cursed mummy he had purchased at Luxor some years earlier. Big game hunting toys were usually produced as target games and **Chad Valley** also produced a **Big Game Target** shooting game as late as the 1970s. Tigers and lions were worth fifty points each – elephants only fifteen.

As this chapter draws to a conclusion, it is not surprising to find the legendary maker of the **Sinnet** and **Big Game Hunt** board games, **Chad Valley,** could itself be historically accused of exploitation and infringement of human dignity. In the 1920s the company dressed a 'little person' (dwarf) in a **Bonzo** dog outfit at their trade stand during the annual industries fair in England. He was instructed to yap, prance and bounce around, much to the amusement of the patrons who included King George V and Queen Mary.[132] 'Dwarves' or 'midgets', as they were commonly called then, were used extensively in circus acts and freak shows in the nineteenth and twentieth centuries. This is no longer considered appropriate, in fact it is illegal in some countries and regarded as a breach of human dignity.

Who would have thought innocent and beautiful games such as **Chad Valley's Sinnet, Hasbro's Mr Potato Head, Shell Company's Rugger, Cutler and Saleeby's** counters, or a game of cards could be steeped in so much controversy and social history. Every toy does indeed tell a story and these classic collectibles and their makers should perhaps be forgiven for their transgressions as these toys were produced in largely good faith from different times and eras.

WIND-UP

A friend who read part of an early draft of a chapter of this book exclaimed with surprise, 'This is not just about toys,' and he was correct. It is also a book that is based largely on my collection, so I apologize now for toys and games that do not appear in this book – space does not allow for the inclusion of all categories of toys and others have been reserved for perhaps a further volume. Several collectors, auctions houses and museums have been most generous in providing images for toys I felt were important in relation to some of the chapters in this book. They are acknowledged separately. I trust at this point the 'whys' and 'wherefores' of my collection have now become clearer and explain in some way how the vast information and history surrounding toys, games, books, other ephemera and even movies, songs and poems have somehow found a place in toy-making history and this book.

The discovery of Tutankhamun's tomb, the traveling exhibition which followed and the Moon landing forty-seven years later provided quite unprecedented consequences and the impetus for not only toy making but distinct changes in other aspects of our culture. It is also possible by revealing some of the developments, events and stories surrounding these toys and games that their spirit and history will be upheld. While this history has only been touched upon it is my hope that an interest in toy collecting, similar to the Wright Brothers' interest in a toy helicopter, or Steve Wozniak's interest in *Tom Swift* stories, will inspire new collectors or readers to at least appreciate a rich and wonderful hobby.

Rear view of Hubley Toys US mail bike.

ACKNOWLEDGMENTS

» Bertoia Auctions, USA, Michael, Lauren and Jeannie Bertoia
» Dale Kelley, *Antique Toy World* magazine, Founded by Dale Kelley, 1971, USA – still going strong
» Griffiths Institute, Oxford University, Archaology department for Tuttoom images
» David Brash, Sarah Beresford, Liz Hardy and the team at New Holland Publishers
» Hakes Americana Collectibles, USA
» Lloyd Ralston Auctions, USA, Glen & Terry Ralston
» Anne Gifford, wonderful designer (and wife)
» Shirley Henderson, NZ, Shirley Temple doll photo
» Mikado Skoda locomotive, photo R. Stettinger
» Kathy Healey – wonderful typist
» Hugh Schofield, NZ, image of DC-3 aircraft
» Egypian Museum, photo of table for Senet board game, Ayman Khoury.

The toys, games and collectibles reproduced in this book from my collection have been reproduced for identification purposes. Every effort and communication has been made to trace any existing copyright holders for items reproduced in this book and we apologize in advance for any unintentional omission. Any omissions will be acknowledged in future volumes or editions of this book.

BIBLIOGRAPHY

Adams, J M 2013, *The Millionaire and the Mummies*, St Martin's Press, NY.

Antique Toy World magazine, publisher Dale Kelley, Chicago, USA.

Aune, A 1990, *Arcade Toys*, Robert F Mannella, USA.

Barrett Noel, Antique & Auctions Ltd, The Siegel Collection of Games and Toys, June 5–6, 1992, USA.

Bertoia Auctions, Signature Sale, USA Nov 11–12, 2017.

Bertoia Auctions, The Dick Ford Collection, Sep 17–18, 2004 USA.

Botto, K 1978, *Past Joys*, Prism Editions, Chronicle Books, USA.

Bracken, T 1879, *The New Zealand Tourist*, Union Steam Ship Company of NZ.

Burkett, M 1998, *Pioneers of the Air*, Ticktok Publishing Ltd, UK.

Burness, T 1986, *Monstrous American Car Spotter's Guide 1920–1980*, Motorbooks International Publishers, USA.

Capps, B 1973, *The Indians*, Timelife Books, USA.

Clark, T (ed.) 1977, *Bakelite Style*, Chartwell Books, USA.

Clerici, G (1976) *Tennis*, Octopus Books Ltd, London, 1976.

Cook, P & Slessor, C 1993, *Bakelite, An Illustrated Guide to Collectible Bakelite Objects*, The Apple Press (Quintet Publishing Ltd), London.

Cooper, SF 2001, *The Victorian Woman*, V&A Publications, London.

Corbett, C 2010, *The Poker Bride*, Atlantic Monthly Press, USA.

Costello, J & Finnegan, P 1988, *Tapestry of Turf – The History of NZ Racing, 1840–1987*, Moa Publications, NZ.

Dregni, M (ed.) 2010, *The Ultimate Road Trip*, Voyageur Press.

Every Girls Annual, Stories of School Adventure and Sport, Pilgrim Press, London, 1922.

Fraser, A 1972, *A History of Toys*, Spring Books, London, The Hamlyn Publishing Group Ltd.

Fritze, RH 2016, *Egyptomania:The History of Fascination, Obsession and Fantasy*, Reaktion Books, London.

Geary, J 1990, *Studebaker Toys and Models*, J Geary, USA.

Glancey, J 2006, *The Car, A History of the Automobile*, Carlton Books Ltd, London.

Goodfellow, C 1991, *A Collector's Guide to Games and Puzzles*, The Apple Press (Quintet Publishing Ltd), London.

Graham, F Lanier 1968, *Chess Sets*, Walker & Company, NY.

Grant, D 1994, *On A Roll:The History of Gambling and Lotteries in NZ*, Victoria University Press, NZ.

Hanlon, B 1973, *Plastic Toys*, Schiffer Publishing Ltd, USA.

Harry, L 2000, *Slinkey – The Fun and Wonderful Toy*, Running Press, USA.

Haylett, J & Evans, R 1989, *The Illustrated Encyclopaedia of World Tennis*, Golden Press Pty Ltd, Australia/NZ.

Hutchinson,K & Johnson, G 1997, *The Golden Age of Automotive Toys 1925 – 1941*, Collector Books, USA.

Israel, A & Swain G 2014, *Mah Jongg: The Art of the Game*, Tuttle Publishing, Hong Kong.

Jaffe, D 2006, *The History of Toys*, Sutton Publishing, England.

Jarrott, C 1906, *Ten Years of Motors and Motor Racing*, E. Grant Richards, London.

Keating, B 1977, *Famous American Cowboys*, Rand McNally & Company, USA.

Kendall, T 1978, *Passing through the Netherworld*, Kirk Game Company, USA.

Kirsten, SA 2007, *Tiki Modern*, Taschen, Germany.

Kitahara, T 1985, *Cars, Tin Toy Dreams*, Chronicle Books, San Franciso, USA.

Kitahara, T & Shimizu, Y 1996, *1000 Tin Toys*, Taschen, Japan,1996.

Knowles, T 2009, *100 Years of Motoring, Twentieth Century in Pictures*, Ammonite Press, England.

Laban, Brian 2011, *Cars The Early Years*, Ullmann Publishing, Germany.

Lang, J 1909, *The Land of the Golden Trade*, Caxton Publishing, London.

Leopard, Dave, *Rubber Toy Vehicles*, Pub David Leopard, USA, 1994

Lind, C 1996, *The People and the Power: The History of the Tiwai Aluminum Smelter*, New Zealand Alumimium Smelters Ltd, Invercargill.

Love, B 1984, *Play the Game*, Guild Publishing (Roxby Productions Ltd), London.

Mackett-Beeson, AEJ 1973, *Chessmen*, Octopus Books Ltd.

Maddocks, M 1978, *The Great Liners*, Timelife Books, Amsterdam.

Meccano Magazines, 1930s–1960s

Miller, J & K 1995, *Texas Stories*, Chronicle Books, USA.

Miller, J 2006, *Metal Toys*, DK Publishing, London/NY.

Modellers' World magazines, 1974–1980, Modellers World Productions.

New Zealand as a Tourist and Health Resort, 3rd Edition, Thomas Cook, NZ, 1899.

Nicolson, M 1948, *Voyages to the Moon*, The Macmillan Company, Canada.

O'Brien, R 1990, *The Story of American Toys*, New Cavendish Books, London.

O'Brien, K 2008, *O'Brien's Collecting Toys*, 12th Edition, Krause Publications, USA.

Opie, R 2016, *The Fun of the Fifties: Ads, Fads and Fashion*, Michael O'Mara Books Ltd, London.

Pitts, R 2009, *Pepys the Story of the Company and Its Games*, 4th Edition, self published.

Putt, G & McCord, P 2009, *Phar Lap: The Untold Story*, Equus Marketing and BAS Publishing, Australia.

Richardson, S 1981, *Minic Lines Bros, Tin plate Vehicles*, Mikansue, England.

Seddon, P 2001, *Tennis's Strangest Matches*, Robson Books, London.

Smith, R & Gallagher, WC 2004, *The Big Book of Tin Toy Cars*, Schiffer Books, USA.

Tabak, T 2009, *Dreams and Demon's of a NZ Cycling Legend*, Kennett Brothers, NZ.

The Nash Times, Nash Car Club of America, Vol. 37 No. 1, Jan/Feb 2006.

Tumbusch, TN 1990, *Space Adventure Collectibles*, Wallace-Homestead Book Company, USA.

Tyldesley, J 2007, *Egyptian Games and Sports*, Shire Publications Ltd, London.

Tyldesley, J 2008, *Cleopatra: Last Queen of Egypt*, Profile Books, London.

Tyldesley, J 2012, *Tutankhamen: The Search for an Egyptian King*, Basic Books, NY.

Weltens, A 1977, *Mechanical Tin Toys in Color*, Blandford Press, England.

Whitehill, B 1992, *Games: American Boxed Games and Their Makers 1822–1922*, Wallace-Homestead, USA.

Whittaker, N 2001, *Toys Were Us*, Orion, London.

Wilkinson, M 1983, *The Phar Lap Story*, Budget Books, Australia.

Young, Duin, Richardson 2012, *Blast Off!: Rockets, Robots, Ray Guns, and Rarities of the Golden Age of Space Toys*, Dark Horse, London.

Zarnock, M 2015, *Hot Wheels: How to Pick Antiques Like a Pro*, Krause Publications, USA.

ENDNOTES

INTRODUCTION

1   *Antique Toy* World magazine,press release, Katonah Museum, April 1994.

2   'Toy World Highlights New Jersey's Rich Industrial [and Fun] History', PR release from New Jersey State Museum, published in *Antique Toy World* magazine, December 2016.

3   Louis Benech, Christies Auctions, France April 2015, press release.

4   Email to the author 22 February 2018.

5   Proust, M, *In Search of Lost Time Volume 6: Time Regained*, first published by Grasset and Gallimard, Paris, 1913.

6   Botto, K, *Past Joys*, Chronicle Books, 1978.

7   Bertoia Auctions, Vineland, New Jersey, USA, Donald Kaufman collection.

8   Fisher, C, *NZ Herald,* 13 April 2017, p. 15.

9   Bryson, B, *The Lost Continent*, Secker and Warburg, 1989.

CHAPTER 1: FUN AND SERIOUS GAMES IN THE PYRAMIDS

10   Tyldesley, J, *Tutankhamun: The Search for an Egyptian King*, Basic Books, New York, 2012, p. 67.

11   ibid., p. 64.

12   Painting of Queen Nefertari (c. 1295–1255 BC) playing Senet, royal wife of Akhenaten an Egyptian pharaoh,possible Egyptian ruler prior to Tutankhamun's reign.

13   Mackett-Beeson, AEJ 1967, *Chessmen*, first published by G Weidenfeld, London, 1967.

14   *Art Deco 1910 to 1939*, Introduction, V&A Museum, London March 2003.

15   Catalog of Am-Duat (The Egyptian Board Game) by Chad Valley Co Ltd, England. Taken from *Play the Game* by Brian Love, Guild Publishing London, Roxby Press and Book Club Associates 1984, p. 16.

16   Ehrlich, D 2017, 'The Mummy Is the Worst Tom Cruise Movie Ever', IndieWire, 7 July.

17   Kamp, D 2013, 'The King of New York', *Vanity Fair,* April.

18   Peter A Piccione, Introduction to the rules, on reverse of the box cover to Cadaco's Senet, game.

19   Riordan, R, *The Red Pyramid*, 2010, *The Throne of Fire*, 2011, *The Serpent Shadow*, 2012, Disney Hyperion and Puffin.

20   'Imhotep, Builder of Egypt' board game by Thrones and Kosmos Games, designed by Phil Walker-Harding, Australia

21   Tyldesley, J 2012, *Tutankhamun: The Search for an Egyptian King*, Basic Books, New York, 2012, pp. 140–141.

CHAPTER 2: GO WEST YOUNG MAN, GO WEST!

22   Stevens, V 1970, *Great Western TV Themes*, EMI, Super Tunes Production.

23   The origin of this phrase is debated still, however, it is variously attributed to John Soule in 1851 and Horace Greely in 1865.

24   Omeara, D 2003, *The Guns of the Gunfighters*, Krause Publications.

25   'Remember the Alamo!' was a famous battle cry which motivated Sam Houston's Texans during their victorious battle of San Jacinta in 1836.

CHAPTER 3: TOY HORSES FOR TOY COURSES

26   Grant, D 1994, *On a Roll: A History of Gambling and Lotteries in New Zealand*, Victoria University Press.

27   Blew, WCA 1901, *A History of Steeple Chasing*, John C Nimmo, p. 293.

28   Costello, J & Finegan, P 1988, *Tapestry of Turf – A History of New Zealand Racing*, Moa Publications, 1988, p. 136.

29   ibid.

30   Costello, J & Finegan, P, op. cit., p.136.

31   Whitehill, B 1992, *American Boxed Games and their Makers 1822–1992*, Radnor, USA, p. 142.

32   Keating, B 1977, *Famous American Cowboys*, Rand McNally & Co, USA, p.75.

CHAPTER 4: ENDURING FOLK ART, DREAM CARS AND TOYS IN ALUMINUM

33   'What Happened to Dreamworld', *Fortune* magazine, 1 February 1947, p. 92.

34   Bohn Aluminum and Brass Corporation, Detroit, Michigan in *Fortune* magazine, 1 February 1947.

35   Frank Hoess, Hoess Siding and Roofing, in *American Builder*, October 1946.

36   Premier Aluminum Windows advertisement in *Fortune* magazine, February 1947.

37   'Henry J Kaiser', https://www.britannica.com/biography/Henry-J-Kaiser

38   Kirsten, SA 2007, *Tiki Modern*, Taschen, pp. 132–133.

39   *Science and Mechanics* magazine, October 1995, p. 45.

40   Young, BGB, 'Underwood, Harold Jack', Te Ara Encyclopaedia of New Zealand, teara.govt.nz/en/biographies/5u1/underwood-harold-jack.

41   Melton, W & Wagner, R 2003, *Barclay Toys: Transport & Cars 1932–1971*, Schiffer Publishing, USA.

42   Fun Ho! history: www.funhotoy.co.nz

43   Young, E 1979, 'Nostalgia for Collectors in New Zealand Toyshops', *Autocar*, March.

44   Quote from an ex-employee of Underwood Engineering in conversation with the author at the opening of the Fun Ho! Museum in 1990.

45   Fun Ho! history: www.funhotoys.co.nz/funhotoys/streamlux-australia.aspx

46   Lines Brothers: www.triang.nl/historynew.htm

47   Department of Statistics, Overseas merchandise trade 2012 statisphere.govt.nz

48   Young, BGB, op. cit.

49   https://en.wikipedia.org/wiki/Aluminum_Model_Toys; 'Santa Claus' Workshop'; http://iagenweb.org/allamakee/history4/santaworkshop.htm.

50   See the series of books by Jean-Michel Tisné.

CHAPTER 5: TOYS, BOOKS AND GAMES IN A RACE TO THE MOON

51   Wells, HG *The War of the Worlds*, first published in 1895.

52   Gibson, CR 1921, *The Stars and their Mysteries*, Seeley, Service & Co Ltd, London.

53   Verne, J *From the Earth to the Moon*, first published in 1865; *Around the Moon*, the sequel to *From the Earth to the Moon*, first published in 1870.

54   Fournier, R 2017 'Tiny Toy Corner: Adventures of Baron Munchausen', *Antique Toy World*, 3 October, p. 62.

55   Lot 181, Old Salem Toy Museum & TA Gray Collection, Pook & Pook Inc. with Noel Barrett Auctions, 20 November 2010.

56   Lofting, H 1928, *Dr Dolittle in the Moon*, Jonathon Cape, London, p.25.

57   Keeline, JD, 'Tom Swift on the Silver Screen', http://www.keeline.com/Tom_Swift_Silver_Screen.pdf.

58   Appleton, V 1911, 'Tom Swift and his Electric Rifle', Grosset & Dunlap, USA.

59   Robby the Robot type toy designed by Robert Kinoshita.

60   Coggins, J and Pratt, F 1952, *By Spaceship to the Moon*, Random House, NY.

61   *Tom Corbett, Space Cadet*, Dell Comics, number 400, 1952.

62   Vivid Imagination Toy Company, Surrey, England est. 1992 by ex-Matchbox employees Nick Austin and Alan Bennie. Beginning with borrowed capital of £380,000, the company eventually sold for £62 million in 2003.

63   *Captain Scarlet and the Mysterons* jigsaw puzzle, Waddington UK/Holdson Products NZ, 1967.

64   *Star Trek Annual* 1970, World Distributors Manchester Ltd and BBCTV.

65   *Star Trek* Captain's Log collectible trading cards, seventy-two card set produced by Topps Chewing Gum Inc., 1976.

66   'High prices for Star Wars at Auction', *Otago Daily Times*, 18 January 2016.

67   Reynolds, D 1998, *Star Wars: The Visual Dictionary*, Dorling Kindersley, p.58.

CHAPTER 6: EARLY PERIOD–LATE PERIOD PLASTIC TOYS

68   'Ivory Carving', Encyclopaedia Britannica Online, www.britannica.com/art/ivory-carving; chess piece c. 12 AD, Collection Des Médailles et Antiques, Bibliothèque Nationale de France.

69   Chou dynasty (112–256 BC).

70   Fraser, A 1966, *A History of Toys*, Hamlyn, London, p. 31.

71   Grant, D 1994, *On a Roll: A History of New Zealand Gambling and Lotteries*, Victoria University Press, pages 34, 35.

72   ibid.

73   ibid.

74   'Maintaining Leadership' advertisement, *Punch Almanack for 1930*, 4 November 1929.

75   Moulded Products Australasia Ltd, plastic products advertising brochure, c. 1952.

76   Hanlon, B 1993, *Plastic Toys: Dimestore Dreams of the 50s and 60s*, Schiffer Publishing Ltd, USA, p. 30.

77   ibid.

78   Advertisement, Marquis Toys for Boys and Girls, *The Retailer*, June 1949, Australia.

79 (i) Monsanto Plastics advert in *Fortune* magazine, August 1939; (ii) 'Plastic' – General American advert in *Fortune* magazine, October 1949; (iii) 'Lucite', DuPont Plastics advert in *Fortune* magazine, October 1945.

80 Hanlon, B, op. cit., p.16, advert 'Playthings' Sept. 1950.

81 100 Piece Toy Soldier Set, Lucky Products Inc, New York; advert, *Dark Shadow's Gold Key Comics*, rear cover, February 1974.

82 Interview: Mr Mark Lusty, LEGO builder, 22 October at the Auckland Brick Show, New Zealand.

CHAPTER 7: TWO WHEELS, FOUR WHEELS, HOT WHEELS

83 *8 Automobiles*, MOMA, New York, 1951, Introduction to catalog.

84 'Amos E Northup', http://www.coachbuilt.com/des/n/northup/northup.htm; Keller, ME 1998, *The Graham Legacy: Graham-Paige to 1932*, Turner Publishing, USA.

85 Hayden, W 2008, 'Remembering Wyandotte Toys', *The News Herald*, 5 December, Michigan, USA.

86 Burness, T 1986, *Monstrous American Car Spotter's Guide 1920–1980*, Motorbooks International, USA, p. 183.

87 Nash advertisement for 1942, in Burness, T (1986), op. cit., p. 232.

88 Nash advertisement from a series of twelve by Ed Zern, Nash Motors, 1950.

89 ibid.

90 Pininfarina, established 1930. Famous Italian design firm who have designed for Ferrari, Alfa Romeo, Maserati and Peugeot

91 Nash-Healey sports cars, clad in aluminum bodies performed well at Le Mans, finishing first in class in 1952.

92 Chrysler advertising brochure 1939, Chrysler Dealers brochure 1939, Chrysler advertisement 1939.

93 Lincoln Zephyr advertising brochure, 1936.

94 Butler, S 2016, 'Marchesini Fords Update', *Antique Toy World*, vol. 46, October, p.47.

95 BMC Mini Countryman review, *Modern Motor* magazine, Australia, November 1960, p.25.

96 1969 American Motors Plymouth advertising brochure for Plymouth Barracuda sports coupe (mod top) and Plymouth Satellite.

97 Zarnock, M 2015, *Pickers Pocket Guide: Hot Wheels*, Krause Publications, p. 113.

CHAPTER 8: TRAINS AND BOATS AND PLANES

98 1975, *The Railroaders*, Time Life Books, p. 19.

99 2014, *The Train Book: The Definitive Visual History*, Dorling Kindersley, p.55.

100 McGavin, TA 1971, *NZR Locomotives and Railcars to 1970*, NZ Railway and Locomotive Society; Wikipedia, NZR RM Class (Standard), https://en.wikipedia.org/wiki/NZR_RM_class_(Standard).

101 Heath, E & Stott, B 1993, *Classic Railcars, Electric & Diesel Locomotives of New Zealand: Volume two*, Grantham House, NZ.

102 Sold by Bertoia Auctions USA, Richard T Claus collection, July 2012.

103 Maddocks, M 1978, *The Great Liners*, Time Life Amsterdam, p. 34.

104 ibid., p.28.

105 Humphreys, A 2017, *Journey – The Age of Steam 1800–1900*, Dorling Kindersley, pp. 222–223.

106 'New Zealand as a Tourist and Health Resort', Thomas Cook & Son, 3rd Edition 1899 – advertisement.

107 Maddocks, M 1978, *First Visions of a Golden Age at Sea*, Time Life, Amsterdam, p. 34.

108 Priestley, JB 1970, *The Edwardians*, William Heinemann Ltd, p. 135.

109 Chirnside, M 2009, *RMS Aquitania The Ship Beautiful*, The History Press, p. 86.

110 Maddocks, M 1978, *The Queens at War*, Time Life , p. 143.

111 ibid, p. 150.

112 www.tourismnewzealand.com/markets-stats/sectors/cruise/sector.

113 www.statista.com/statistics/385445-number-of-passengers-of-the-cruise-industry-worldwide.

114 Burkett, M 1998, *Pioneers of the Air*, Ticktock Publishing Ltd, p. 8.

115 ibid.

116 www.thefirstairraces.net/rules.php.

117 The Brighton Toy and Model Museum, www.brightontoymuseum.co.uk/index/category:Rovex_plastics.

118 www.britannica.com/technology/Concorde.

CHAPTER 9: TOY MAKERS PLAY CAT AND MOUSE

119 Pederson, J 1999, 'Brio History'in *International Directory of Company Histories: Vol. 24*, St James Press, Michigan.

120 Playthings Jan 1928, 'Gong Bell News'.

121 Playthings Jan 1928, 'Gong Bell News'.

122 Mueller Jnr, Richard 'Gong Bell Trix Toys', www.oldwoodtoys.com/trix.htm.

123 '10 New Creations', Alderman Fairchild Company, Rochester, New York, advert New York Toy Fair 1928.

124 'Nasty sting in the tail of the Bee', *New Zealand Herald*, 8 July 1996.

125 'Buzzy Bee and Friends', http://buzzybeetv.com/about-buzzy-bee-and-friends-history/.

126 Fritz, R 2017, *Egyptomania*, Reaktion Books, p. 333.

CHAPTER 10: ALL CHANGE – TENNIS, TARGET GAMES AND OTHER TOYS REFLECT SOCIAL CHANGE

127 Clerici, G 1976, *Tennis*, Octopus Books, London, p 229.

128 Whittaker, N 2001, *Toys Were Us*, Orion House, London, p 183.

129 ibid., p 97.

130 ibid., p 160.

131 Fritze, RH, op. cit., pp. 229–230.

132 Fraser, A, op. cit., p 210.

ABOUT THE AUTHOR

Warwick Henderson is a long-term gallerist, Art Fair pioneer, toy collector and author based in Auckland, New Zealand. Warwick curated two major public museum touring exhibitions of antique toys and games in New Zealand the 1990s. He has written essays for various publications since the 1980s and wrote a seminal history of the New Zealand art market *Behind the Canvas* in 2012. He shares the enjoyment of collecting with his ever-helpful wife and two adult children.

First published in 2018 by New Holland Publishers
London · Sydney · Auckland

131–151 Great Titchfield Street, London W1W 5BB, United Kingdom
1/66 Gibbes Street, Chatswood, NSW 2067, Australia
5/39 Woodside Ave, Northcote, Auckland 0627, New Zealand

newhollandpublishers.com

A catalogue record for this book is available from the National Library of New Zealand.

ISBN 9781869664855

Group Managing Director: Fiona Schultz
Publisher: Sarah Beresford
Project Editor: Liz Hardy
Designer: Sara Lindberg
Production Director: James Mills-Hicks
Printer: Toppan Leefung Printing Limited

10 9 8 7 6 5 4 3 2 1

Keep up with New Holland Publishers on Facebook
facebook.com/NewHollandPublishers

UK £14.
US $19.